Report Writing for Law Enforcement and Corrections Professionals

By

Ken Morris
and
Michael R. Merson

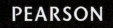

Boston   Columbus   Indianapolis   New York   San Francisco
Amsterdam   Cape Town   Dubai   London   Madrid   Milan   Munich   Paris   Montreal   Toronto
Delhi   Mexico City   Sao Paulo   Sydney   Hong Kong   Seoul   Singapore   Taipei   Tokyo

Editorial Director: Andrew Gilfillan
Executive Editor: Gary Bauer
Editorial Assistant: Lynda Cramer
Director of Marketing: David Gesell
Marketing Manager: Thomas Hayward
Product Marketing Manager: Kaylee Carlson
Marketing Assistant: Les Roberts
Program Manager: Tara Horton
Project Manager Team Lead: Bryan Pirrmann
Project Manager: Susan Hannahs
Operations Specialist: Deidra Smith
Creative Director: Andrea Nix
Art Director: Diane Six

Manager, Product Strategy: Sara Eilert
Product Strategy Manager: Anne Rynearson
Team Lead, Media Development & Production: Rachel Collett
Media Project Manager: Maura Barclay
Cover Designer: Melissa Welch, Studio Montage
Cover Image: Halfdark/Getty Images
Full-Service Project Management: Chandrasekar Subramanian, SPi Global
Composition: SPi Global
Text Printer/Bindery: LSC Communications/Harrisonburg
Cover Printer: LSC Communications/Harrisonburg
Text Font: Palatino LT Pro, 11.5/13.5

Credits and acknowledgments borrowed from other sources and reproduced, with permission, in this textbook appear on the appropriate page within the text.

Acknowledgements of third party content appear on page with the borrowed material, which constitutes an extension of this copyright page. Unless otherwise indicated herein, any third-party trademarks that may appear in this work are the property of their respective owners and any references to third-party trademarks, logos or other trade dress are for demonstrative or descriptive purposes only. Such references are not intended to imply any sponsorship, endorsement, authorization, or promotion of Pearson's products by the owners of such marks, or any relationship between the owner and Pearson Education, Inc. or its affiliates, authors, licensees or distributors.

Many of the designations by manufacturers and sellers to distinguish their products are claimed as trademarks. Where those designations appear in this book, and the publisher was aware of a trademark claim, the designations have been printed in initial caps or all caps.

Library of Congress Cataloging-in-Publication Data

CIP has been requested but not yet received at time of print

17 2023

ISBN 10:   0-13-335045-2
ISBN 13: 978-0-13-335045-6

Dedication

To Maureen, Kristen, Pat, Tim, Sean and Maggie for allowing me the time to get this finished . . . now, wax up the ski's! — Ken Morris

Stefanie, Michaela, and Mackenzie . . . for all of you! — Michael R. Merson

Brief Contents

Contents

Preface

This textbook is intended to serve students considering a career in the field of criminal justice. They range from students attending a college or university to students enrolled in a law enforcement or corrections academy. Our focus is on the universality of the criminal justice system regarding reports. There is significant overlap of the law enforcement and correctional aspects of the criminal justice system. A criminal case report completed by a patrol officer often mirrors an incident report completed by a correctional officer. The basic concepts of report writing cut across criminal justice career fields. This textbook is designed to provide instruction in all aspects of the criminal justice profession.

The structure of this textbook is based on a holistic approach that tries to address all of the aspects of the intricacies of the criminal-justice report-writing system. That is, writing a good report must address a variety of issues to be successful. For example some of these issues include establishing proper jurisdiction, documenting the legal elements of the crime, and ensuring proper procedural steps are followed while collecting evidence and interviewing suspects. These are just a few examples of why procedural and statutory information has been incorporated into this textbook. Good report writing does not occur in a vacuum; there are numerous legal requirements that must be met that are driven by case law and statutory requirements.

ORGANIZATION OF THE TEXT

Law enforcement agencies across the nation use various software and forms to assist their sworn personnel in collecting the facts and circumstances of a specific crime or other situation. The software and forms are a valuable resource for ensuring that the correct information for a crime or other situation is collected and is placed in a specific location on the report form.

The concept of our textbook is to present an all-inclusive system of report writing that is characterized by following a methodical process from arrival at a crime scene to presentation in court. The book's method of instruction utilizes presentation of information, video scenarios, and practical exercises. We take you through the report-writing process in three methodical phases. We like to call these phases the "crawl, walk, and run" method. Each phase builds on the knowledge gained from the previous phase.

In the crawl phase, we cover the basics of report writing. The book begins with procedures when first arriving at a crime scene. Next, we transition into securing the scene and then the art of note-taking. Basic English grammar skills are also presented in this phase of the textbook, and the general structure of the narrative report is also examined. Completed case reports are offered that are illustrative of the tenor and content of well-written case reports. Practical exercises are given to reinforce the concepts presented in the crawl phase.

In the walk phase, the student is introduced to the myriad types of calls for service and some of the more common forms of paperwork that the law enforcement professional will encounter. In this phase, we also offer instruction on the various forms the student may encounter if employed in the corrections setting (jails, prisons, probation). Building upon the crawl phase, the student is faced with more practical exercises to hone his or her skills and become familiar with the technical requirements of the various types of law enforcement forms.

The textbook concludes with the run phase. The intent here is to provide extensive practice working through the technical challenges of the narrative case report. This is the phase in which the application of the knowledge gained during the previous phases is applied to practical exercises. The practical exercises are more intense and challenging. A homicide case challenges the student to apply all of the concepts presented in the textbook in an extensive exercise. The textbook finishes with techniques for presentation of your case report in a court of law.

PEDAGOGICAL FEATURES

We have created a unique learning system for the criminal justice student. The chapters are designed to present the student with the structure and techniques of report writing supported by the following key features:

- The *Right* Way to *Write* focuses on the specifics of "how" to approach professional law enforcement writing. This section emphasizes the essential writing principles to help guide you through the report-writing process. Each chapter is examined in matters germane to writing skills and strategies necessary to accomplish the task of professional law enforcement writing.
- **Tips for Success** are presented to provide focus and structure to the chapter concepts.
- **Forms and Document Examples** are provided for all type of reports. The examples relate to the common forms frequently presented and explained.
- **Chapter Summary** reinforces the vital material presented in the chapter.
- **Practical Exercises** conclude the chapter to reinforce the concepts presented in the chapter by providing realistic and challenging exercises for the student.
- **Video Scenarios** provide context for assignments, where the student must apply his or her observational skills, take notes, and then write the case report. The videos are built into assignments within the REVEL eText. This "hands-on approach" benefits the student by providing real-world applications to the textbook material.

FORMS AND DOCUMENT EXAMPLES

It should be noted that the forms used throughout this textbook are intended to be generic in nature although there are numerous references to the "State of Colorado." The general application of the form and content of these forms and documents are applicable to any jurisdiction in the country. Some of the required verbiage may vary from state to state, there are extensive commonalities in the preparation of these forms, which have been reflected in this textbook. With regard to how and what writing style to use in preparing these legal documents, your agency's policy and procedure manual, or standard operating procedures, will offer specific guidelines for preparing these documents. Follow the general guidelines offered in this textbook and then apply the appropriate jurisdictional or agency requirements, and you will be in compliance with the requirements of whatever document you are preparing.

INSTRUCTOR SUPPLEMENTS

Instructor's Manual with Test Bank. Includes content outlines for classroom discussion, teaching suggestions, and answers to selected end-of-chapter questions from the text. This also contains a Word document version of the test bank.

TestGen. This computerized test generation system gives you maximum flexibility in creating and administering tests on paper, electronically, or online. It provides state-of-the-art features for viewing and editing test bank questions, dragging a selected question into a test you are creating, and printing sleek, formatted tests in a variety of layouts. Select test items from test banks included with TestGen for quick test creation, or write your own questions from scratch. TestGen's random generator provides the option to display different text or calculated number values each time questions are used.

PowerPoint Presentations. Our presentations offer clear, straightforward outlines and notes to use for class lectures or study materials. Photos, illustrations, charts, and tables from the book are included in the presentations when applicable.

To access supplementary materials online, instructors need to request an instructor access code. Go to **www.pearsonhighered.com/irc**, where you can register for an instructor access code. Within 48 hours after registering, you will receive a confirming email, including an instructor access code. Once you have received your code, go to the site and log on for full instructions on downloading the materials you wish to use.

ALTERNATE VERSIONS

eBooks This text is also available in multiple eBook formats. These are an exciting new choice for students looking to save money. As an alternative to purchasing the printed textbook, students can purchase an electronic version of the same content. With an eTextbook, students can search the text, make notes online, print out reading assignments that incorporate lecture notes, and bookmark important passages for later review. For more information, visit your favorite online eBook reseller or visit **www.mypearsonstore.com**.

REVEL™ is Pearson's newest way of delivering our respected content. Fully digital and highly engaging, REVEL replaces the textbook and gives students everything they need for the course. Seamlessly blending text narrative, media, and assessment, REVEL enables students to read, practice, and study in one continuous experience—for less than the cost of a traditional textbook. Learn more at **pearsonhighered.com/revel**.

ACKNOWLEDGEMENTS

We would like to thank the El Paso County Sheriff's Office in Colorado Springs, Colorado, for all of their enthusiastic assistance regarding this textbook. Specifically, the use of their forms, policy and procedures, and SOPs. Additionally, Sergeant Cy Gillespie deserves many kudos for being our "hands-on" source of information; his responsiveness to our numerous requests is demonstrative of the consummate criminal justice professional.

REVIEWERS

David Bentz, San Joaquin Delta College

John W. Bolinger, MacMurray College

William P. DeFeo, Western Connecticut State University

M. George Eichenberg, Tarleton State University

Roy W. Heringer, Grossmont College

Raymond Hsieh, California University of Pennsylvania

Jay Kramer, Central Georgia Technical College

Jeffrey F. Majewski, Bristol Community College

Chris McFarlin, Tri-County Technical College

Catherine Sanders, Triton College

Diane Sjuts, Metro Community College

Anne Strouth, North Central State College

Ronald R. Thrasher, Oklahoma State University

Tammy Thurman, Lewis University

Kelly Treece, Glenville State College

ABOUT THE AUTHORS

The authors of this textbook have a combined total of 36 years' experience working for law enforcement agencies and more than 17 years of instruction at the college level. Michael Merson was employed by a major law enforcement agency, the Colorado Springs Police Department, and Ken Morris was employed by the EL Paso County Sheriff's Office (Colorado Springs, CO). Ken also served as a United Nations police officer in the war-torn country of Kosovo for over a year. Combined they bring patrol, jail, and international policing applications to their current educational careers.

KEN MORRIS

My criminal justice career spans more than 28 years. Prior to my retirement, I was serving as the Patrol Division Commander for the El Paso County Sheriff's Office. As the Division Commander, I exercised supervision and control of 106 sworn and civilian employees. In 1999, I took a 15 month leave-of-absence from the Sheriff's Office and worked as a United Nations Peacekeeper (police officer) in Kosovo, Yugoslavia. I attained the rank of station commander of the third largest city in the province before returning back to work for the Sheriff's Office. I have done consulting work for the Bureau of Indian Affairs, The National Institute of Corrections, and the Department of Justice.

Working most of my criminal justice career employed by a sheriff's office afforded me the opportunity to work both in the law enforcement and detention divisions of the profession. My career in detentions entailed every detention assignment from "floor deputy" to warden of a 600-bed inmate capacity facility. I was the Sherriff's Project Manager for the construction of a new county jail in 1987 and served as the first warden of that facility when it opened in 1989. Our new detention facility received national recognition by the National Institute of Corrections as a "resource center," hosting their Planning of New Institutions (PONI) program, which entailed a one-week seminar on how to build a new detention facility. Our new detention facility served as a "model" jail, and I served as a consultant for those seminars.

I feel that having worked in both detentions and law enforcement has provided unique insight into the intricacies of criminal justice report writing. Teaching has been my passion; I enjoy the teaching environment. I earned a bachelor's degree in 1973 from the University of Memphis. In 1992, I graduated from the University of Colorado with a master's degree in public administration. I also earned a law enforcement certificate from the University of Colorado. I have taught at the Sheriff's Office Law Enforcement Academy for numerous years. My educational background and "hands-on" experiences largely contributed to my desire to write this textbook.

Additionally, I have done extensive consulting work for the Department of Justice, the Bureau of Indian Affairs, and the National Institute of Corrections.

MICHAEL MERSON

I joined the U.S. Army in January of 1991 and served in the Military Police Corps until March of 1998. It was in the U.S. Army where I first started writing police reports for crimes committed on the various army posts where I was assigned. The first police reports I wrote were in the third person, and I quickly found them to be difficult to write and not very reader-friendly for other people. In the U.S. Army, I also began taking classes in criminal justice, which led to completing a BS in sociology (criminology) at Colorado

State University. I completed my master's degree in criminal justice at the University of Colorado.

I left the U.S. Army in March of 1998 and was quickly hired by the Colorado Springs Police Department that same month. During the hiring process, I was one of the top five candidates from an applicant pool of more than 1,000 applicants selected for the academy that consisted of only 24 future law enforcement professionals. While working for the Colorado Springs Police Department, I was assigned to the patrol division, traffic division, the neighborhood police unit, the commercial vehicle unit, and the evidence cadre. I also was assigned to the Major Accident Unit and, on occasion, trained new officers while patrol.

Currently, I'm employed by Pikes Peak Community College and Colorado State University, where I teach criminal justice classes to future law enforcement professionals. I have also served as the Interim Director of the Pikes Peak Regional Law Enforcement Academy and previously served as a Citizen at Large for the El Paso County Community Corrections Board for three years.

During my tenure at Pikes Peak Community College, I was assigned, by Ken Morris, to create a report-writing class for our Criminal Justice Program. While completing my research for the class, I discovered that the available textbooks dealing with report writing were simply inadequate in several areas. I felt that Ken and I could write a better textbook. I decided to approach Ken with the idea of creating a new report-writing textbook. Soon, the two of us were sending emails back and forth sharing ideas. After two agonizing years of writing, research, and revisions, we had created what we thought was a great textbook. We approached representatives from Pearson Publishing, and I guess you can say "the rest is history."

People often ask, "Why didn't you write a report-writing textbook years ago?" I simply say, "Well, I had to read and write a couple of thousand police reports before I thought I was ready to teach someone else how to do it the right way!"

We have both taught law enforcement report-writing classes to college students for many years in both lecture and online distance education classes. The Criminal Justice Advisory Board at our school, composed of members of local law enforcement leaders, consistently requested that we send candidates for employment to them "who can write a good report. We can teach them the other skills." After using and reviewing many report-writing textbooks, we found that none truly fit our student's needs, so we decided to write a new text based upon the best current practices in the field.

1

REPORTS, THE ENGLISH LANGUAGE, AND POLICE JARGON

LEARNING OBJECTIVES

- Enhance knowledge and understanding of the English language as it applies to completing law enforcement written reports.
- Recognize the various procedural issues in completing a law enforcement written report.
- Understand the unique style, flow, and content of a law enforcement written report.
- Apply your knowledge to practical examples by successfully completing the chapter exercises.

INTRODUCTION

Law enforcement report writing is one aspect of the law enforcement profession that most officers look upon with disdain, dread, and a reluctance to accept. It doesn't have to be that way. Report writing is an acquired skill that can be mastered in a relatively short period of time. By following some simple guidelines, one can become proficient in the mastery of the complexity of operating in a law enforcement environment that is characterized by elusive solutions to very complex and challenging problems. Report writing is a skill that will improve with practice and experience. You don't have to reinvent the wheel to acquire these skills but you do need basic English language writing proficiency and an ability to put actions into words. Your task is to develop a writing style that is comfortable to you and complies with agency guidelines.

The first officer on the crime scene knows the specific elements of that incident (environment) more thoroughly than anyone else will ever comprehend. The officer has immersed himself or herself into a situation that requires the utmost skill and professionalism to bring some type of order and direction for the impending investigation. The officer has arrived on the scene, taken control of the incident, and developed some type of course of action to begin to resolve the situation. As the first officer on the scene, your response to the incident is not finished until a complete and thorough case report has been written and submitted for filing. The police case report will be the focal point and the central repository of the criminal investigation and eventual prosecution. *It may be easy to arrest somebody, but when you do, you need to have a case that you can prove in court.*

THE CASE REPORT

The case report is critical in capturing every significant detail of the incident. The case report is an investigative tool utilized to find perpetrators and begin to bring some type of closure to a criminal incident. It is a legal document which can be subpoenaed into court; your case report is a piece of evidence. You must be able to defend in court every word written about the incident. You will refer to this document when the case comes to court. Report writing is the major form of communication within a law enforcement agency.

Picture yourself on the witness stand testifying in court and having to justify everything contained in your case report. Make no mistake, this is a challenging and hostile environment. Defense attorneys are well trained in picking apart weak case reports. Additionally, it may be a year or longer before the case ever gets presented in court. There is no way you will be able to recount the events of the case without a well written case report.

Best Practices: When preparing your case report, always be thinking about your future courtroom testimony.

The case report is where the details of the incident are professionally documented and maintained. As first responder, you were the only person to really understand the dynamics and complexity of the incident. You arrived on the crime scene, observed the incident, experienced the emotions of the participants, and took appropriate action to begin to resolve the incident. Your case report will be the focal point of the investigation of the incident. Whatever is contained in the report should be an accurate reflection of what happened during the incident. Capturing essential information in an understandable fashion is essential to the success of the investigation.

IMPORTANCE OF THE CASE REPORT

Your case report is a permanent record of everything that transpired in a criminal incident. A good case report captures and maintains significant details of a specific incident. The case report enables others who were not at the crime scene to understand the specific facts that occurred at the scene. You typically have only one chance to detail the crime scene into a comprehensive and thorough case report. Remember, if it isn't written, it doesn't exist.

WHO MIGHT EXAMINE YOUR CASE REPORT?

Your case report is a permanent record and you never know who might be examining it. Your writing style should be driven by who reads your report and why. Law enforcement officials interact with different types or groups of individuals every day, and effective communication with these groups is essential. You may have a wide and varied audience and your writing style should reflect this. Below is a partial list of the persons and reasons why someone would examine your case report.

- Your initial supervisor will thoroughly scrutinize the report for accuracy and completeness. This initial supervisor is probably the same individual who will do your performance evaluations. Thus, professionalism in preparing your report will contribute to good performance reports. Your performance ratings will be highly influenced by the quality of your case reports. The future success of your law enforcement career may be measured by the caliber and professionalism of those reports.
- If the report entails a major case, it may be reviewed by the chain of command, which may include command staff and other supervisory personnel. Additionally, this will help you to recall the specifics of the case when testifying in court at a future date, which could be months or years after the incident.
- Follow-up investigators might be utilizing your initial case report if the case requires additional investigation. A well written report will ensure a smooth transition of critical information that will be transferred to these investigators who probably have little or no information of the specifics of the incident without your case report.
- Any officer of the court may be reviewing this case report. This includes the judge, the district attorney, defense counsel, and possibly jurors. Remember, your case report is a legal document and a piece of evidence.
- The media. Parts of your case report may be released to members of the media by the public information officers of your agency.

WHEN COMPOSING YOUR CASE REPORT

- Be thinking about how you would describe all of the activities that took place.
- What are the elements of the crime that will help prove your case in court?
- Is it written in proper English? Poor word choice affects the meaning and understanding of the case report.
- Keep it simple. Do not use a complicated or sophisticated word when a simple one will work.
- Were you careful of grammar and punctuation? Errors here could change the meaning of your case report.
- Ask the question, "How do you know?"

HOW DO YOU KNOW?

When responding to the incident, you will probably be interviewing the reporting party, victims, witnesses, and perhaps suspects. A crime scene is anything but a controlled environment; it is typically chaotic and confusing. You have just responded to a call for service and will undoubtedly meet victims and witnesses on one of the worst days of their lives. Collecting essential and reliable information is extremely important. Asking the right questions and verifying the information is critical and will contribute to the closure of the case. You want to determine how reliable all information you obtain at the crime scene is before you prepare your case report. When you are unsure of a victim/witness's information, ask the follow-up question "How do you know?"

Example

A practical example might help clarify this statement. Let's examine hypothetical statements from two victims who gave a statement regarding a vehicle observed leaving the scene of a burglary case.

Victim one: "I saw the burglar drive away in a 1995 blue Chevy Impala."

Ask the question, **"How did you know** it was a 1995 blue Chevy Impala?"

Victim one: "I used to own a 1995 Chevy Impala and it looks identical to the one I owned."

Victim two: "I saw the burglar drive away in a 1995 blue Chevy Impala."

Ask the question, **"How did you know** it was a 1995 blue Chevy Impala?"

Victim two: "I don't know, it looks like it could be a Chevy or Ford, I guessed on the year and model of the car but I think it was either a Chevy or Ford."

In the statement of victim one, you know you can confidently put out an all-points bulletin over the dispatch radio for a 1995 blue Chevy Impala vehicle. Additionally, if the perpetrator is apprehended, you have pretty reliable vehicle identification by a reliable witness when the case comes to court.

In the statement by victim two, your radio dispatch will probably be describing either a mid-nineties blue Chevy or Ford sedan. This victim's observation of the suspect's vehicle will be weaker testimony when the case comes to court. By simply asking "How do you know?" this statement will help to clarify the veracity and weight in court of the victim's statement. You don't want a defense attorney to be asking the "How do you know?" questions in court that might challenge the credibility of your witness. It is best to have the answers to these types of questions in advance and share them with the prosecutorial staff in advance of courtroom testimony.

AGENCY REQUIREMENTS

The information on case report writing in this textbook is intended as a general guideline for producing well-written documents that can be tailored to apply to all department requirements. Your agency policy and procedure manual or standard operation procedures will dictate specifics on style and other nuances of the case report. Each agency has a specific format and style, which will be contained in their case reports. All agencies have individual requirements. There is no single comprehensive system of report writing that is universally accepted. This textbook contains the many common characteristics and writing techniques that can be tailored to fit the requirement of any law enforcement agency.

For example, some agencies' policy and procedure manuals may require the use of all upper-case lettering in lieu of both upper- and lower-case lettering. Some agencies require the use of military time, whereas others require the use of a.m. and p.m. Just about every agency's face sheet (or cover sheet) is different, yet usually contains some common elements. These common elements include most of the essential times, locations, and demographics of involved individuals. It doesn't matter. This textbook focuses on the common elements of writing a good case report. These specific elements can be transferred to any style and format that your agency may require.

BASIC PRINCIPLES OF THE ENGLISH LANGUAGE

It is assumed that you have a basic competency in writing the English language. This textbook is not intended to do extensive remedial English grammar and punctuation exercises. This textbook is intended to enhance your understanding and communication of basic English writing skills with some simple and reliable exercises. Remember that good case report writing is an acquired skill that can be learned and improved with some basic knowledge and practice.

STYLE

The case report should be written as a free-flowing type of document that reads like a short story. It should be designed to use complete, simple sentences and paragraphs. The wording should be simple and easy to understand. Eliminate needless words. There should be no headings, Roman numerals, labels, or other items that break up the continuous flow of information. Write the case report to inform and communicate information, not to impress the reader with abstract, ambiguous, and confusing wording.

KEEP IT SIMPLE!

The basic goal of any well-written case report is to compress all of the critical events of a crime scene into a concise yet thorough document. Use plain and understandable English that will effectively communicate what occurred to any audience who may read the report. Use the shortest words possible as they are eaiser to spell and comprehend. Avoid using abstract words and contractions. This document should contain information utilizing the most efficient amount of words while not compromising critical details of the crime. Your writing style should be the closest to the way that people talk to each other. Think of the words that you utilize in everyday conversation. Keep it simple!

ABSTRACT WORDING

Abstract wording should be avoided in preparing your case report. Your challenge in writing a good case report is to put into words what you have observed. Take the time to explain abstract words such as uncooperative, intoxicated, depressed, and so on. This will help clarify to the reader exactly what you observed.

Example

Don't simply state that "The suspect was **uncooperative and belligerent**." Explain what you mean by the word uncooperative. A better way of detailing the encounter might be: "Upon arrival, the suspect clenched his fist, took a fighting stance, and stated 'I'm not going to jail.' The suspect then picked up a baseball bat and said, 'Come and get me!'"

FIRST PERSON SINGULAR

Unless agency requirements dictate something else, it is best to use the first person singular style of writing in case reports. Use the word "I" instead of "this officer" or "he/she." The first person singular style utilizes simple language as if you are speaking to someone. This makes it very clear to the reader who is doing what. Your agency will dictate what style of writing is required in the case report. If given the choice, use the first person singular style.

Example

"I arrived on the scene at 3 p.m. and I observed who appeared to be the victim, Mr. John Smith, standing on the front porch of the residence."

PAST TENSE

Use the past tense when writing case reports. This makes common sense as the incident did occur prior to the completion of the case report. Your case report is recounting events that have already transpired and thus the past tense is the appropriate writing style to utilize. Always be cognizant that you are recording events that have already occurred. Skipping tense from past to present should be avoided unless you are using quotes or statements of victims, witnesses, or suspects.

CHRONOLOGICAL ORDER

Your case report should always be written in chronological order. Always state what events happened first and then proceed on with the rest of the case report. Your case report should detail how the incident unfolded in sequential order.

A side benefit of placing things in chronological order is that you now know where to begin writing your report. Many authors struggle with where to start their writing. Putting things in chronological order eliminates this dilemma and gives you a great starting point and understandable flow for your report. Your case report will have a logical progression of how the events of the incident unfolded. The goal of chronological order is to give the reader an accurate overview of the incident in simple and understandable words. It should read like a book.

Beware that chronological order does not dictate that you write the exact time for every action you took during the incident. Listing the exact time of every event will assume all you were doing was recording times. The exact time only needs to be contained in the case report when you are emphasizing the most important details of the incident. For example, you would always want to document: when you were first dispatched to the incident, your arrival time, your departure time, when you administered first aid, when someone was transported to the hospital or jail, and so on.

PASSIVE VERSUS ACTIVE VOICE

Using the passive voice is often confusing and ambiguous to the reader. Avoid using the passive voice. For the sake of clarity and understanding, the active voice should be used in writing your case report. In the active voice, you always put the "who" in front of the "what." It is much easier to follow and you gain more information by putting the "who" first. The active voice normally requires fewer words, which contributes to the brevity of the report.

Putting things in the active voice is a fairly simple process:

- First, identify the action of the sentence.
- Next, identify who or what is performing the action.
- Finally, put who or what is performing the action in front of the action.

Example of the passive voice: (Avoid)

The knife was placed into evidence.

Example of active voice: (Use)

Sgt. Smith placed the knife into evidence.

By reading the first example, written in the passive voice, the reader cannot be sure who the individual was who placed the knife into evidence. The active voice eliminates confusion by making it clear who placed the knife into evidence. Using the active voice simplifies the case report and leaves no doubt *who* did *what*.

FACTUAL STATEMENTS

You are the "fact finder" with regard to the criminal incident. You are recording the facts of the case, what you observed, what actions you took, and documenting statements and evidence found at the crime scene. Be objective! Your case report will include factual statements. Use your five senses, when appropriate, in composing your case report:

- what you observed
- what you heard
- what you stated
- what you smelled
- what you touched

USE OF NAMES

If possible, don't refer to individuals as "suspects" or "victims." Use their names and titles (if you know them). Using the names of the involved individuals makes it very clear who is doing what. Using surnames such as "Mr." and "Ms/Mrs." when appropriate is the preferred method of listing names. Beware, though, that some agencies delete the surname, choosing to simply use the last name of the individual. Read the example below to understand why using names is important.

Example: (Bad)

I interviewed suspect #1, who stated he did not bring the gun. Suspect #1 stated that suspect #2 had brought the gun to the pawn shop. Suspect #1 stated that victim #1 contributed to the incident by not opening the cash register. That is when victim #2 came around the corner of the pawn shop and hit suspect #2 on the head with a glass bowl. Suspect #2 then shot victim #2.

Example: (Good)

I interviewed the suspect, Mr. John Black, who stated that he did not bring the gun to the pawn shop. Mr. Black stated that the second suspect, Mr. Michael Jones, had brought the gun into the pawn shop. Mr. Jones stated that Mr. Tom Dugan, the pawn shop manager, contributed to the incident by not opening the cash register. That is when Mr. Joe Jersey, assistant pawn shop manager, came around the corner of the pawn shop and hit Mr. Jones on the head with a glass bowl. Mr. Jones then shot Mr. Jersey.

Thus, by this example, we can see that anyone who picks up the completed case report can clearly visualize what occurred and understand who the participants were. Once you have identified the players (for example, suspect #1, Mr. John Black), don't repeat the words "suspect" or "victim." Continue to reference him throughout the case report as simply Mr. Black. Normally when introducing the name of a victim, witness, or suspect you will list their full name initially and then simply use their last name prefaced by either Mr. or Ms. In using their proper names, it makes the report less wordy, easier to understand, and displays neutrality and professionalism.

USE OF QUOTES

The use of quotes is something that you want to use sparingly, but quotes are often important to include in your case report. You want to capture the emotions and the drama of the incident, and often the use of quotes is an excellent way to document these circumstances. It is best to use quotes in the following circumstances:

- Use quotes when the suspect's statement is incriminating, embarrassing, or you would lose the impact of the statement without the use of quotes.
- Use quotes when the suspect, victim, or witness makes a statement that results in a refusal, denial, consent, waiver, or confession.
- Use quotes to avoid using subjective statements like the suspect used profanity, obscenity, or other ambiguous terms. Use quotes to capture the suspect's exact words—although it may appear embarrassing, it paints a picture of the incident.
- Use quotes when using your own words would sound improper. For example, when questioning a child, and the child's response is "the man put his hand on my pee-pee."
- Use quotes when the statement itself constitutes a criminal offense.

RUN-ON SENTENCES

The run-on sentence is probably one of the most common errors in case report writing. A run-on sentence is a sentence that goes on too long without helping to clarify the events being described. The longer the sentence, the more trouble the reader will have understanding the meaning. Overlong sentences cause you to use too many words. Thus, the goal of brevity is sacrificed. Always put a period at the end of any complete thought. Edit your sentences down to the bare minimum. Use short sentences followed by a period. Although you may be tempted to use a comma or a dash, in most cases use a period.

POLICE JARGON

Law enforcement officers have some unique words and phrases that are appropriate to use during certain activities in their daily routines. Police jargon is basically a type of hybrid language used for a specific purpose for a specific audience. For example, while communicating with the dispatch center, they may utilize the "Ten Code" or other technical terms for the sake of brevity and efficiency.

An example of this use of police jargon could be something like this radio broadcast:

"10 Adam 2, on-scene, 10 Adam 2 requesting a BOLO, MVT, on a white Chevy Impala, northbound on Easy Street, occupied two times. Nothing further at this time."

This type of police jargon is proper in this circumstance. It is *not* appropriate in your case report. Always remember your audience when writing your case report—it is *not* solely for fellow law enforcement officers. Court officials, attorneys, and perhaps jurors will have access to your case report. Your case report will be read by individuals outside of your law enforcement agency who will not understand your agency's jargon and abbreviations. It is critical that a "civilian" audience can read and understand your case report. Again, keep it simple and understandable.

ABBREVIATIONS

Most law enforcement policy and procedure manuals discourage or even prohibit the use of abbreviations. As with the use of police jargon, not every reader will understand the meaning of the abbreviation. Spell out the entire word, which will aid in the understanding and comprehension of the sentence.

SIMPLE VOCABULARY

Keeping things simple is essential in any well-written case report. Trying to impress your reader with overcomplicated and sophisticated wording will confuse the reader. Keep things simple to avoid frustrating the reader's comprehension of what you are intending to communicate. Remember that many readers (jurors, for example) may not have even a high school education. Don't forget your total audience when composing your report. Simple wording and sentences are easy to understand and are the best way to convey the facts of the investigation. The objective of case report writing is to communicate information. Communicate this information as clearly and precisely as possible.

Example: (Bad)

The situation was exasperated by the fact that Mr. Lasher was using ambiguous phrases and elusive terminology. I suggested that he should take a moment and compose his equilibrium and then continue with the interview.

Example: (Good)

Initially, Mr. Lasher was unable to communicate effectively. I suggested he take a minute and then speak in clear and simple words.

OBJECTIVE VERSUS SUBJECTIVE WORDS

As the investigator of a criminal case, you are a "fact finder," and as such you are searching for the truth. For the most part, objective wording is essential in writing a good case report. Your role is to document the facts of the case. Subjective wording should rarely be contained in a case report. Stay away from value judgments and give brief factual details instead. Perhaps this will become clearer with the following example, which details events that allegedly transpired in a homicide investigation.

Example—Subjective wording: (Bad)

Mr. Jones had a motive to kill his wife, as he had taken out a $500,000.00 life insurance policy from the Acme Insurance Corporation on her two weeks prior to her murder.

Example—Objective wording: (Good)

I discovered that Mr. Jones had taken out a $500,000 insurance policy from the Acme Insurance Corporation on his wife two weeks prior to her murder.

In the first example, you are inferring that Mr. Jones killed his wife for the money. In the second example, you are just stating the fact that Mr. Jones had taken out a life insurance policy on his wife recently. Remember, you are a fact finder searching for the truth. Let the jury decide if this fact (the $500,000 life insurance policy) has any bearing on the criminal case.

Although it must be used sparingly, there is a proper time to use subjective wording. For example, suppose you encountered a robbery suspect who pointed his revolver at you and you had to use force. Then subjective language might be appropriate. Your case report may contain the following verbiage:

Appropriate use of subjective wording. I observed Mr. Jones hiding behind the teller's counter of the bank. *Fearing for my safety and the safety of others*, I drew my service sidearm and ordered Mr. Jones to drop the gun.

Objectivity in your case report is essential, but there may be rare instances where you want to relate your emotions. In the example above, you are conveying an emotion (fear for officer/civilian safety) that documents why you had to take an appropriate course of action. Emotions are normally not something that applies in case reports, but in this instance it is proper. It illustrates to the reader the severity of the situation and documents why you had to use the necessary force: for the protection of lives.

STATING CONCLUSIONS OR USING DEDUCTIVE LOGIC

What you observe is a fact; a conclusion or deduction based on an observation is a guess, opinion, or an assumption. Take the time to describe what the suspect was doing.

Example: (Bad)

I saw the suspect trying to break into the house.

Example: (Good)

I observed the suspect with a flat-nosed screwdriver wedged between the front door lock and the door frame. I next observed the suspect use a prying motion on the door lock, which appeared to force the door open.

"IT SHOULD BE NOTED"

Avoid using the phrase "It should be noted." Everything in your case report should be noted.

PROOFREADING

It is always best to compose your case report as soon after the incident as possible. This may not always be possible if you are backed up with other calls for service that must be handled. If at all possible, though, write your case report the same day that the incident occurred. Many agencies' policy and procedure manuals require that the case report be completed prior to finishing your shift. Start to prepare the case report as early as possible. This is advantageous because the critical events are still fresh in your mind. Organize your writing and take the time necessary to complete an understandable and professional product.

Create good proofreading techniques. Proofreading your case report is essential. Re-read your case report and revise it as necessary. You might find it best to print out the completed report rather than trying to proofread the case report from a computer screen. Take the time to review your wording and grammar. Does your report accurately paint a picture of the incident? It may be best to proofread the report once and then take a break and re-read the case report later. Using software like spell-check is also helpful. It also might help to review previous case reports that you had submitted of similar incidents for ideas. Read over your case report several times. You will be surprised at the mistakes you will catch doing this exercise.

As with any other skill you are attempting to master, practice will lead to improvement. The more case reports you complete, the more your skills and professionalism will improve. Additionally, you can really improve your technique by simply doing more reading. It doesn't matter if you read fiction novels, biographies, or the newspaper—just do more reading. Recreational reading contributes to your understanding of sentence and paragraph structure and composition. It will improve your knowledge of basic grammar skills. The more you read, the better you'll become at preparing case reports.

When beginning your law enforcement career, it is good to get the advice of a fellow officer on the quality of your early case reports. Select an experienced officer from the agency that is known for their expertise in preparing good case reports. Don't simply ask the officer,

"What do you think?" Ask an experienced officer specific, open-ended questions that require some feedback. For example:

- Please note any wording that you found confusing or vague.
- What words, sentences, or phrases are improper or have grammatical errors?
- Where should I edit down the report?
- Did I incorporate every element of the crime and use of force correctly?
- Would you feel confident testifying in court on the contents of this report?
- What would you change?

In getting feedback from a fellow law enforcement officer, it is best to not ask several other officers from the agency for their opinions. It may appear to be seen as a sign of disrespect or perhaps that you don't value the first officer's opinion. Pick the best person first and you will avoid starting off on the wrong foot.

ETHICAL CONSIDERATIONS

Always remember that you are not the judge and jury. You are the fact finder. Your mission is not to prove a suspect's guilt, but to gather the facts and let the judicial system determine the outcome. You must report all facts of the case, not just those that point in one direction. Your ethical directive is to always be fair, objective, and honest. If you have a suspect in a particular incident and you discover evidence favorable to helping the suspect, list it in the case report. Your moral compass should guide you through what is right and wrong in any investigation. You are a rule follower, and you must set aside your personal feelings and stay professional.

THE *RIGHT* WAY TO *WRITE*

Professional law enforcement writing is a very specific form of writing. You are writing for several different audiences: your peers, supervisors, attorneys, juries, judges, and others. The writing style needs to be focused on all of these potential readers. Your report will be considered a legal document that can be closely scrutinized in the judicial process. This judicial process includes the judge, jury, and attorneys. Members of the jury may not have graduated high school. Judges and attorneys obviously will have advanced degrees. Your writing style challenge is to convey critical information that will be understandable to these varying participants in the criminal justice process.

The best writing approach is to keep things simple. Simple and complete sentences are the best way to ensure all of the various readers can understand what information you are trying to convey. The purpose of your report is to convey information, not to impress the reader with your mastery of sophisticated and possibly ambiguous vocabulary. Remember to stay focused on the task at hand, which is to document essential information that is simple and understandable to the myriad of educational levels of potential readers.

The writing style needs to place emphasis on objectivity and professionalism. You are a fact finder reporting on all of the important aspects of the incident. This style of writing has no place for speculation or opinion. Keep your personal theories out of the report and stick to the facts of the case. Your report will bridge the gap between the investigation and the prosecution of suspects. The focus, philosophy, and approach to good report writing should be simple sentences that are grammatically correct and contain only factual information.

TIPS FOR REPORTS, THE ENGLISH LANGUAGE, AND POLICE JARGON

Some Frequent Errors in Case Report Writing. The following is a compilation of some of the most common mistakes in preparing a case report. Be sure and keep these shortcomings in mind when you proofread your case report.

- Not establishing proper jurisdiction. As mentioned previously, your case report is a legal document and the exact location of the incident must be included in the case report.
- Leaving out significant details
  - Review your state statutes on what are the "legal" elements of a crime and be sure to include each legal element of the crime in your case report.
  - Leaving out significant details can be minimized by taking good notes.

- Failure to write clearly
  - Keep things clear, concise, and understandable.
  - Remember your audience may not have a college education.
  - Keep it simple.

- Using improper English
  - Use simple sentences and paragraphs and make sure your case report is grammatically correct.
  - Sentence and paragraph structure should be simple and complete.
  - Beware of punctuation errors.
  - The "spell check" function of your computer system will assist you in ensuring words are spelled correctly in your case report.

- Not maintaining your objectivity
  - You are a fact finder and as such you should maintain objectivity (with a few rare exceptions).
  - Stick to the facts.
  - Opinions have no place in your case report.
  - Don't guess or make deductions.

- Jumping tense
  - Stick to the past tense.
  - Although sometimes the present tense is appropriate—when including statements of victims, witnesses, or suspects, for example—try to keep things in the past tense as much as possible.
  - Keeping things in the past tense will make the case report easy to follow and understand.

- Chronological order
  - Your case report should read like a book. List things as they have occurred from the time of your arrival on the crime scene until the time of your departure.

SUMMARY

Most law enforcement officials view report writing as the bane of their existence, which keeps them from doing the *real work of policing*. This assumption is wrong. The quicker you assume a professional approach to case reports and hone your writing skills, the more your value as a competent law enforcement officer will improve. Multiple errors in writing and grammar will cause you to lose credibility and the confidence of your supervisors.

The task of report writing is to organize the facts of the case in a logical and understandable fashion. This is accomplished by using correct grammar and composing simple sentences and paragraphs to write an accurate and complete narrative.

Composing the narrative portion of a report is probably the most challenging part of bringing a successful investigation to resolution. Develop a pattern of writing in a methodical and orderly manner. Your goal is to document the incident from the starting point to the conclusion of your involvement in the case. As with anything else that occurs in life, effective report writing is accomplished by practice and a sincere effort toward professionalism. Practice makes perfect and your skills will improve with experience.

When writing your case report, you must be aware of your limitations. The case report should be brief without sacrificing critical elements. The case report must also be objective and complete. The old adage from the TV show "Dragnet" applies when completing your case report. On the show, detective Joe Friday often said, " Just the facts." Your goal is to provide a comprehensive case report that contains specific details of the case, is well written, and easy to understand. Know your audience, which could range from highly educated attorneys to common jurors. Keep it simple and understandable. Use simple sentence and paragraph structure. The report should be an accurate reflection of what happened in the incident. It should read like you are telling a story.

EXERCISES

The goal of these exercises is to get an idea of your writing style and competency with the English language.

1. Compose a narrative report detailing a specific event that occurred to you during any previous day of the week. Use the narrative style of report writing that is presented in this first chapter. Do not try to create a face sheet. It will probably help the accuracy of the report if you do some note-taking. Limit this narrative to two typed pages in length.

or

2. Write a short chronological story on your life beginning with your early childhood memories through the present day. Remember to utilize the concepts and style outlined in this chapter.

or

3. In this chapter you learned what *not* to do when completing a report. The art of being a good writer involves the ability to recognize bad writing. In this next exercise, Officer E. Literate completed a supplement report for a robbery that had occurred. Officer Smith has completed the Face Sheet, so Officer E. Literate was required to complete a supplement report explaining his actions and involvement in the robbery case. The supplement contains many errors and it is up to you to identify at least fifteen (15) mistakes.

List the mistakes here.

1. _____
2. _____
3. _____
4. _____
5. _____
6. _____
7. _____
8. _____
9. _____
10. _____
11. _____
12. _____
13. _____
14 _____
15. _____

Lynn City Police Department Continuation/Supplement		Case Number 15-32456			
Offense Title Criminal Mischief		City/State Statute Number 18-4-501			Date of this Report 01/17/2015

Codes RP = Reporting Party AV = Additional Victim W = Witness LO = Law Enforcement Officer A = Arrestee S = Suspect O = Other

Code	Last, First, Middle	Date of Birth	Age	Sex	Race	Occupation
A	Jordan, Richard, William	01/17/2000	15	M	H	Waiter

Residential Address	City	State	Zip Code	Home Phone	Other Phone
4320 North Weber St.	Mersonville	KS	88088	913-555-0179	913-555-0186

Clothing Description	Alias	Summons Number
Blue Jeans, White t-shirt, and white running shoes		1908456

Identifying Marks/Scars/Tattoos	Height	Weight	Build	Hair	Eyes
	6'03"	325	L	BRO	BRO

Elements/Narrative

Officer Statement:

On 01-17-2015 at approximately 1700 I, Officer E. Literate 1789P, and Officer Smith 1980P were dispatched to 4330 North Weber in reference to a criminal mischief that involved a rock that had been thrown threw a window of the residence.

Upon arrival I an Officer Smith made contact with the victim, Mr. Henry Sawyer who informed us that he was sitting in his recliner in the living room at approximately 1645 on 01-17-2015 when a rock came threw his front window that faces North Weber St.

Mr. Sawyer stated that when he looked out the window he observed Richard Jordan, who lives a few houses away, lie down on the grass next too the sidewalk with a slingshot in his hand. Mr. Sawyer said that when Mr. Jordan realized that he was caught an he took off running toward his home because he knew he could not hanged around.

Denise Jordan, Richard Jordan's mother, arrived as we were speaking to Mr. Sawyer and she wanted to know what had happened. I explained to her that Mr. Sawyer believed that her son had used a slingshot to brake his front window with a rock and that Mrs. Sawyer had observed her son with the slingshot in front of his home after it had occurred.

Mrs. Jordan stated that her son had in fact broken the window and that he came home an told her about it a few minutes ago and that he had told her that it was an accident. Mrs. Jordan offered to pay for the damage an asked Mr. Sawyer not to press charges against her son.

Mr. Sawyer told Mr. Jordan that he was going to have her son arrested based on the principal of the situation an that he did not believe it was an accident to.

Mr. Jordan told Mr. Sawyer that she would contact there family attorney an then stated to Mr. Sawyer "Your wrong for doing this" an than she turned and walked away.

Officer Smith competed the original report an served and released Richard Jordan for Criminal Mischief under $500.

See Officer Smith's report for more information.

Officer Name/Employee Number	Supervisor Name/Employee Number	Page 1 of 1
E. Literate 1789P	J. Thomas 3089P	

2

THE ART OF
NOTE-TAKING

LEARNING OBJECTIVES

- Understand how to recall your actions and compile them into an accurate and comprehensive case report.

- Understand the guidelines to the process of note-taking, creating an outline, and then transferring that information into a professional case report.

- Understand the importance of creating a workable format and style of note-taking that will assist you in completing a clear and accurate report.

- Apply your knowledge to practical examples of note-taking by successfully completing the chapter exercises.

INTRODUCTION

Note-taking is a skill that must be mastered by report writers working in the field of criminal justice. The information you collect in your notes will be the foundation of your completed written report. The skills an individual needs to be a good note taker can be learned. Individuals who learn the basics of note-taking from this chapter can eventually expand on their note-taking skills by incorporating a style that is uniquely their own.

THE PROCESS OF NOTE-TAKING

Think of note-taking as a type of shorthand to prompt your memory of what actions you have taken, as well as what has been observed and stated. Your mind works faster than your ability to document a word-for-word recounting of a specific incident. Additionally, you don't have the time to accomplish this detailed and labor intensive task. The goal of note-taking is to record key phrases or words that will trigger your memory, resulting in an accurate, factual, and complete case report.

OFFICER SAFETY ISSUES WHEN TAKING NOTES

Note-taking should never be attempted until the crime scene is rendered safe. Once you place a tablet in one hand and a pencil or pen in the other you are placing yourself in a vulnerable position. Always be conscious of the scene and aware of your surroundings. Be careful to locate yourself in a safe and defensible position. Take the time to place victims, witnesses, and especially suspects where they are at a strategic disadvantage. Remember that a crime scene, no matter how safe it appears, can turn into a volatile situation in a matter of seconds. Remember your officer survival skills at all times. Be safe!

STEP-BY-STEP APPROACH TO NOTE-TAKING

The basic first step in note-taking is documenting initial findings in a notebook. Thus, the first decision to be made is what type of notebook is best suited for this specific incident. There is no one-size-fits-all answer to the question of what type of notebook to utilize. Each type has specific advantages, disadvantages, and applications. A brief summary of these types of notebook tablets follows. It is recommended that every officer have access to each of these types of tablets when responding to an incident.

Types of Note-Taking Tablets

- **Pocket Type:** This can best be described as a small pocket-sized tablet that conveniently fits into the officer's top pocket. They typically measure three by five inches. Sometimes there is a need to write down only a few notes concerning a pressing issue or incident. The pocket type of note pad is easily accessible and great for jotting down short suspect or vehicle descriptions that call for an immediate dispatch transmission. Due to the small size of the pages, the pocket type of note pad is not practical for extensive interviews or observations.

- **Steno Pad:** These tablets are larger than the pocket type of note pad but smaller than a legal pad. They typically measure six inches by nine inches. These types of note pads are great to use when interviewing victims, witnesses, or suspects at a secure crime scene, when there is no longer a sense of urgency, and the officer needs to record a detailed outline of the incident. Like the pocket type of notebook, the steno pad is a bound notebook. The pages are not removable; if you eventually have to testify in court, and you bring your notebook, the whole notebook must be taken and could possibly be subpoenaed into evidence.

- **Preprinted Note Sheets:** These sheets are preprinted sheets of paper that officers use in note-taking. The many forms that you will complete as a law enforcement official have many of the same blocks that need to be filled in with information. These preprinted note sheets can be useful and speed up the collection of vital information. These types of notes are not really suited for in-depth investigations but rather for misdemeanors and smaller class felonies.

- **Legal Pad:** These types of note pads are the largest sized notepads that you will probably use. They provide much more writing space for more detailed note-taking. Legal pads are typically the note pad of choice for officers interviewing victims, witnesses, or suspects at a law enforcement office or in an interview room. These types of note pads are also good when having a victim, witness, or suspect write out their own statement. A legal pad may be difficult to hold and is thus best suited for use when a desk or table is available.

- **Loose-Leaf Notebook:** Loose-leaf notebooks are the preferred tool to use for major cases where the body of work requires an extensive narrative report and numerous supplemental and follow-up items. Major criminal cases may require the use of several notebooks, A loose-leaf notebook is not recommended for field notes (notes taken at a crime scene) for several reasons. While at the crime scene, the ease and the utility of note-taking is a must. A loose-leaf notebook is cumbersome, intimidating, and presents storage problems. Additionally, pages can be easily removed, damaged, or lost which could expose you to accusations of tampering or negligence. If your department policy and procedure manual requires the use of a loose-leaf notebook, ensure that the pages are numbered consecutively to guard against any allegations of missing or deleted documentation.

TAKING NOTES

Quite simply, note-taking helps document your actions and observations when responding to a call for service as a law enforcement officer. What you are attempting to accomplish is recording the names, locations, and key events of the incident at a time when these events are fresh in your mind. This general guideline is designed to develop a simple and practical method to record and process crime scene notes. These are guidelines that will become engrained in your report writing techniques with practice.

START AT THE BEGINNING

First and foremost, if your agency requires that you keep your notes, on the first page of the notebook, list your name and contact information just in case the notebook is lost or misplaced. Some law enforcement professionals tape their department business card onto the inside cover of the notebook specifically for that reason.

It is recommended that you write only on one side of the page in any notebook. This helps to prevent "bleeding" or smearing of the ink. It is also advisable to have some 3" x 5" index cards (or scrap paper) in your notebooks in case you have to give information to subjects while at the crime scene. These index cards eliminate tearing out pages of your notebook, which could raise unnecessary questions when bringing your notebook to court. You always want to minimize any allegations of tampering or withholding information in any criminal proceeding. Keep the notebook in its original condition with no pages missing.

Your field notes can be used as legal documents. It is important to remember that it is essential that all of the information contained in your notes is accurate. This means that names are spelled correctly, addresses and phone numbers are current, and all statements accurately document the facts of the case. Also, remember that keeping things in chronological order will help simplify the process.

Now let's break things down into a useable guideline for field notes on preprinted note sheets:

Case #:				Title:		
Dispatch:		Arrival:				Cleared:
Date:		Time:		Location:		
Suspect/Victim/Witness/Other:						
Name:						
DOB:	Race:	HGT:	WGT:		Hair:	Eyes:
POB:		Sex:	Male		Female	
Clothing Description:						
Address:		City:			State:	Zip Code:
Contact Numbers: Home:					Cell:	Wk:
Employer:			Occupation:			
Business Address:		City:			State:	Zip Code:
Business Phone:			Business Victim: Yes	No		

The information listed above can be found on most forms that need to be completed by law enforcement officials during an investigation. Experience has taught that during investigations a more accurate case report resulted when an officer completed this sheet and wrote out his or her notes on the bottom portion of the page during the interview process.

Best Practices: Collect all the information necessary for an accurate report. It eliminates the need to contact someone again because you forgot to collect the information the first time.

Forgetting to collect important information during your investigation can create more work for you, another officer, or a detective who is assigned to follow up on the original investigation. Forgetting to collect information may also lead victims, or others, to think that you do not care about the circumstances of their case.

BEGIN TO LIST EVENTS/ELEMENTS OF THE CASE

The next step is to document the key elements of the case. Start by using a word or words that describe each point that you want to document later into your case report. The key point here is to utilize "buzzwords" or phrases that will jog your memory. The facts do not necessarily have to be in the order that your report will be written. Placing these facts into chronological order will occur later in the process. Your goal is to create an outline that you can organize and compile into a comprehensive, chronological case report at a later time.

For example: Following are the notes of a simple assault that occurred at a shopping mall.

Case #:   **14-08362**   Title: **3 Assault**

Dispatch: **1540**   Arrival:**1550**   Cleared: **1630**

Date: **10-01-2014**   Time: **Approx. 1530**   Location: **4220 Lincoln Ave. (Mall)**

~~Suspect~~/Victim/~~Witness/Other~~:

Name: **Nathan Robert Jackson**

DOB: **07-26-70**   Race: **W**   HGT: **6'01"**   WGT: **215**   Hair: **BRO**   Eyes: **BRO**

POB: **N/A**   Sex: Male   Female

Clothing Description:

Address: **1192 Willow Rd.**   City: **Mersonville**   State: **TX**   Zip Code: **88088**

Contact Numbers: Home: **972-555-0189**   Cell: **972-555-0178**   WK: **972-555-0172**

Employer: **Drakes Brakes**   Occupation: **Mechanic**

Business Address: **3090 Winter Rd.**   City: **Mersonville**   State: **TX**   Zip Code: **88088**

Business Phone: Business Victim: Yes   No

Circumstances: The following information would be on the bottom or reverse side of the previous sheet.

At approx: 1530 Jackson @ mall shopping obsv. fight start between 2 people

#1 = Susp. H M 5'08" – 5'10" /BRO hair/ 165-180/ BLU jeans/ RED sweat shirt hoody/ UNK shoes/ 16-17 YOA

#2 – H M BRO hair/ BRO pants/ WHT t-shirt/ 5'08"- 5'09" / UNK shoes / also 16-17 YOA

Jackson attempted 2 stop fight/ susp. turned & looked @ Jackson and w/out warning with a closed R fist punched him on the L side of his face and then ran away toward S-ENT. & EXIT of mall.

#2 male also ran away toward N-ENT. & EXIT of mall.

Both males also had UNK # of friends who also left (No Descrip)

Mall Sec. ARR. Short time later but all parties GOA

Jackson Pain but no severe injury No video/ No photos/ No evid./no wit.

This case can be recorded in another way during the interview process with the victim by using a 5.5" x 3.87" notebook.

The notes in Figure 2.1 have all the same information that the preprinted sheet has but it is not as neat due to the small size of the notepad.

The notes in Figure 2.2 involve the crime of graffiti, but there are many things left open to question, and a defense attorney may ask later if an arrest is made.

1. Why is there a shopping list?
2. What do tickets to the fair have to do with the graffiti?

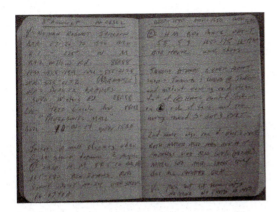

Figure 2.1   (*Photo by: Michael Merson*)

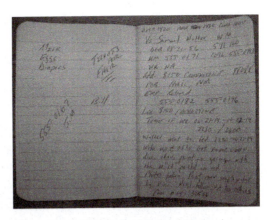

Figure 2.2   (*Photo by: Michael Merson*)

3. Who is Jim? Is he a suspect?
4. Who is Bill? Is that another suspect as well?
5. Are those Bill's phone numbers on the opposite page in the graffiti notes section?

Best Practices: Use your notepad for investigations *only*, especially if you are required by your agency to retain your case notes.

OTHER ISSUES IN NOTE-TAKING

USING A TAPE RECORDING DEVICE

Using a tape recorder can help capture essential details when documenting your actions and the facts of the case. Using a tape recorder permits you to gather a lot of information in a very short period of time. It can be used as you are jotting down field notes or independently, which makes it a versatile tool. It is also a good tool to archive victim, witness, and suspect statements. These recordings may become critical, especially when played before a jury, in capturing the emotion and intensity of crime scene participants, which may be lost in the written word.

There are several issues to consider when using a tape recorder. Never utilize a tape recorder as the sole source of information on a crime scene. The recorder can malfunction, resulting in the permanent loss of vital case information. Additionally, background noise and other types of audible interference can delete some, or all, of the recorded information. You really have no way of determining the quality of the recorded information until it is played back in its entirety. Remember to transcribe your notes exactly, as discrepancies between the recorded information and the written field notes, or case report, could pose issues in court.

USING DISPATCH INFORMATION

Using information from your agency's communication center (i.e., dispatch) can be a valuable tool in the note-taking process. First, it is always advisable to synchronize your wristwatch at the beginning of each shift to the clock utilized by dispatchers working in the communication center. For the sake of uniformity, all officers at the shift briefing should follow suit and synchronize their individual wristwatches. This simple action will help minimize discrepancies between your field notes, dispatch communications, and other officers on the scene. Bear in mind that individual timepieces may be a maximum of 59 seconds off, but this is much better than being off by two minutes or more because no one took the time to synchronize their watch prior to shift change.

Best Practices: Officer safety is paramount! Some officers may look at the wristwatch as an "outdated" method of tracking time. The cell phone and some other devices used to keep time may be popular or trendy but they could compromise officer safety. Officers should not be placing their hands into their pockets to retrieve cell phones or other items when interviewing or contacting people that are involved in possible criminal activity.

Most law enforcement agencies have a "computer-aided dispatch" system. This system affords the officer the luxury of obtaining a "hard copy" of all dispatch transmissions on a particular call-for-service. At the end of a shift, if not earlier, the officer can retrieve a printed copy of the critical times/activities, which can be included in the case report. Thus, there is no need to take field notes at critical times like: arrival, requesting wants and warrants, assuming command of the scene, giving vehicle/suspect information, and so on. Everything transmitted over the radio will be documented in the printed copy of the dispatch transmissions.

ABBREVIATIONS

While abbreviations are best avoided in writing the narrative case report, they can be useful in note-taking. It is important to always make sure you understand the meaning of the abbreviations when you are writing a report.

The notes taken by the officer during an investigation should be consistent in regard to the abbreviations, codes, and symbols used while taking notes. Below is a list of some commonly used abbreviations, codes, and symbols that officers have used.

ACC	Accident Number
ADD	Address
ADV	Advised
AKA	Also known as
ARR	Arrival Time
CRN	Case Report Number
DOA	Dead on Arrival
DOB	Date of Birth
DT	Dispatch Time
DL	Driver License or DL# Driver License Number
EYE	Eye Color
FEL	Felony
FST	Field Sobriety Test

FTA	Failure to Appear
GOA	Gone on Arrival
HAI	Hair Color
HGT	Height
ID	Identification
LIC	License Plate Number
LKA	Last Known Address
LOC	Location
MIS	Misdemeanor
MPH	Miles Per Hour
OBSV	Observed
ODT	Offense Date or DOF Date of Offense
OFF	Offense
OTM	Offense Time
POB	Place of Birth
POI	Point of Impact
POR	Point of Rest
RAC	Race
RO	Restraining Order or PRO Permanent Restraining Order
RP	Reporting Party
SSN	Social Security Number
SUS	Suspect or PERP Perpetrator
TRO	Temporary Restraining Order
VIC	Victim
VIN	Vehicle Identification Number
WIT	Witness
WGT	Weight

OTHER ABBREVIATIONS

Colors

RED	Red
BLU	Blue
WHT	White
BLK	Black
GRN	Green
YEL	Yellow
ORG	Orange
BRO	Brown
BLO	Blonde

Race and Sex

WF/WM	White Female/White Male
BF/BM	Black Female/Black Male
AF/AM	Asian Female/Asian Male
HF/HM	Hispanic Female/Hispanic Male

SYMBOLS:

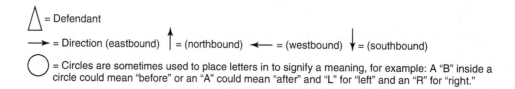

These examples are just a few of the many ways that a law enforcement professional can save time when collecting information for reports. Once again, most officers will develop their own style and format. Don't let all the examples listed confuse you and lead you to believe that you must use every one of them. The truth about shorthand is that many of you are currently using shorthand in one way or another. In the world of today, technology has afforded us with a new style of written communication.

The majority of people have used, or currently use, text messaging. This new style of written communication has reduced the English language from "laughing out loud" to simply LOL. Take the below text abbreviations for example.

OMG	Oh my gosh
BRB	Be right back
G2G	Got to go
TTYL	Talk to you later
IDK	I don't know
BBL	Be back later
BTW	By the way
IIRC	If I recall correctly

By using what you already know, you can develop your own style of shorthand to create a format that you are comfortable with while taking notes during an investigation. The notes taken by officers during an investigation can take many forms.

THE *RIGHT* WAY TO *WRITE*

Note-taking requires a different style of writing. Gathering information and then writing a comprehensive law enforcement report from your notes has its challenges. Time and logistics do not permit the law enforcement professional the luxury of sitting down in a comfortable and relaxed setting and completing the report while on the scene of the incident. Thus, documentation and recall play an important part in what style of writing is best for note-taking. The goal of note-taking is to document basic essential words or phrases that will later be translated into a comprehensive law enforcement report.

Good note-taking is characterized as a fast-paced endeavor which requires you to take notes quickly and efficiently. You need to capture as much information as possible; your focus should be on important facts and significant elements of the incident. Be a good listener and identify the most relevant information. Try to absorb the information you are given in the initial interview. This will minimize any confusion when you ask the individual to repeat the story. Write down specific words and key phrases that pertain to the incident, focus on the most important details and eliminate all filler words and insignificant conversations.

Write your notes legibly. Sloppy or illegibly written notes make it hard to read, or possibly useless, when you attempt to write up the incident. Make a mark in your notes when you start a new topic. New topics could include: interviewing a new witness, describing new evidence, or documenting the arrival of additional officers, supervisors, medical professionals, and so on. Next, document each subcategory of events as it unfolded. Use wide margins when note-taking. This prevents the note pad from becoming too crowded and allows you to add additional information if it is discovered, or when you review your notes.

Your writing style must be accurate and complete while also balancing your other duties at the crime scene. The law enforcement professional may be in an environment characterized by potentially volatile and dangerous individuals. This compounds the challenges of taking good notes. Find a writing style of note-taking that maximizes your recall yet also keeps the task at a manageable level. The key to an effective writing technique is to find a balance between accurate, reliable note-taking and officer safety.

Always take notes on the critical aspects of the incident. It is often permissible to use tape recording or video camera devices to support note-taking. Again, never rely on these recording devices solely for documentation purposes as they can experience technical problems, resulting in lost evidence. Additionally, many law enforcement agencies (including correctional agencies) are equipping their personnel with body cameras. These devices also can add depth to your note-taking strategy, but should never be used in lieu of written note-taking. Studies have shown although while recording devices are convenient, note takers retain facts and information better when they take notes by hand. As mentioned previously, it is always a good practice to take written statements from the involved individuals (e.g., victims, witnesses, suspects) if possible.

TIPS FOR NOTE-TAKING

- Leave some room in your notes, make sure your notes are not crowded.
- If you are in doubt about including something, put it in your notes; often these little, insignificant details help solve cases.
- Document key words and phrases expressed by a victim, witness, or suspect.
  - If the victim, witness, or suspect states something that amounts to a refusal, denial, consent, waiver, admission, or confession, document the exact words in your notes.

- Mechanical pencils are handy if the weather is too cold as ballpoint pens often freeze up.

- Summarize as soon as possible after the event, while your memory is fresh.
  - This gives you an opportunity to organize the information in some meaningful way.
  - It also allows you to use your short-term memory.
- Try to keep things in chronological order.
- Crime scene note-taking is an essential element in preparing your case report.
- Your notes are the first step in completing a professional case report.
- It is essential to organize your actions and the facts of a case into a logical and comprehensive outline utilizing a method which is understandable and retrievable at a later time.
- You need to break down the information in your field notes into logical categories of manageable size.
  - Don't forget the main purpose of the report.
  - Consider general topics then subdivide them into usable groupings.
- Use clear and concise words whenever possible, standard abbreviations are permissible.
- Use good penmanship, notes should be readable and able to be understood by other readers.
- Leave personal information of yours out of any notebook—it can be subpoenaed.
- Number the pages of the note book.
- Use some type of organizational method, preferably an outline, to help prepare your case report.
- Your notebook is a permanent record, not just a tool to refresh your memory.

SUMMARY

The nature of law enforcement work does not facilitate an environment where an officer can respond to a call for service, take whatever action is required to resolve the call, and then sit down, and at a leisurely pace write a case report. Calls for service are frequently backed up and the officer finds himself running from call to call. Often, report writing is delayed until the end of the shift, or even delayed until the next day.

Most law enforcement agencies require documentation of felony cases to be completed prior to dismissal from work, some allow reports for misdemeanor cases to be turned in the following day. Being able to recall your actions and compile them into an accurate and comprehensive case report is a challenge. This makes the process of note-taking a critical skill to master.

Methodical note-taking contributes to being overwhelmed at a crime scene. There are specific steps to note-taking that will help expedite the process. Once the field notes are recorded, they should be retrieved at a later time and organized into a simplified and usable outline. The process of transferring your notes into a useful outline is essential. Your outline will help with the challenge of reducing a myriad of facts, often captured in a hurried and disjointed fashion in your notes, into a legible case report. This chapter provided proven guidelines to aid in the process of note-taking, creating an outline, and transferring that information into a professional case report. As with any process, this is an acquired skill which will be improved with practice.

EXERCISES

1. Divide yourselves into pairs in the classroom and interview each other in regard to the misdemeanor theft of the ceramic gnome that you had in your front yard. Both of you should take turns being the victim and the officer. Both of you should select a third student in the class as the suspect that you observed running from the scene carrying your ceramic gnome.

   Follow these rules during this exercise:

   Try to use some of the abbreviation examples listed earlier, and come up with some of your own.

   You both should use your real information so that you do not get confused during the interview.

   The only things you should make up in this exercise are the description of the ceramic gnome and its value (misdemeanor).

   Currently you do not know the name of the suspect and have never seen him or her before.

   You heard a noise this morning and opened the front door and observed the suspect pick the gnome up and yell something at you. (What he or she yelled can be made up so that each of you has something different.)

   Do not get too carried away with this exercise by trying to make it difficult for each other, because later, you will need to write a report on this case. The case number is 14-00001 and you should use this additional information:

   Date: Your current date

   Dispatch time: 0530

   Arrival time: 0540

   Time of occurrence: 0515

   Title: Theft (Your state statute number)

   You should use the preprinted interview sheets that can be found in the "Appendix: Sample Forms" for this exercise.

2. Video interviews.

   Watch the video of a law enforcement official interviewing a witness to a crime and complete your own notes as the witness explains what she observed. *(Video Scenario of an Interview 2.2 Domestic Assault)* You should use the preprinted interview sheets, which can be found in the "Appendix: Sample Forms" of this book for this exercise.

   Retain your notes for further exercises in the following chapters.

   Additional Information:

   Case Number: 14-56090

   Zone: 4

   Sector: 3

Date: Your current date

Time: Your current time

Mrs. Jackson's information:

Occupation: Bottle label maker

Phone Numbers: Cell: 719-555-0163

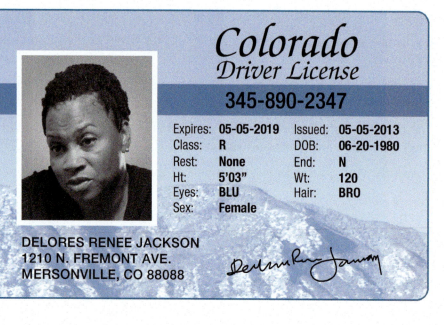

3

THE PARTS OF THE NARRATIVE CASE REPORT

LEARNING OBJECTIVES

- Recognize that the narrative case report is an essential legal document that directly contributes to the prosecution of criminals.

- Identify the various parts of a narrative case report.

- Understand the basics of narrative report writing.

- Apply your knowledge to practical examples by successfully completing the chapter exercises.

INTRODUCTION

The completion of the narrative report is the final step in documenting what transpired with regard to the incident. This document, more than any other written correspondence you produce, is a reflection of your training, skills, and abilities as a law enforcement officer. Additionally, your annual evaluation will certainly reflect your competency in preparing professional narrative case reports.

This document should be prepared using the English grammar skills referenced in Chapter 1. If your writing skills are weak, consider taking a remedial college level English class—it is time well spent and certainly worth the money and effort. Many law enforcement agencies offer tuition assistance for their officers to take higher education classes. This will pay high dividends in your evaluations and enhance your possibilities for promotion.

This textbook is not intended to be a remedial English grammar primer. The old adage, "Live by the sword, die by the pen" applies here. It is always advisable when first starting your law enforcement career to select someone in your agency who is known for writing good reports and have him/her proofread your first draft. As mentioned earlier in Chapter 1, this individual could be a valuable resource for you to utilize. Never be afraid to ask for help.

Remember the basics of narrative report writing. Keep the sentences simple and understandable. Various individuals will be reading parts of this report and it is essential to have a document that can be easily understood. The educational level of those exposed to this report will vary from lawyers with doctorate degrees to jurors who may have an eighth grade education. The narrative report is a legal document that can be subpoenaed into court. Again, simplicity and readability are critical elements to communicate your actions.

Professional report writing is an acquired skill that can be learned and mastered over time with experience and a sincere effort to hone your skills. Practice, Practice, Practice!

MAJOR PARTS OF THE CASE REPORT

The chronological order of the case report should resemble the simple outline described below. Follow this simple guide and you will have a clear and concise replication of the incident.

- **Face Sheet** (sometimes called the cover sheet)
  - The purpose of the face sheet is to organize facts and gather statistics.
  - This is usually a preprinted form produced by the law enforcement agency that details demographic and offense information.
  - Law enforcement agencies vary in the style and content on the forms that they utilize. There is no universal "standard" form.
  - Typically, you are just filling in names and checking the appropriate boxes to complete the face sheet.
  - The face sheet is a quick checklist for critical information involving the incident.

- **Introduction**
  - Introduce the events of how you responded to the incident.
    - For example: *While on routine patrol, I was dispatched to 2242 Elm Street, Colorado Springs, CO 80902, in reference to a residential burglary in progress.*
    - The introductory section of the case report may not be a complete paragraph. It is intended merely to set up the body of the case report.

- **Reporting Individual/Victim Statements**
  - Typically you will be greeted at the crime scene by the victim or the reporting party. Continue the case report with the initial information that you gained from these individuals.

- **Witness(es) Statements**
  - If there were any witnesses, be sure and include their statements in chronological order.

- **Facts of the Case**
  - Your observations of the incident
    - These are your facts of the case.
    - Did you observe a broken window?
    - Did you observe pry marks on the locks?
  - This is where you would document the elements of the crime committed.

- **Suspect(s) Statements**
  - It is usually best to interview the suspect after all pertinent information on the incident has been obtained if possible.

- **Conclusion**
  - o Did you make an arrest?
  - o Was the suspect transported to the county jail?
  - o What charges were filed?
  - o When was your final departure time from the crime scene?
  - o Is the case closed, unfounded, or does it require some type of follow up investigation?

Follow these guidelines when composing your report and it will read like a logical, sequential document. Please note that this is not an absolute format. For example, upon arrival at a crime scene you could possibly be met first by the suspect, who makes an incriminating statement ("I just shot the fool."). In this case, putting the suspect's statement toward the end of the case report would sacrifice the chronological order of events.

SYNOPSIS

Some law enforcement agencies require a synopsis or "synops" of the incident—this is typically found at the bottom of the face sheet. A synops is basically a brief summary of the incident, which informs the reader of the essential facts and the disposition of the case. The synops portion of the face sheet should state the facts, be understandable, and should have an emphasis on brevity.

Best Practices: The synopsis should support the title of the report. If the crime committed is an assault, then the elements of an assault should be briefly and accurately documented in the synopsis.

THE NARRATIVE REPORT (THE PART OF THE CASE REPORT WHERE YOU TELL THE STORY)

This is the main body of the report written in paragraph format using complete sentences and basic English grammar skills. It gives an overview of the criminal incident. A report usually is preceded by forms. Typically, the first form is called the "face" sheet or "cover" sheet. This consists of a series of fill-in-the-blank type information or boxes to check. The purpose of the face sheet is to offer a quick reference to the reader as to what is contained in the packet.

The body, or the narrative portion of the report, contains a flowing narrative of the incident and what actions the officer accomplished. This is usually the second sheet of the packet. Often, the narrative portion of the case report may entail more than one page.

Use paragraphs to help paint the picture of how the incident unfolded. Always start a new paragraph when you change locations, individuals, or significant events. The paragraphs should usually contain five or six sentences. Some paragraphs may be longer, some paragraphs may only be one sentence long (for example your introductory statement). Each paragraph should have one central idea or theme.

Your goal here is to guide the reader through the incident. The narrative report should tell the story in simple and understandable language. The quality of the narrative report does not depend on the length. The length of the narrative report is determined by clearly and precisely documenting the events of the incident. Some reports will be short and others may take several pages. Supplemental reports may also be added to the original packet.

SUPPLEMENTAL AND FOLLOW UP REPORTS

A supplemental report is a general phrase that refers to any one of the numerous types of subsequent narratives or attachments that will be added to the original case report. It may include: witness statements, waivers, laboratory findings, or other forms connected with the incident.

Follow up reports are usually authored by someone other than the writer of the initial case report. These typically involve issues that arise at a later date after the case report has been filed. These follow up reports are usually attached to the initial case report. It is expected that initial case reports be filed in a timely manner. As a result of this, additional information concerning the case often materializes. Adding information to the body of the initial case report after it has been filed is prohibited. Any additional information should be written as a supplemental report and attached to the initial case report. When appropriate, explain why the information was not contained in the initial case report. Figure 3.1 shows a harassment Face/Cover Sheet report.

The first portion of the Face/Cover Sheet involving this particular Harassment identifies the following information to others who read the report:

1. The crime committed
2. Victim information
3. Suspect information (which also includes the summons number issued to him)

The preceding victim and suspect information was copied from the interview sheets that were completed during the initial interviews.

The following information is the Elements/Narrative section from the Face/Cover Sheet (Figure 3.1), which identifies information others need to read the report.

Elements/Narrative

On 01-27-2014 at approximately 1055 I, Officer Smith 1616, was dispatched to 119 Beech St. in reference to a Harassment complaint. Upon arrival I made contact with Glenn Lincoln, the victim, who stated that he observed his neighbor Michael Raye putting trash into his garbage can that was sitting next to the street.

Mr. Lincoln confronted Mr. Raye about putting his trash into his cans and this confrontation turned physical when Mr. Raye pushed Mr. Lincoln to the ground. Mr. Lincoln stated he was not injured during this confrontation.

> Neighborhood Follow-Up/YES
>
> Witness Information/NO
>
> Suspect Information/YES
>
> Arrest/YES
>
> Evidence/NO
>
> Photos/NO

The first sentence in the included narrative identifies the officer completing the report and how he or she became involved in the situation and the date and time of involvement.

Mersonville Police Department Face Sheet	☒ Offense ☐ Supplement ☐ Other	Case Number 14-01234

Offense Title	City/State Statute Number	Date of this Report
Harassment in the First Degree	*16-3-1700*	*01/27/2014*

Zone 2	Date and time Reported				Date and Time of Occurrence			
	Month	Day	Year	Time	Month	Day	Year	Time
Sector 6	*01*	*27*	*2014*	*1050*	On or Between	*01* *01*	*27* *27*	*2014* *2014*	*1030* *1045*

Victim's Name Last, First, Middle	Date of Birth	Age	Sex	Race	Occupation
Lincoln, Glenn Walter	*11/05/1968*	*45*	*M*	*W*	*Retired*

Residential Address	City	State	Zip Code	Home Phone	Victims ☒ Yes
119 Beech St.	*Mersonville*	*CO*	*88088*	*719-555-0199*	Brochure ☐ No

Business Address	City	State	Zip Code	Work Phone	Cell Phone
None					*719-555-0198*

Business Name	Business Address	City	State	Zip Code	Business Phone

Codes RP = Reporting Party AV = Additional Victim W = Witness LO = Law Enforcement Officer A = Arrestee S = Suspect O = Other

Code	Last, First, Middle	Date of Birth	Age	Sex	Race	Occupation
S	*Raye, Michael Robert*	*09/26/1971*	*43*	*M*	*W*	*Security*

Residential Address	City	State	Zip Code	Home Phone	Other Phone
121 Beech St.	*Mersonville*	*CO*	*88088*	*719-555-0188*	*719-555-0186*

Clothing Description	Alias	Summons Number
Blue Jeans, White T-shirt, Black shoes	*N/A*	*10090038*

Identifying Marks/Scars/Tattoos	Height	Weight	Build	Hair	Eyes
Tattoo left arm of pirate skull	*6'01"*	*215*	*M*	*BRO*	*BLU*

Elements/Narrative

On 01-27-2014 at approximately 1055 I, Officer Smith 1616, was dispatched to 119 Beech St. in reference to a Harassment complaint. Upon arrival I made contact with Glenn Lincoln, the victim, who stated that he observed his neighbor Michael Raye putting trash into his garbage can that was sitting next to the street.

Mr. Lincoln confronted Mr. Raye about putting his trash into his cans and this verbal confrontation turned physical when Mr. Raye pushed Mr. Lincoln to the ground. Mr. Lincoln stated he was not injured during this confrontation.

Neighborhood Follow-Up/YES

Witness Information/NO

Suspect Information/YES

Arrest/YES

Evidence/NO

Photos/NO

Case Disposition	Patrol Investigation	Assigned to:
☐ Open ☐ Closed ☒ Cleared by Arrest ☐ Unfounded	Continued ☐ Yes ☒ No	

Officer Name/Employee Number	Supervisor Name/Employee Number	Page 1 of 2
Smith 1616	*Carter 090*	

Figure 3.1 *Harrassment Face Sheet/Cover Sheet Report* (continued on next page)

The second sentence identifies who the victim or reporting party is and what he reported to the responding officer.

The third sentence supports the crime of "Harassment." In Colorado, pushing someone without injuring them would meet the elements of Harassment.

The word "YES" beside Neighborhood Follow-Up informs the reader that the officer spoke to the residents near the location of the reported crime.

Mersonville Police Department Face Sheet		☒ Offense ☐ Supplement ☐ Other			Case Number 14-01234	
Offense Title *Harassment*			City/State Statute Number 18-9-111		Date of this Report 01/27/2014	

Zone 2	Date and time Reported				Date and Time of Occurrence			
	Month	Day	Year	Time	Month	Day	Year	Time
Sector 6	01	27	2014	1050	On or Between	01 / 01	27 / 27	2014 / 2014	1030 / 1045

Victim's Name Last, First, Middle *Lincoln, Glenn Walter*		Date of Birth 11/05/1968	Age 45	Sex M	Race W	Occupation *Retired*	
Residential Address 119 Beech St.	City Mersonville	State CO	Zip Code 88088	Home Phone 719-555-0199	Victims ☒ Yes	Brochure ☐ No	
Business Address None		City	State	Zip Code	Work Phone	Cell Phone 719-555-0198	
Business Name	Business Address		City	State	Zip Code	Business Phone	

Codes RP = Reporting Party AV = Additional Victim W = Witness LO = Law Enforcement Officer A = Arrestee S = Suspect O = Other

Code A	Last, First, Middle *Raye, Michael Robert*		Date of Birth 09/26/1971	Age 43	Sex M	Race W	Occupation *Security*
Residential Address 121 Beech St.	City Mersonville	State CO	Zip Code 88088	Home Phone 719-555-0188	Other Phone 719-555-0186		
Clothing Description *Blue Jeans, White T-shirt, Black shoes*			Alias N/A		Summons Number 10090038		
Identifying Marks/Scars/Tattoos *Tattoo left arm of pirate skull*			Height 6'01"	Weight 215	Build M	Hair BRO	Eyes BLU

Figure 3.1 *Harrassment Face Sheet/Cover Sheet Report*

The word "NO" beside Witness Information informs the reader that there were no witnesses to this reported crime.

The word "YES" beside Suspect Information informs the reader that there was a suspect identified in this reported crime.

The word "YES" beside Arrest informs the reader that an arrest was made in this reported crime.

The word "NO" beside Evidence informs the reader that there was no evidence associated with this reported crime.

The word "NO" beside Photos informs the reader that there were no photos taken during the investigation of this reported crime.

After the responding officer writes the report, the first line supervisor will be the first person to read the report and then pass it along to the detective bureau. This Face/Cover Sheet informs the detective assigned to the case that the crime of Harassment occurred, who the victim and suspect are in the case, and a brief explanation about the offense. The detective also knows that there are no witnesses, evidence, or photos associated with the reported crime.

Best Practices: It is helpful to provide information in the synopsis about the victim, the suspect, and the witness along with their disposition at the time of the report. Other information in the synopsis could include evidence, neighborhood follow-up, and photos. The overall goal of the synopsis is to support the elements of the crime and to inform the reader about what is and what is not included in the report.

Additionally, the detective knows that a suspect was identified, an arrest was made, and, from the last few boxes on the Face/Cover Sheet, that the patrol investigation is not continuing and that the case was closed by an arrest. The detective can then take the report and file it with the District Attorney knowing that there is no additional investigative follow-up required by him or her in relation to this reported crime.

On the following pages you will find the completed Harassment report (Figure 3.2).

Mersonville Police Department Continuation/Supplement			Case Number 14-01234 Date of this Report			
Offense Title Harassment			City/State Statute Number 18-9-111		Date of this Report 01/27/2014	

Codes RP=Reporting Party AV= Additional Victim W=Witness LO= Law Enforcement Officer A=Arrestee S=Suspect O=Other						
Code	Last, First, Middle	Date of Birth	Age	Sex	Race	Occupation

Residential Address	City	State	Zip Code	Home Phone	Other Phone

Clothing Description	Alias	Summons Number

Identifying Marks/Scars/Tattoos	Height	Weight	Build	Hair	Eyes

Elements/Narrative

Victim Statement:

Mr. Lincoln stated that he was contacted by his waste service on 01-18-2014 and was informed that the trash he left for pick-up in front of his residence on 01-17-2014 had hazardous material (oil) in it and that this type of waste needed to be disposed of differently according to EPA standards.

Mr. Lincoln stated that he did not put oil in his trash that day but he had observed his neighbor, Michael Raye, changing the oil in his car that was parked on the street the previous night. Mr. Lincoln did not confront Mr. Raye at that time because he did not see him place the oil in his trash.

Mr. Lincoln did however observe Mr. Raye changing the oil in his wife's car last night and when he placed his trash next to the street this morning he observed from his living room window Mr. Raye walk over to his trash cans carrying a plastic milk bottle containing a black liquid.

Mr. Lincoln stated that he walked outside and asked Mr. Raye what he had placed into his trash cans. Mr. Raye who was now in his own yard said "just some trash, my trash service does not come until next week." Mr. Lincoln stated that he then lifted his trash can lid and removed the milk jug with the black liquid and tossed it back into Mr. Raye's yard and told him he could dispose of his hazardous material properly and not put it in his trash.

Mr. Lincoln stated that Mr. Raye became angry and walked over aggressively with his hands clinched into a fist and pushed him down and said "you want to fight me!" Mr. Lincoln stated he got up and walked into his home and called the police. Mr. Lincoln stated that he was not injured and that no one observed the altercation.

Officer Statement:

I spoke to Michael Raye and he stated that he did put trash into Mr. Lincoln's trash can but thought it was not a problem because he had done it before and Mr. Lincoln did not object. Mr. Raye denied pushing Mr. Lincoln down and stated that when Mr. Lincoln tossed the milk jug back into his yard he did walk over toward him and yell "are you trying to start a fight with me?" He then observed Mr. Lincoln trip over his own sidewalk and fall onto the ground as he backed away from him.

Mr. Raye then decided not to make any further statements concerning the incident. He was served on summons number 100900038 for Harassment and released.

Neighborhood Follow-up was conducted but no witness could be located. No evidence or photos were taken.

No further information.

Officer Name/Employee Number Smith 1616	Supervisor Name/Employee Number Carter 090	Page 2 of 2

Figure 3.2   *Completed Harassment Report*

In the Supplement/Continuation of the Harassment report, the information documented follows the reported crime in chronological order from contacting the victim/reporting party to the officer contacting the suspect. The entire report will be forwarded to the District Attorney's Office after a short review in the Detective Bureau. The District Attorney can now make a decision whether to prosecute the suspect, offer a plea deal, or even drop the charges altogether.

THE *RIGHT* WAY TO *WRITE*

The writing style of the narrative case report is where it all comes together. The writing style must focus on well-constructed paragraphs and sentences using proper English grammar skills. Regarding the "Right Way to Write," the emphasis of the narrative report is on presenting clear, concise, and comprehensive information that is grammatically correct and understandable to readers with a wide variety of educational levels. Additionally, the document must survive the potential legal ramifications in a courtroom. Always remember that compliance with standard English grammar skills and comprehension count heavily in a courtroom setting.

Proper writing skills are a necessary component to an effective narrative report. This style of writing entails "telling the story" to the reader in chronological order in simple, understandable words. You need to "paint the picture," using words, of what occurred at the incident. The purpose of this chapter is not to provide fundamental writing skills but rather to focus on the technique and style of applying these writing skills.

Writing a good narrative report requires practice and feedback rather than extensive explanation and directions. There is an assumption by the authors that you have acquired proper basic English grammar skills. It is recommended that if you intend to make a career in law enforcement you need to obtain mastery of English grammar skills at the college level. If you have not already taken a Basic English Composition class at the college level, plan to do so in the near future.

TIPS FOR THE PARTS OF THE NARRATIVE CASE REPORT

By way of review, here is a brief outline of critical things to remember when preparing your narrative case report.

- Use proper English (be aware of sentence and paragraph structure).
- Use careful punctuation and grammar.
- Keep it simple (be aware of who the potential reader may be).
- Keep things in chronological order (you are telling a story, start from the beginning and proceed on to the conclusion).
- Do not forget to include who, what, when, where, how, and why.
- When interviewing victims, witnesses, or suspects, ask the question: "How did you know" (this will pay dividends in later courtroom testimony).
- Do not neglect your agency's requirements when dealing with issues such as format and style.
- Use clear and concise wording.
- Avoid abstract words.

- Keep things in the active voice.
- Use the first person singular.
- Keep things in the past tense.
- Use the involved persons names (don't get trapped into using "victim 1, victim 2, etc.).
- Use the surnames (for example, "Mr. and Mrs.") when referring to victims, witnesses, and suspects.
- Use factual statements, don't guess or use deductive statements.
- Be sure to include your observations.
- Use quotations sparingly.
- There are only two kinds of writers in this world: those who use too many commas and those who don't use enough commas; be aware of this dilemma and adjust your style as needed.
- Avoid run-on sentences.
- Don't use police jargon.
- Avoid abbreviations.
- Check for spelling and grammatical errors.
- Remember your ethical considerations.
- Don't be afraid to ask a competent officer to proofread your report.

SUMMARY

The narrative case report is probably the most important document that every law enforcement officer will prepare. It is an essential legal document that directly contributes to the prosecution of criminals. Additionally, your annual evaluations always rate your proficiency in writing skills.

Preparing a well-written narrative case report should not be a daunting task. By following the steps contained in this chapter you are well on your way to becoming a proficient and competent writer. Officers who can prepare a professional narrative case report will contribute to the professionalism of their organization. At our college, we have a "Criminal Justice Advisory Board" which is comprised of numerous law enforcement chiefs, commanders, and other high-ranking law enforcement officials. The one common request they consistently make is: "Send us candidates who can write!" Although it requires a bit of skill, it is a skill that can be mastered with practice and hard work.

EXERCISES

1. The notes you took earlier from Chapter 2 concerning the theft of the gnome need to be documented on a Face/Cover Sheet and Supplement/Continuation. Use the correct report forms, found in the "Appendix: Sample Forms" of this book, to complete this exercise.

2. The notes you took during the witness interview video in Chapter 2 Exercise 2.2, *(Video Scenario of an Interview 2.2)* concerning the domestic assault, need to be documented on the Supplement/Continuation sheets. Use the correct report forms, found in the "Appendix: Sample Forms" of this book, to complete this exercise.

4

THE BASICS OF ENGLISH GRAMMAR

LEARNING OBJECTIVES

- Understand the importance of using proper English grammar skills in preparing criminal justice documents.

- Understand the basics of English grammar.

- Analyze your writing style and how to apply this style to criminal justice documents that comply with your agency's requirements.

- Apply your knowledge to practical examples by successfully completing the chapter exercises.

INTRODUCTION

Knowing how to express your observations clearly and correctly when writing a narrative police report is essential. The purpose of your case report is to communicate information. In order to facilitate effective communication, some basic rules of English grammar and punctuation must be followed. Your case report should be written using a form of speech that is composed of simple and understandable sentences. This chapter presents some of the basic principles of the English language. It is strongly recommended that, as aspiring police officers, you consider taking a college level English class if you have not already done so. This will pay big dividends toward a successful career in law enforcement.

Although this chapter may seem somewhat basic, it is intended to give you a refresher on the proper structure of sentences and paragraphs. Being able to use the English language properly is critical in report writing. You must be able to convey exactly what happened with no other possible interpretations or misconceptions. As stated in earlier chapters, composing simple, understandable sentences is always best in report writing. Court cases have been lost due to grammar mistakes.

THE BASICS OF ENGLISH GRAMMAR

TYPES OF WORDS

Nouns are words for people, places, or things.
Examples of nouns:

People: suspect, witness, victim, Mr. Jones, and Police Chief Smith

Places: City Hall, Denver, and America

Things: gun, knife, wrench, and bullet

Common nouns are not names of specific names of persons, places, or things.
Examples of common nouns:

suspect

victim

witness

weekday

Proper nouns are specific names of persons, places, or things and they are capitalized.
Examples of proper nouns:

El Paso County Sheriff's Office

Pikes Peak Community College

Commander Morris

Officer Merson

Pronouns are words that substitute for a noun or noun phrase.
Examples of pronouns:

I found the gun.	"I" is the pronoun in this sentence.
Who found the knife?	"Who" is the pronoun in this sentence.

Verbs are words that are used to express action or a state of being. The verb emphasizes something about the subject of your sentence.
Examples of verbs: hit, strike, punch, bite, and throw

The burglar **crept** by the window.

"Crept" is the verb that expresses action.

The driver **appeared** to be intoxicated.

"Appeared" is the verb that expresses a state of being.

Verb Tense: Most reports cover situations that have occurred in the past. Therefore, most report writing should be written in first person and in past tense.
The following is an example of the proper use of verb tense in report writing.

I entered the residence and discovered that the suspect had beaten Ms. Smith, the victim, who was unconscious.

The following is an example of poor use of verb tense in report writing.

I am enter the residence and discover that the suspect beat Ms. Smith, the victim, who is unconscious.

When you write a case report, you are using a form of technical writing. In the two examples above, it is clear that both sentences are telling a story. The first example refers to a situation that occurred in the past. The second example refers to a situation that is described as if it is currently happening. The difference is that the latter sentence is of a style that is used for creative writing in novels or storytelling. The goal of these types of writings is to keep the reader on the edge of their seat. This is not appropriate in case report writing. For the majority of the case report, you will be using the past tense.

PARTS OF A SENTENCE

A sentence has two parts: the **subject** and the **predicate**. Simple sentences could be:

The victim cried.   The "victim" is the subject and "cried" is the predicate.

The crime occurred.   The "crime" is the subject and "occurred" is the predicate.

A more complex sentence could be:

The upset victim of the robbery cried uncontrollably during the testimony.

The "upset victim of the robbery" is the subject and "cried uncontrollably during the testimony" is the predicate.

PUNCTUATION

Punctuation is very important for the law enforcement professional in report writing. Punctuation can demonstrate the myriads of personalities, moods, or even the emotions that took place at the incident. Often these feelings are critical both from an evidentiary perspective for the appropriate charges and/or for court proceedings. Again, you want to "capture the moment" in your case report to justify how you handled the case.

Periods are placed at the end of sentences or statements, abbreviations, decimals, and initials.
Example of a period in a sentence:

The suspect decided not to render a written statement.

Examples of periods needed in abbreviations:

Dr., Mr., Ms., Ph.D., and time a.m./p.m.
Dr. Williams stated that Ms. Smith had a fractured radial head.

Examples of periods not needed in abbreviations:

El Paso County Sheriff's Office (EPSO)
Federal Bureau of Investigation (FBI)
Central Intelligence Agency (CIA)

Question marks end an interrogative sentence.
Examples of question marks:

Do you understand your rights?
Did you murder your neighbor?

Direct quotations and questions. When using direct quotations, the question mark will go inside the quotation marks when the quotation asks the question and outside the quotation marks when the entire sentence poses the question.

Example of question mark inside the quote:

I asked her, "Did you slap your husband?"

Example of a question mark outside the quote:

Who yelled "Get off of my property"?

Exclamation points will end sentences that show emotion or excitement or a sense of urgency.

Examples of an exclamation point:

Call 911 now!
I heard the gunshots and I just ran!

Commas are used to clarify a relationship within a sentence and may be used for *a list, coordinating adjectives, with an introductory phrase, and with coordinating conjunctions.* There are only two kinds of writers in this world: those that use too many commas and those who don't use enough commas. Try to strike a balance in using commas.

Example of commas that list items:

"The burglar stole a DVD player, television, clock radio, and my wristwatch."

Example of a comma used to coordinate adjectives:

Mr. Jones stated he had a slow, painful recovery.

Example of a comma used in an introductory phrase:

Because Mr. Jones had followed the doctor's instructions, he had a quick recovery.

MISUSED WORDS

Misused words in report writing can confuse and mislead the reader. Below is a short list of common words that can be misused in writing reports.

Advice and advise
The word "advice" is a noun.
The word "advise" is a verb.
*Mr. Lawrence followed Officer Smith's **advice** and moved his car out of the fire zone. Officer Smith **advised** Mr. Drake of his Miranda Rights.*

Affect and effect
The majority of the time, the word "affect" is a verb that means to influence.
The word "effect" is a noun which means the result.
*How did the burglary **affect** your family?*
*What is the **effect** of this speeding ticket in regards to my license?*

Among and between

The word "among" should be used in language relating to many things, and the word "between" is used for just two things.

*Mr. Johnson was **among** the victims. The unidentified robbery suspect stood **between** Mr. Roberts and Mr. Davis when he ordered them to hand over their wallets.*

As and like

The word "as" is a subordinating conjunction and it introduces a subordinate clause.

The word "like" is a preposition and it is followed by the object of a preposition.

*Mr. Smith stated that Carl Travis acted **as** if he were intoxicated.*

*Mr. Smith stated that the robbery suspect looked **like** a white male.*

Bad and badly

The word "bad" is an adjective.

The word "badly" is an adverb.

*Mr. Williams stated that he felt **bad** for striking his wife in the face during their argument.*

*Mrs. Williams stated that she was not **badly** injured when her husband struck her face.*

Elicit and illicit

The word "elicit" is a verb that means to draw out.

The word "illicit" is an adjective that means illegal.

*During my investigation I attempted to **elicit** a statement from Mr. Smith.*

*The confession was determined to be **illicitly** obtained.*

Good and well

The word "good" is generally an adjective.

The word "well" is generally an adverb.

*Mr. Smith stated that he thought it was a **good** idea to kill his wife, but it was not planned **well**.*

Hang, hanged, hanging, and hung

The words "hang," "hanged," and "hanging" should generally be used in reference to people, whereas the word "hung" should be used when referencing objects.

*In the past, Mr. Smith had expressed vocally to his friends that he would **hang** himself if his wife ever left him.*

*When I entered the residence, I discovered the body of Mr. Smith **hanging** from the balcony.*

*The evidence indicated that Mr. Smith **hanged** himself in his residence.*

*The apartment appeared to be clean, with the exception of the bedroom, where curtains were found on the floor that had once **hung** over the window.*

Imply and infer

The words are verbs but "imply" means to suggest and "infer" means to draw a conclusion.

*Mr. Smith stated that he did not mean to **imply** that he thought his wife deserved to be slapped, just that she would not stop accusing him of having an affair even after he asked her to leave him alone.*

*Based on the statements of all parties it was **inferred** that Mr. Smith was the one who first used physical violence during the argument.*

Lay and lie

The word "lay" means to put something down.

The word "lie" means to recline.

*I ordered Mr. Smith to **lay** his weapon on the ground.*

*Mr. Smith stated he was feeling dizzy and decided to **lie** down.*

Principal and principle

The word "principal" is used when referring to the head of a school.

The word "principle" is a truth or belief.

*Mr. Jackson, the school **principal**, led me to the locker where he had discovered the marijuana.*

*He wanted to teach the **principle** of moral integrity.*

Prove, proved, and proven

The word "proved" is the past participle of "prove," and "proven" is the adjective form.

*I could not locate evidence to **prove** that Mr. Smith was involved in the theft.*

*I **proved** Mr. Smith was involved in the theft by locating the car used in the commission of the crime.*

*It was later **proven** that Mr. Smith had participated in the theft by driving the car used during the commission of the crime.*

Their, there, and they're

The word "their" is used to show possession.

The word "there" is an adverb and is used to indicate a place.

The word "they're" is a contraction of they and are.

*The suspects parked **their** car near the entrance to the bank.*

*Mr. Smith, the suspect, stated that he parked his car over **there** next to the entrance. **They're** going to the bank.*

To, too, and two

The word "to" is a preposition.

The word "too" is an adverb.

The word "two" is a number.

*Mr. Smith stated that he wanted to go **to** the store at around **two** o'clock, but decided it was **too** late.*

Who, whom, that, and which

The words "who" and "whom" should be used for people whereas the words "that" and "which" should be used to refer to objects.

***Who** is the main suspect in the case?*

*To **whom** is the evidence pointing?*

***That** car was used in the bank robbery.*

***Which** car was used in the bank robbery?*

Who's and whose

The word "who's" is a contraction of who is.

The word "whose" is a possessive pronoun.

Who's the focus of the investigation?

Whose turn was it to watch the suspect?

Your and you're

The word "your" is a possessive pronoun.

The word "you're" is a contraction of you are.

*It was **your** turn to watch the suspect.*

You're going to watch the suspect tonight.

Best Practices: Ensure that your grammar, spelling, and use of specific words in the report are correct. Others who read the completed report may view the continued or repeated errors in your report as a reflection of your commitment and dedication to your chosen profession.

THE *RIGHT* WAY TO *WRITE*

The substance of this chapter provides a review of the necessary aspects of English language grammar skills and writing rules as they apply to report writing. The writing style and technique is extremely important—use proper English! There is a need to express what you observed clearly and correctly when composing your document. As mentioned previously, the importance of grammar skills with legal ramifications in a courtroom cannot be overstated

Writing "style" counts. Although this chapter provides a broad base of instruction in fundamental skills–based written language, it is not intended as a primer on basic English grammatical competency. Instead, the chapter was designed to remind the student in a brief, clearly presented format of the basics of proper English grammar skills. These skills are simple enough to be adopted and applied by the reader of this textbook. Law enforcement and correctional professionals are expected to be well acquainted with the writing components of fundamental language arts. Once again, if you have not already taken a basic English composition class at the college level, plan to do so in the near future.

TIPS FOR THE BASICS OF ENGLISH GRAMMAR

SENTENCE STRUCTURE

Now that you have an idea of some very basic English grammar terminology, you must put the words into sentences. The most natural sentence structure is the simple sentence: it is the type of language that is typically used in conversation. Simple sentences are the easiest to master, and they enhance reader comprehension. Here are a few simple rules for constructing your sentences.

1. Be sure every sentence contains a noun and a verb.
2. Be sure your sentence is able to stand on its own.
3. Identify the main characters in your sentence; that is, who or what is the sentence going to be about?
4. Build your sentence by placing the subject (noun) first, then follow it with a verb that expresses action, and then add the object (if one is needed).
5. Check to ensure that the verb(s) agree with the subject(s) in number, person, and tense.

Below is a short outline of basic sentence structure that was given in Chapter 1.

- Keep it simple: use simple, short sentences.
- Use complete, simple sentences and paragraphs.
- For the most part, use the past tense. You are writing a report on things that happened previously.
- Use a style of writing that conforms to your department guidelines and to your comfort level.
- Use the first person singular style of writing.
- Use clear and concise wording. Avoid abstract and ambiguous wording.
- Keep things in chronological order.
- Use the active voice.
- Avoid police jargon and run-on sentences.
- It is always a good idea to have someone proofread your report.

SUMMARY

Using correct English grammar, punctuation, word choice, and spelling is essential in professional police report writing. Poorly written case reports, besides being embarrassing, could have very dire results in the criminal prosecution of individuals. Focus on style, using correct grammar and word choice to enhance your ability to communicate ideas. Your professionalism is reflected in the words you choose and the way in which you convey ideas. Good grammar is what makes sense to the reader. Good use of grammar conveys both comprehension and understanding. Proper English does take time, skill, and perseverance.

The more you practice writing, the higher the quality of your case report will be. Using basic English skills will enhance your overall clarity of ideas and content. Proper English grammar is a skill that you can master. Work on the most important rules of grammar for providing clarity in writing, and emphasize those rules that will best fit your report writing style. Using correct English not only gives the readers a good impression of your professionalism, but will also pay big dividends in your fitness evaluations, future promotions, and raises. If you are going to be successful in law enforcement, you must possess a good grasp of the English language.

EXERCISES

1. Write a two-page paper on what you did last weekend. Describe in detail what specific activities you engaged in over the weekend. Pay special attention to sentence and paragraph structure and the basic rules of English grammar that were covered in this chapter. Use the active voice and place things in chronological order. After completing this task, have a classmate proofread your paper. Did they discover any grammatical/ spelling or other errors? Were they able to understand what transpired over the weekend?

2. Go to the Internet and research the "most common grammatical mistakes." You will find numerous websites to examine. After completing your research, write a short paper on what you discovered. Were you guilty of any of those errors in the past? Were you at all surprised by your research? Did you learn anything new by conducting this research?

3. Officer E. Literate has completed another supplement for a different crime and you need to find three of his mistakes and explain why they are mistakes.

List the mistakes here.

_____

_____

_____

Glenn Valley Police Department Continuation/Supplement		Case Number 15-32456			
Offense Title *Criminal Mischief*		City/State Statute Number 18-4-501		Date of this Report 01/17/2015	

Codes RP = Reporting Party AV = Additional Victim W = Witness LO = Law Enforcement Officer A = Arrestee S = Suspect O = Other

Code A	Last, First, Middle *Jordan, Richard, William*		Date of Birth *01/17/2000*	Age *15*	Sex *M*	Race *H*	Occupation *Waiter*

Residential Address *4320 North Weber St.*	City *Mersonville*	State *KS*	Zip Code *88088*	Home Phone *709-555-0179*	Other Phone *709-555-0186*

Clothing Description *Blue Jeans, White t-shirt, and white running shoes*		Alias *N/A*	Summons Number *1908456*		

Identifying Marks/Scars/Tattoos		Height *6'03"*	Weight *325*	Build *L*	Hair *BRO*	Eyes *BRO*

Elements/Narrative

Officer Statement:

On 01-17-2015 at approximately 1700 I, Officer E. Literate 1789P, and Officer Smith 1980P were dispatched to 4320 North Weber in reference to a criminal mischief that involved a rock that had been thrown threw a window of the residence.

Upon arrival I an Officer Smith made contact with the victim, Mr. Henry Sawyer who informed us that he was sitting in his recliner in the living room at approximately 1645 on 01-17-2015 when a rock came threw his front window that faces North Weber St.

Mr. Sawyer stated that when he looked out the window he observed Richard Jordan, who lives a few houses away, lie down on the grass next too the sidewalk with a slingshot in his hand. Mr. Sawyer said that when Mr. Jordan realized that he was caught an he took off running toward his home because he knew he could not hanged around.

Denise Jordan, Richard Jordan's mother, arrived as we were speaking to Mr. Sawyer and she wanted to know what had happened. I explained to her that Mr. Sawyer believed that her son had used a slingshot to brake his front window with a rock and that Mrs. Sawyer had observed her son with the slingshot in front of his home after it had occurred.

Mrs. Jordan stated that her son had in fact broken the window and that he came home an told her about it a few minutes ago and that he had told her that it was an accident. Mrs. Jordan offered to pay for the damage an asked Mr. Sawyer not to press charges against her son.

Mr. Sawyer told Mr. Jordan that he was going to have her son arrested based on the principal of the situation an that he did not believe it was an accident to.

Mr. Jordan told Mr. Sawyer that she would contact there family attorney an then stated to Mr. Sawyer "Your wrong for doing this" an than she turned and walked away.

Officer Smith competed the original report an served and released Richard Jordan for Criminal Mischief under $500.

See Officer Smith's report for more information.

Officer Name/Employee Number *E. Literate 1789P*	Supervisor Name/Employee Number *J. Thomas 3089P*	Page 1 of 1

5

FIRST OFFICER ON SCENE

LEARNING OBJECTIVES

- Recognize how to prioritize your actions as the first officer on the scene when responding to an incident.
- Identify and understand the three major tasks that need to be completed upon arriving to a crime scene.
- Understand the first responder's role in processing a crime scene.
- Understand the steps and techniques in the interview process.
- Apply your knowledge to practical examples by successfully completing the chapter exercises.

INTRODUCTION

A crime scene is anything but a controlled environment. A crime has occurred, and there is an expectation that the arriving law enforcement official will bring some semblance of order and control to an intense and possibly volatile situation. Victims, witnesses, and often suspects add to the confusion and chaos. Upon arriving at a crime scene, the responding officer needs to determine what should be done first to secure the scene and make the scene safe for citizens and law enforcement officials. Once these priorities are accomplished, the note-taking process typically begins.

Unless you have a photographic memory, you do not have the ability to recall everything that has occurred at a crime scene. Relying on you short-term recall is a roadmap to failure. Studies have shown the simple act of writing something down helps to imprint the incident in your memory. Additionally, the longer the time span between the incident and the documentation process, the greater the chance of inaccuracies or omissions. The purpose of note-taking is to refresh your memory in preparing your case report.

Crime scene note-taking is an essential element in preparing your case report. Writing a complete and accurate case report requires methodical documenting, organizing, and presentation of the facts of the case. You should take notes that allow anyone who reads them to understand what they mean. Writing a professional case report requires several important steps. Taking good crime scene notes and then transforming this information into an accurate and complete case report is the basis of every successful criminal prosecution.

Note-taking provides the transition from securing the crime scene to writing the case report. When time allows you to sit down and write the case report, reviewing your notes will keep you focused on the facts and details of the incident at a later time. There are some basic rules that serve as guidelines to help simplify the note-taking process. This chapter will make the note-taking process more efficient, consistent, and understandable. Good note-taking is an art that can be mastered.

THE VALUE OF THE FIRST RESPONDER TO A CRIME SCENE

- Your initial actions are critical to the successful resolution of the incident.
- You are the best source of information regarding this incident.
  - You may be the only person to "see" and "feel" the crime scene in its original condition.
  - If the case is transferred to other officers/detectives, your initial case report will be the basis for further investigation and follow-up.
- You are the person responsible for thoroughly documenting your observations and the facts of the case by creating a complete and thorough narrative case report, collecting and preserving evidence, and bringing some type of resolution to the incident.
- Your testimony will be a critical part of the criminal prosecution of any suspects.
- Your narrative case report will be the foundation of your courtroom testimony.

THE THREE MAJOR TASKS TO COMPLETE UPON RESPONDING TO A CRIME SCENE

1. Ensure that the scene is safe.
2. Render first aid (if required).
3. Secure the crime scene.

These three tasks are prioritized and sequentially listed by order of importance.

1. **"Ensure That the Scene Is Safe."** If there is a threat or a dangerous situation, it needs to be neutralized. For example, imagine you are responding to a domestic violence call, and the husband, who is holding a butcher knife, meets you in the front yard. You observe what appears to be blood on the knife. Your first priority should be to quickly survey the immediate environment adjacent to the subject for other potential threats or hazards. You can then have the subject put down the knife and secure him in handcuffs. The elimination of potential threats to yourself and others takes precedence over first aid to those already at the crime scene. If you get injured, you have now compounded the problem.

   Now, let's examine another crime scene where you are the first responder. This scene entails a reported robbery at a neighborhood convenience store. As you arrive at the scene, exit your vehicle, and approach the entrance of the store, you observe what appears to be the store clerk lying on the floor by the cash register. The clerk is bleeding from the mouth and appears to be unconscious. You continue to survey the scene and quickly search all areas of the location where a suspect could be hiding or where additional victims could be located. The area is now safe, and you call for a medical response and begin to administer first aid to the clerk.

In both of the previously mentioned scenarios, the first priority in approaching any crime scene is to make the scene safe. Some skeptics examining the second scenario might say, "Why didn't you begin first-aid procedures immediately upon seeing the bleeding man in the convenience store robbery?" The answer is simple: if there is a suspect still on the scene of the robbery, who subsequently shoots the police officer administering first aid to the victim, we now have two problems (victims), not just one. Your first responsibility upon arriving at any crime scene, as a police officer, is to make the scene safe.

2. **"Render First Aid."** The next priority upon arriving at a crime scene is to render first aid. This may sometimes entail compromising the evidentiary value of the crime scene. This is ok; if you need to walk through bloody footprints to render aid to an injured subject, do so. The preservation of life has the highest priority once the crime scene is rendered safe. This does not mean you are not scene-conscious. If there is another quick way to approach the bleeding victims, other than walking through potentially important evidence, such as footprints, take the alternate route.

As the first responder you have been trained in assessing the situation and calling for medical attention, if required. When in doubt, call for medical assistance anyway—this is not an area where you want to second-guess your decision. Do what you have been trained to do and render first aid to any and all victims that you may observe. Call for additional back-up and medical support as the situation dictates. Keep the dispatch center appraised of your situation. Be scene-conscious.

3. **"Secure the Crime Scene."** Now that the crime scene is safe and any first-aid activities have been attended to, it is time to secure the scene. This includes:

   a. Mark off and secure a crime scene perimeter. This is frequently accomplished by using a "crime scene—do not cross" type of tape. As mentioned previously, each crime scene is unique. It is impossible to know the exact boundaries of the crime scene. The rule of thumb in marking off a crime scene is to be generous. It is better to mark off more area around which you think there may be some evidentiary or safety value than to mark off less of an area. Additional police officers may be needed to accomplish this task.

   b. Remove unauthorized persons from the crime scene. These unauthorized persons may include victims, suspects, witnesses, uninvolved bystanders, or perhaps members of the media. Use common sense when removing unauthorized persons from the crime scene. You obviously want to secure any potential suspects while ensuring that witnesses or victims do not simply walk away or depart the scene by other means. It is best practice to separate witnesses from each other and from the victim or suspect as soon as reasonably possible. This separation prevents intimidation or compromising of information.

   c. Be aware of "evidence contamination and preservation" when processing the scene. Try to keep the scene as pristine as possible. Avoid moving or altering any potential item of evidence while processing the scene. If you do have to move a potential item of evidence, do not return it to its original location; just simply notate in your field notes that the object was moved and process the object in its current location.

ARRIVAL OF ADDITIONAL PERSONNEL

Additional personnel or resources may be required at the scene. These may include emergency first aid technicians, firefighters, detectives, crime-lab processors, other police personnel, and so on. You need to use the "Team Approach" when dealing with other agencies and personnel who may arrive at the crime scene. Every professional called into a crime scene has a job to accomplish and they must all work as a team if efficiency is to be accomplished.

Everyone at the crime scene should be as scene-conscious as possible while accomplishing their duties. This is not always the case. Again, the preservation of life and administering first aid have the highest priority, but it is primarily up to you as the first responder to maintain as much crime scene preservation as possible—given the circumstances and practicality of the situation. Try to ensure that evidence is protected and preserved as much as possible.

As the first responder, you remain in charge of the crime scene until properly relieved by a supervisor. When relieved by a higher authority at the crime scene, always notify that the crime scene has been turned over to the supervisor. Notify the dispatch center of the change of command and then note this formal transformation of authority in your field notebook.

PROCESSING THE CRIME SCENE

Every crime scene is unique. If you are the first responder at a minor crime scene, you will probably be doing all of the crime scene processing and investigation. If it is a major crime scene, then you are the first part of a sophisticated team of responders, each with his or her own specific tasks to accomplish. As mentioned previously, the team approach will always pay dividends. Be empathetic to the other duties required by the various agencies. Communicate and cooperate with these other responders in a courteous and professional manner. These individuals will probably be producing valuable documentation to include in your case report.

The definition of a criminal investigation is "the lawful search for things or people." Anything and everything should be initially considered to have evidentiary value. Your goal at any crime scene is to find the truth. Typically, you will have only one opportunity to process this specific crime scene. When processing the crime scene, always *think court*. Ensure that every action you take will be sustainable in a court of law. Maintain a chain of custody for each piece of evidence from the time of discovery until presentation in court. A well-documented narrative case report will be your strongest asset in preparing your court testimony—never assume that this case will never make it to the courtroom.

You need to ensure that all potential evidence is preserved. The first officer on the scene should try to find the point of entry and/or exit of the suspects and victims, and direct the emergency personnel or other crime scene players to enter via an alternative path or a route that the officer on the scene has already established as the least likely to disturb any potential evidence. The goal here is to minimize any future contamination of evidence.

The crime scene itself is often an elusive concept. It is often impossible to know the exact boundaries of a crime scene. The initial crime scene is best described as the point where the subject turned his criminal intent into actions. The crime scene could continue into various escape routes. There could be secondary crimes scenes that may need to be processed, as well as the initial crime scene. An example of a secondary crime scene could be where a body was dumped after a homicide was committed at a different location.

Time is on your side once you have secured the crime scene. You basically have only one shot at processing the crime scene. Once a crime scene is released to the public, any further evidence discovered at the scene would be compromised and difficult to justify in court. The best procedure is to take all the time you need to process the crime scene thoroughly. Initially, anything and everything should be considered to be evidence.

Make sure that you have proper legal standing to process the crime scene. That is, did you receive proper consent to search the location? Did you acquire a proper search warrant? Did someone waive his or her constitutional rights regarding the search? Always ask these and other questions, as appropriate, before processing any crime scene. When in doubt, *get a search warrant*! Improper legal standing will probably result in eliminating any evidence that you obtain from the crime scene. Thus, you have wasted your time and resources trying to cut corners or by second-guessing the legal system. Once again, the best advice is, when in doubt, *get a search warrant*! Be sure to document the specifics of your legal standing in your case report.

In processing the crime scene, your goal is to be methodical and thorough, following an approved crime scene processing system and using flexible guidelines and common sense. Most good investigators use a simple, methodical process (not rigid) that follows a logical set of principles to complete a thorough crime scene search. Most of these principles will be included in the agency's standard operating procedures. As every crime scene will be unique, approved crime scene processing techniques, which are flexible enough to be applied to any crime scene scenario, are always the best approach. Be methodical and systematic in processing the crime scene. Always keep an open objective mind in processing a crime scene. You are a fact finder and your role is to go where the facts take you.

Your first step in processing any crime scene is determining the boundaries of that crime scene. Where does it start? Where does it end? Do I have the crime scene area secured? Once these questions are answered you are ready to begin to process the crime scene. Look for transient evidence first. Transient evidence is any evidence on scene that could lose its evidentiary value if it's not preserved and protected. Examples of nonvisible transient evidence that could diminish over time include odors of smoke and perfume. Examples of visible transient evidence that can be degraded are footprints in the snow and blood or other biological evidence on a sidewalk when it is raining. Also look for fragile evidence, which could be destroyed or perhaps blown away. A small piece of glass or a hair fiber might be examples of fragile evidence.

CRIME SCENE SURVEY

The crime scene survey often consists of an initial "walk-through" of the crime scene by the first responder (and the lead investigator if it is a major crime scene). Prior to this walk-through, assess the scene for the need of additional personnel. If more personnel are needed, ask for them. Upon starting your crime scene survey, note any transient (temporary) evidence. Mark and photograph this type of evidence first. Communicate to investigators all movements and alterations you may have made to the crime scene. Do not attempt to "re-create" the crime scene with a piece of evidence you have moved; just be sure to note the original location in your case report. As we have learned, record all initial observations of who, what, when, where, and how as you proceed through the crime scene.

Evidence collection should not occur until all photos and sketches have been accomplished. Always photograph every piece of evidence before it is placed in an evidence container. It is best to photograph the evidence at least once as it is discovered, and then at least a second time with a numeric scale displayed alongside of the piece of evidence. Most crime lab photographers recommend that you then photograph the same area where the evidence was located after you have placed the item into an evidence container. The value of this photograph is to demonstrate that there was nothing below this piece of evidence that could have gone unnoticed.

Sketching is another task that may be required at a crime scene, especially at a major crime scene. Each item of evidentiary value must be measured from fixed points for inclusion in your sketch. Be sure to note all points of entry and exit. You don't have to be a great artist, but you do have to know how to take exact measurements. Your note-taking steno pad or some "blocked type" graph paper will be useful in creating the crime scene sketches. Most agencies today have the first responding officer or crime lab technician take precise measurements and then feed that data into a sophisticated computer program that produces a true-to-life sketch of the crime scene.

Most police agencies today utilize a video recorder when processing a crime scene. Video cameras are easy to operate, and you get instant feedback on the clarity and quality of the scene being filmed. Video recordings can be extremely useful in documenting the nuances of any crime scene. You also have the ability to narrate while filming the crime scene. This allows you to highlight certain aspects of the scene that may be critical to the investigation. Juries love video recordings as they place them at the scene without having to leave the courthouse!

EVIDENCE COLLECTION AND PRESERVATION

Proper collection and packaging of evidence is critical in any crime scene investigation. The first step is to be cognizant of what might be considered to be evidence. Basically, anything and everything could have evidentiary value. Be objective and open-minded while progressing through a crime scene. Always document the collection of any piece of evidence. Ideally, this documentation should both be in the narrative case report with photos attached. Each piece of evidence should be collected and individually stored in some type of evidence envelope. Your agency will have specific guidelines as to the proper procedures for collecting, storing, and preserving evidence. Know these guidelines and always document each step in the process of placing an item(s) into evidence.

INTERVIEWING VICTIMS, WITNESSES, AND SUSPECTS

Taking statements from the key players at a crime scene is usually the responsibility of the first police responder who arrived at the scene. Initially, a crime scene is anything but a controlled environment. The first officer on the scene must immediately begin to restore order and control over all of the individuals who may be present at the crime scene. Once order is restored and no officer safety issues exist, you may begin to gather information and take statements as necessary.

When interviewing anyone at a crime scene, always be cognizant of officer safety issues. Always wait until complete order is restored before beginning the interview process. Once you pull out your notepad and pen, you have compromised your safety, as your hands are no longer free to protect yourself. When taking notes, always place yourself in a defensible position. Never sit down if the person you are interviewing is standing. If a secondary officer is available, have him or her stand strategically by the person being interviewed.

Always try to obtain some type of valid photo identification card from any subject you interview. If they don't have identification readily available, jot down specific demographic information and attempt to confirm that information by way of contacting the dispatch center. You should accomplish this prior to the subject's departure. Always ask if the information on the identification card is current and correct. You will also need to acquire the subject's cell phone number and the name, address, and phone number of the subject's place of employment.

Usually the best way to begin any law enforcement interview is to introduce yourself and tell the subject the purpose of the interview. You want the person being interviewed to relax and become comfortable in confiding in you. Ask open-ended questions first. Open-ended questions get the subject talking. The most commonly used approach by good interviewers is to simply state, "Tell me what happened?" Most officers let the individual tell the entire story and then, once the story is completed, will ask some follow-up questions. Most officers simply listen to the story the first time and then break out the notepad and ask the subject to repeat the story.

It is generally a good practice to ask the subject to repeat the story a second time. This may be prefaced with follow-up clarification types of questions. You want to be sure to clarify any issues involving the statutory elements of a crime with the subject. As the subject is repeating the story, you are taking notes. Beware if anything has changed since the telling of the first story. If some facts have changed upon retelling the story the second time, the subject may be trying to deceive the interviewer.

During the last phase of the interview, the officer usually reads his or her notes back to the subject. This is designed to ensure the information is correct and accurate and that there have been no omissions. In certain cases, it is appropriate to have a subject write out a statement. This will be attached to your narrative case report. Some preprinted law enforcement forms will include space for victim or witness statements.

THE STEPS IN THE INTERVIEW PROCESS

1. The individual simply tells the story of what happened.
    a. Ask open-ended questions, get them talking.
    b. Use your body language to comfort and encourage conversation.
2. The individual tells the story again, and the officer takes notes.
    a. Check this story for consistency with the first telling of the events.
    b. The officer can ask follow-up clarification questions during this phase.

3. The officer reads back his notes to the subject.

   a. This is where you have the opportunity to catch any errors or perhaps discover if something has been left out.

If you follow these simple guidelines, you will have a great start on building your narrative case report.

THE *RIGHT* WAY TO *WRITE*

Addressing the writing style of this chapter, which is dedicated to the first officer on the scene, is an elusive topic. The main issue in this chapter is the application of situational knowledge, which is critical to a comprehensive understanding of how and what to document. Attending to officer safety and scene control overlap into the arena of report writing. Your observations upon arrival at the scene are a critical ingredient of the narrative report. Applying what you observed into a clear and concise narrative report is essential to any resolution to the incident.

What occurs upon the arrival of the first officer at a crime scene does help build the elements of a solid written report that will capture the most critical elements necessary to document the incident. The responding officer is charged with identifying and later documenting key distinctions regarding the validity and significance of all aspects of the crime scene. Multitasking and your observational skills are paramount at this stage of the investigation. Your goal as the first officer on the scene is to process the scene effectively while documenting the events in a logical order that will later be translated into an effective and efficient narrative report.

You should be cognizant that there is a strong relationship between arriving on the scene, your observations, note-taking, interviewing and the finished narrative report. All of these concepts are intertwined. A holistic approach to a crime scene characterized by accomplishing a multitude of challenges and procedural functions should be your goal. Your multitasking skills are essential to the proper documentation of the crime scene. Tactical and procedural matters do impact the writing style of the narrative report. What you did and what you observed are critical elements in any professional narrative report.

TIPS FOR THE FIRST OFFICER ON SCENE

- Ensure the scene is safe.
- Render first aid.
- Secure the crime scene.
- Arrest the offender if he or she is on scene.

- Separate and identify possible witnesses.
  - Use your preprinted note sheets or note pad.

- Identify additional emergency responders on scene.
  - Record their names, police/deputy division, fire station, and EMS crew number.

- Take notes.

SUMMARY

The first officer who responds to a crime scene has a phenomenal responsibility for the successful investigation and prosecution of perpetrators. His or her expertise in handling the initial activities of the scene will affect the overall efficiency in resolving the often complex and elusive issues that characterize almost every crime scene. As the first officer at the scene, you are expected to demonstrate a sophisticated understanding of the incident and then take appropriate action to bring some closure to the victim(s).

A crime scene is anything but a controlled setting. As a first responder your initial actions are critical to bringing stability to the situation. You may be the only law enforcement official to see the crime scene in its original shape. Among the myriad of duties you may have to accomplish to stabilize the situation, YOU will have to write a case report detailing the facts and circumstances involving the case. You can't possibly record everything that transpires at a crime scene. You are not expected to. You are responsible for documenting what was observed, what actions you took, and who was at the crime scene. What you are doing is capturing critical elements, at critical and specific moments that relate to the commission of a criminal offense.

The purpose of this chapter is to give general guidelines for what needs to be accomplished by the first responder to any crime scene. Some crime scenes are simple; others are much more complicated. Some cases are pretty straightforward; others can be quite elusive and challenging. This chapter provides a quick overview of some basic concepts, strategies, and ideas on what is required of a first responder. Numerous textbooks have been written about each of the specific tasks to be accomplished. You should consider doing some additional reading regarding crime scene processing.

EXERCISES

1. Describe a hypothetical crime scene to a classmate. Have the classmate take notes as you are recounting the hypothetical crime. Have a third classmate (who was not present) write a narrative case report on the case, based solely on the notes the second classmate wrote. Is all of the critical information contained in the final case report? Were all of the legal elements of the crime clearly listed in the report? Were there any omissions pertaining to the case? Use the preprinted interview sheets that can be found in the back of this book to complete this exercise.

2. Design an outline of each step that a first responding police officer will need to accomplish when responding to a crime scene. Compare your list to a classmate's. What similarities and differences (omissions) did you observe? A blank step list has been provided for you to complete on the following pages.

3. Write a short narrative case report involving any hypothetical crime scene. Next, using the same crime scene scenario, write a short newspaper article chronicling the incident. Now compare the two documents. How are they the same? How are they different? A blank case report and newspaper article have been provided for you to complete on the following pages.

A first responding police officer must accomplish the following steps when responding
to a crime scene.

1.

2.

3.

4.

5.

6.

7.

8.

9.

10.

11.

12.

13.

14.

15.

16.

17.

18.

19.

20.

21.

22.

23.

24.

25.

26.

27.

28.

29.

30.

MERSONVILLE POLICE DEPARTMENT COVER SHEET

Offense ☐	Supplement ☐	Other ☐	Case Number

Offense Title	State/City Statute	Date of this Report

Zone/Sector	Date and time Reported				Date and Approximate Time of Occurrence			
	Month	Day	Year	Time	Month	Day	Year	Time

Victim's Name Last, First, Middle	Date of Birth	Age	Sex	Height	Weight	Build	Hair	Eyes	Race

Residential Address	City	State	Zip Code	Home Phone	Cell Phone

Business Address	City	State	Zip Code	Business Phone	Occupation

Location of Offense	City	State	Zip Code

If a business is the victim complete the information below

Name of Business	Business Address	City	State	Zip Code	Business Phone

Codes RP = Reporting Party AV = Additional Victim W = Witness LO = Law Enforcement Officer A = Arrestee S = Suspect O = Other

Code	Name: Last, First, Middle	Date of Birth	Age	Sex	Height	Weight	Build	Hair	Eyes	Race

Residential Address	City	State	Zip Code	Home Phone	Cell Phone

Business Address	City	State	Zip Code	Business Phone	Occupation

Clothing Description	Alias

Identifying Marks	Summons Number

Narrative

Report Completed by:	Signature:	
		Page of Pages
Report Completed by:	Signature:	

MERSONVILLE DAILY NEWS

_____

_____

_____

_____

_____

_____

_____

_____

_____

_____

_____

_____

_____

_____

_____

_____

_____

_____

_____

_____

6

TYPES OF REPORTS

LEARNING OBJECTIVES

- Understand some of the various types of reports utilized by criminal justice agencies and how to choose the appropriate type of report given the circumstances of the incident.

- Capturing essential information by utilizing specialized forms that are designed to help guide the officer through specific types of incidents, thereby minimizing needless verbiage and maximizing efficiency.

- Understand how the various forms trap critical information and help to guide you through the documentation process.

- Understand the distinguishing elements in various types of reports.

- Apply your knowledge to practical examples of various types of reports by successfully completing the chapter exercises.

INTRODUCTION

A career in law enforcement requires that you document crimes, to which you are dispatched, accurately and professionally throughout your shift. Many of these calls for service will require different departmental forms that must be completed in order to document these incidents correctly. The collection and documentation of information with regard to a specific criminal investigation and the forms or reports needed to accomplish this task can, at times, be very time consuming. However, if you are familiar with the required forms needed for each specific situation, you will be better prepared to accomplish this task successfully.

Best Practices: If there is a particular report form that your agency uses to capture information that involves a specific type of criminal investigation or situation, then use that form! Your agency's SOPs will guide you in the right direction to ensure that you do not forget a required form. Make sure you comply with your agency's requirements regarding the use of the proper forms!

Below is a list of crimes or situations and the departmental forms that may be needed to complete a thorough investigation. These forms are the primary focus of this textbook.

1. Traffic summons (Ticket)
2. Traffic crashes
3. Misdemeanor crimes
4. Felony crimes
5. Domestic violence calls for service
6. Incident reports
7. Suspicious circumstances

1. TRAFFIC SUMMONS (TICKETS)

As a law enforcement professional patrolling and enforcing the laws in your jurisdiction, you may be required to perform directed or proactive traffic enforcement activity in your sector. The directed traffic activity may be to survey the top vehicle crash locations in your sector.

Proactive Traffic Enforcement is an enforcement practice where a law enforcement professional enforces traffic laws in his or her area of patrol without any direction or command order from a supervisor to do so.

An example of proactive traffic enforcement is when an officer during his or her patrol activity observes a vehicle with expired plates and decides to contact the driver and issue a traffic summons or ticket for the violation.

Directed Traffic Enforcement is an enforcement practice where a law enforcement professional is directed or ordered by a supervisor to monitor and enforce traffic violations that are usually found in a specific location within his or her area of responsibility during a shift.

An example of a directed traffic enforcement situation is when an officer is told by a supervisor to monitor and enforce red light violations at a high crash intersection that is found in that officer's area of responsibility.

You may be directed to issue a summons or ticket for all traffic violations in these critical areas in order to improve the traffic safety for all citizens. Many agencies also encourage patrol officers, if time permits, to enforce the traffic laws in construction zones and school zones that may be located in their assigned sectors. In these zones, speeding violations are a significant and dangerous hazard to pedestrians working and walking in those zones.

The Bureau of Justice Statics 2008 survey revealed that in 2008 traffic stops accounted for more than 43% of the contacts between law enforcement and citizens in the United States. Approximately half of those contacts resulted in a traffic summons or ticket. The stopped drivers in this survey represented 8.4% or 17.7 million of the 209 million drivers 16 years of age or older who were on the road that year. The survey also discovered that more than half of the drivers stopped had been stopped for speeding.

It simply makes good sense to enforce the traffic code of your jurisdiction. Good law enforcement academy instructors will emphasize the value and the dangers of the "routine" traffic stop. Always remember that you are operating in an environment characterized by potentially volatile individuals who may display unexpected and perhaps irrational behavior—be safe! Never underestimate the potential risks and benefits when enforcing traffic violations.

Figures 6.1 and 6.2 are an example of the front and back of a traffic summons or ticket.

LYNN CITY POLICE SUMMONS/COMPLAINT

Lynn City Police Department Summons and Complaint Penalty Assessment	☒ Lynn Municipal Court ☐ Lea County Court ☒ Traffic ☐ Non-Traffic ☐ Other	Summons 1800900 Case Number

The People of California, City of Lynn vs.

First	Middle	Last		DOB
Glenn	Walter	Smith		11/05/68

Residential Address		City	State	Zip Code
320 N. Spruce St.		Lynn	CA	88088

Drivers' License Number Presented	☒ Yes ☐ No	State	Race	Sex	HGT	WGT	Hair	Eyes	Alias
99-1100-1600		CA	WHT	M	6'04"	280	BRO	BRO	

Home Phone	Cell Phone	Work Phone	Occupation	Employer
760-555-0199	760-555-0187		Retired	U.S. Navy

Identifying Marks/Scars/Tattoos	Place of Birth
Tattoo Left Shoulder of Anchor with USN over it	Pensacola, FL

Vehicle Information

License Plate Number	Vehicle Year	State	License Year	Last Four of Vehicle Identification Number	Evidence
CHIEF241	2009	CA	15	BLER	☐ Yes ☒ No

Make	Model	Body Style	Damage	Color(s)	Traffic Crash	Photos
FORD	Mustang	CP	N/A	GRY	☐ Yes ☒ No	☐ Yes ☒ No

Towed	Towed	Towed By:	Towed To:
☐ Yes	☒ No		

Charges

City/State Statute Number	Title	Fine	Surcharge	Points
9-34-5234	SPEEDING 10-15 over	$100.00	$20.00	4

Description	
Defendant drove 65MPH in a posted 50MPH zone	☐ Felony ☐ Misdemeanor

City/State Statute Number	Title	Fine	Surcharge	Points
		$	$	

Description	
	☐ Felony ☐ Misdemeanor

Approximate Location of Violation	Violation Date	Violation Time
2300 N. Washington Ave.	01-01-14	1250

Custody/Service Location	Service Date	Service Time
Same	Same	1300

You are hereby directed to appear as indicated

☐ Lea County Court located at 3030 Pembrook Blvd. Ste. 13, Lynn City, CA 88888

☒ Lynn Municipal Court located at 640 Smith Rd. Ste. 303 Lynn City, CA 88888

On the __30__ day of __January__ __2014__ at __1300__ AM/PM

To answer charges of violations of the ☐ 1970 CRS as Amended ☐ California Children's Code
☒ The Code of Lynn City 2014

☐ Non Payable Summons ☐ Traffic ☐ Criminal	☒ Payable Summons ☒ Traffic ☐ Criminal
Without admitting guilt, I hereby promise to appear at the time and place indicated. Failure to appear constitutes a separate offense and will result in a warrant being issued.	Upon signing below I promise to pay the assessed fine within 20 days to the County Treasurer's Office per the instructions on the reverse side. Further, upon payment of this Penalty Assessment I acknowledge guilt of all charges. I am aware that the Penalty Assessment must be paid within 20 days or it becomes by law a Summons and Complaint and REQUIRES my appearance before the court at the time and place indicated above.
X_____	X_Glenn Smith_____

☐ Defendant Held in Custody ☐ Morris County Justice Center ☐ Defendant Released

The undersigned have probable cause to believe that the defendant committed the offense(s) against the peace and dignity of the people of the State of California; and that this summons and complaint was signed and served upon the defendant at the location and on the date referenced above.

Officer: _James_ _1616_ Served by: _Michael James_ Complaining Witness _____

Figure 6.1 *Front of Traffic Summons or Ticket*

Probable Cause Affidavit

On 01-01-2014 at approx 1250 I, Officer James 1616, observed the defendant, Smith, NB in the LL of the 2300 block of N. Washington Ave. Vis: 65 Radar Conf. 65 Posted 50MPH No other veh. No obstr. Smith Stated was late for a party and did not notice that he was that much over the speed limit.

Radar Calib. B and A each stop. No further information

WEATHER: ☒ CLEAR ☐ CLOUDY ☐ RAIN ☐ SNOW ☐ FOG ☐ DAWN ☐ DUSK

TRAFFIC: ☒ VEHICLE ☐ PED ☐ BICYCLE ☐ ONCOMING ☐ SAME ☐ CROSS

DIRECTION OF TRAVEL: ☒ NORTH ☐ SOUTH ☐ EAST ☐ WEST

RADAR: GUN NUMBER *890* TUNING FORKS *123-50MPH/128-35MPH*

ATTITUDE: ☒ EXCELLENT ☐ GOOD ☐ FAIR ☐ POOR

SURFACE CONDITIONS: ☒ DRY ☐ WET ☐ SNOWPACKED ☐ ICY

☐ INTERSECTION ☐ CROSSWALK ☐ STOP BAR

☒ SPEED POSTED ☐ NOT POSTED ☐ SCHOOL ZONE

OFFICER(S) TO BE NOTIFIED FOR TRIAL

OFFICER *JAMES*   BADGE NUMBER *1616*

OFFICER   BADGE NUMBER ____

UNDER PENALTY OF PERJURY, I AFFIRM THAT ALL THE INFORMATION CONTAINED UPON THIS DOCUMENT IS TRUE AND CORRECT TO THE BEST OF MY KNOWLEDGE.

AFFIANT_____ PRINT NAME_____

ADDRESS_____

HOME PHONE_____ WK. PHONE_____

ON THIS DATE, THE AFFIANT SIGNED THIS AFFIDAVIT AND SWORE TO ITS TRUTH

NOTARY PUBLIC_____ MY COMMISSION EXPIRES DATE_____

Figure 6.2 *Back of Traffic Summons or Ticket*

2. TRAFFIC CRASHES (THE TRAFFIC REPORT AND ALL ADDITIONAL REQUIRED SUMMONS AND FORMS)

Traffic enforcement during a shift of duty can involve investigating traffic crashes as they occur. In most medium-to-large law enforcement departments, there are specialized patrol units designated to investigate traffic crashes. This enables other officers to answer more serious or urgent calls for service in their jurisdiction. If your agency does not have a dedicated traffic unit or this unit is busy, there may be a time when you may have to answer a call involving a traffic crash.

Motor vehicle traffic crashes can range in severity from minor property damage with no injuries to severe incidents with major property damage and the possibility of a loss of life. Many departments have stopped using the term "accident" and now use the term "crash" because the latter leads one to believe that there were no contributing driver actions that led to the crash and therefore no fault assigned. Serious motor vehicle crashes can have both criminal and civil implications. Assessing fault at such incidents is of critical importance with regard to future litigation. Additionally, good traffic crash investigations can assist traffic engineers in recognizing potentially dangerous intersections or roadways. Additionally, published media reporting can help alert the general public to potentially dangerous intersections.

Although completing a traffic crash form might not seem as the most glamorous aspect of policing, take the time to get it right! Cutting corners or the failure to put check points in the appropriate reporting boxes of a motor vehicle crash form will result in missing critical crash information. Additionally, take the time to write a comprehensive and professional narrative of the scene. Remember that these are legal documents that can be used in court and will be utilized in insurance investigations. These forms will be scrutinized; sloppy work will have dire consequences.

Figures 6.3 and 6.4 are examples of the front and back of a traffic crash report.

3. MISDEMEANOR CRIMES

Misdemeanor summons and complaint forms are used for criminal cases, which would result in a jail sentence of one year or less plus a possible fine upon conviction. The summons and complaint form can be used for either misdemeanor or petty offenses. In most agencies, it is an acceptable practice to write out these summons and complaint forms by hand. Summons and complaint forms typically provide less information and details than a full-blown criminal felony case report. These forms will usually have all the information needed to include the probable cause affidavit on the reverse side of the summons.

The top portion of the summons and complaint form typically contains boxes to be checked and blank spaces for information such as names, addresses, and other information. These blank spaces help to guide the officer in obtaining critical information needed to complete a thorough investigation.

Additionally, the records section of the agency utilizes the summons and complaint forms to retrieve critical crime information. These forms have a wealth of information on the types and number of crimes occurring in the jurisdiction. The form also makes retrieval of required information for the Uniform Crime Reporting System and other surveys quite simple.

The Federal Bureau of Investigation (FBI) collects information from law enforcement agencies across the nation and places this information in the Uniform Crime Report (UCR), and every year the FBI will present the latest crime trends in America in a detailed report. The information collected is gathered from the reports that law enforcement professionals complete each day.

The front portion of the summons and complaint form typically contains the data that describes the person being charged and the suspect's personal information, along with the charge he or she was arrested for. The narrative portion on the back of the form is often designated with the title "Probable Cause Affidavit." This portion of the summons and

State Department of Revenue Traffic Crash Report

☐ Amended/ Supplement ☐ Under 1,000 ☐ Private Property ☐ Counter Report   Page 1 of 1

DOT CODE	DOR CODE	☐ Interstate HWY HWY Number ___ ___ ___ ☐ State HWY MILE Point ___ ___ ___ . ___ ___ ☒ City State County Road	Case Number 14-02456

Date of Accident 01-26-14	City Mersonville	State FL	Agency Mersonville Police Dept.	County Morris	County # 3

Time (24 Hour) 1500	Officer Number 1616	Officer Name James	Officer Signature *Michael James*	Zone Sector/Detail 4-3

Date of This Report 01-26-14	Agency Code 3	Number Killed 0	Number Injured 0

Location Street, Road, Route _____ Miles _____ Feet ☐ North ☐ South ☐ East ☐ West of:
North Rd.   ☒ At Jackon St.
Latitude _____ _____ _____   Longitude _____ _____ _____

Investigated at Scene ☒ Yes ☐ No	Total Vehicles 2	District Number 4-3	Bridge Related ☐ Yes ☒ No	Public Property or Employee ☐ Yes ☒ No	Railroad Crossing ☐ Yes ☒ No	Const. Zone ☐ Yes ☒ No	HWY Interchange ☐ Yes ☒ No	Photos ☒ Yes ☐ No

Vehicle 1 or _____ ☒ Vehicle ☐ Parked ☐ Bicycle ☐ Pedestrian ☐ Non-Vehicle ☐ Non-Contact Vehicle	Vehicle 2 or _____ ☒ Vehicle ☐ Parked ☐ Bicycle ☐ Pedestrian ☐ Non-Vehicle ☐ Non-Contact Vehicle

Last Name Smith	First Name Glenn	MI W	Last Name Emerson	First Name Steven	MI M

Street Address 320 N. Spruce Sr.	Home Phone 850-555-0199	Street Address 8150 Fort Smith Rd.	Home Phone 850-555-0193

City Mersonville	State FL	Zip 88088	Other Phone 850-555-0187	City Mersonville	State FL	Zip 88088	Other Phone 850-555-0187

Driver License Number 99-1100-1600	CDL	State FL	Sex M	DOB 11-05-68	Driver License Number 98-7608-5432	CDL	State FL	Sex M	DOB 09-13-76

Primary Violation ☐ DUI Careless Driving	Primary Violation ☐ DUI None

Violation Code 42-4-1402	Citation Number 18009001	Common Code	Violation Code	Citation Number	Common Code

Year 2009	Make Ford	Model Mustang	Body Type CP	Year 2010	Make Ford	Model F150	Body Type TRK

License Plate Number CHIEF241	State or County FL	Color Gray	License Plate Number RGHNEK12	State or County FL	Color Red

Vehicle Identification Number 1234567891P12BLER	Vehicle Identification Number 4567FT98765432ZYK

Vehicle Owner Last Name ☒ Same	First	MI	Vehicle Owner Last Name ☒ Same	First	MI

Address	City	State	Zip	Address	City	State	Zip

Towed due to damage ☐ By: To:	Towed due to damage ☐ By: To:

Vehicle 1 damage diagram: _2_ ☒ / _2_ ☒ / _2_ ☒ / _2_ ☒ / _2_ ☒

Vehicle 2 damage diagram: ☒ _2_ / ☒ _2_ / ☒ _2_ / ☒ _2_ / ☒ _2_

Slight = 1 Moderate = 2 Severe = 3 / Shade in areas of Damage | Slight = 1 Moderate = 2 Severe = 3 / Shade in areas of Damage

Insurance Company ☐ None ☐ No Proof All Right Insurance Policy # 945098-ARI-01	Exp. Date 01-31-2015	Insurance Company ☐ None ☐ No Proof Floridas Best Ins. Grp. Policy # ADI 31-039-090	Exp. Date 09-30-15

Owner Damage Property Last Name	First	MI	Address	City	State	Zip

TU #	Pos	Rest	Endo	Saf Eqp	Air Bag	Eject.	Susp Imp	Inj Sev	Age	Sex	Name/Address
1	1	Y	N	N	N	N	N	N	38	M	Same as Driver #1
2	1	Y	N	N	N	N	N	N	46	M	Same as Driver #2

Approved BY: Sgt. Davis	ID. # 2345	Date 01-26-2014

Figure 6.3 *Front of Traffic Crash Report*

Case # 14-02456	DOR CODE	Accident Date 01-26-2014	Agency *Mersonville Police Dept.*

Describe Accident

Vehicle # 2 was northbound on North Rd. stopped at the intersection of Jackson St. at the stop sign.

Vehicle # 1 was also northbound on North Rd. approaching the intersection of Jackson St. behind Vehicle # 2

Vehicle # 1 failed to stop and struck the rear end of Vehicle #2 with its front end causing moderate damage to both vehicles.

Details

Driver Vehicle #2 Statement:

Vehicle #2, Driver Emerson, said that he was northbound on North Rd. and had stopped at the intersection of Jackson St. at the stop sign waiting for traffic to clear so that he could turn left onto Jackson St. when he was hit from behind by vehicle #1.

Driver Vehicle #1 Statement:

Vehicle #1. Driver Smith said that he was northbound on North Rd. approaching Jackson St. when he dropped his cell phone into the passenger floorboard. Mr. Smith said that he reached down to retrieve the cell phone and took his eyes off the road for only a second not knowing that he was that close to the intersection.

Mr. Smith said that when he looked back at the road he saw the truck and he tried to stop but could not and struck the rear end of the truck with the front end of his car.

Officer Statement:

The intersection of Jackson St. and North Rd. is controlled by a traffic sign for traffic moving north and south on North Rd.

Traffic moving east and west on Jackson St. is not required to stop at the intersection and all vehicles moving north and south on North St. must stop before entering the intersection as directed by a visible stop sign.

Both drivers stated that they did not have any injuries and that they were wearing their seatbelts.
Both drivers exchanged information.
Neither vehicle involved in the crash needed to be towed.
No photos were taken.
Damage to Vehicle #1 estimated to be over $1,000.
Damage to Vehicle #2 estimated to be over $1,000.
Driver #1 Mr. Glenn Walter Smith was issued traffic summons #18009001 for Careless Driving.
No further information

Commercial Vehicle Carrier Name	☐ US DOT ☐ ICC ☐ State DOT
Address	Carrier Identification #
Commercial Vehicle Carrier Name	☐ US DOT ☐ ICC ☐ State DOT
Address	Carrier Identification #

Figure 6.4   *Back of Traffic Crash Report*

complaint form is where the law enforcement professional provides a chronological summary of the officer's activities in responding to this incident and the probable cause or the elements of the crime that supports the arrest that he or she made.

Figures 6.5 and 6.6 show an example of the front and the back of a misdemeanor summons and complaint form.

Mersonville Police Department Summons and Complaint Penalty Assessment	MPD	☐ Mersonville Municipal Court ☒ Morris County Court ☐ Traffic ☒ Non-Traffic ☐ Other	Summons 1800900 Case Number 15-45678

The People of Florida, City of Mersonville vs.

First	Middle	Last	DOB
Glenn	Walter	Smith	11/05/68

Residential Address	City	State	Zip Code
119 Beech St.	Mersonville	FL	88088

Drivers' License Number Presented ☒ Yes ☐ No 123-45-6789	State FL	Race WHT	Sex M	HGT 6'04"	WGT 380	Hair BRO	Eyes BRO	Alias

Home Phone	Cell Phone	Work Phone	Occupation	Employer
850-555-0199	850-555-0187	850-555-0191	Retired	U.S. Navy

Identifying Marks/Scars/Tattoos	Place of Birth
Tattoo Left Shoulder of Anchor with USN over it	Pensacola, FL

Vehicle Information

License Plate Number	Vehicle Year	State	License Year	Last Four of Vehicle Identification Number	Evidence
CHIEF24	2009	FL	15	1234	☐ Yes ☒ No

Make	Model	Damage	Body Style	Color(s)	Traffic Crash	Photos
FORD	Mustang		CP	GRY	☐ Yes ☒ No	☒ Yes ☐ No

Towed ☐ Yes	Towed ☒ No	Towed By:		Towed To:	

Charges

City/State Statute Number	Title	Fine	Surcharge	Points
18-4-401	Theft	$Court	$NA	Court

Description	
Defendant stole car stereo valued at $250.00	☐ Felony ☒ Misdemeanor

City/State Statute Number	Title	Fine $	Surcharge $	Points

Description	
	☐ Felony ☐ Misdemeanor

Approximate Location of Violation	Violation Date	Violation Time
1890 W. Jackson St	05-23-2015	1520

Custody/Service Location	Service Date	Service Time
119 Beech St.	05-23-2015	1700

You are hereby directed to appear as indicated

☒ Morris County Court located at 3030 Pembrook Blvd. Ste. 13, Mersonville, FL 88888

☐ Mersonville Municipal Court located at 640 Smith Rd. Ste. 303 Mersonville, FL 88888

On the _20th_ day of _July_ _2015_ at _9:00_ AM/PM

To answer charges of violations of the ☒ 1970 CRS as Amended ☐ Florida Children's Code ☐ The Code of Lynn City 2014

☒ Non Payable Summons ☐ Traffic ☒ Criminal	☐ Payable Summons ☐ Traffic ☐ Criminal
Without admitting guilt, I hereby promise to appear at the time and place indicated. Failure to appear constitutes a separate offense and will result in a warrant being issued.	Upon signing below I promise to pay the assessed fine within 20 days to the County Treasurer's Office per the instructions on the reverse side. Further, upon payment of this Penalty Assessment I acknowledge guilt of all charges. I am aware that the Penalty Assessment must be paid within 20 days or it becomes by law a Summons and Complaint and REQUIRES my appearance before the court at the time and place indicated above.
X _Glenn Smith_	X _____

☒ Defendant Held in Custody ☐ Morris County Justice Center ☒ Defendant Released

The undersigned have probable cause to believe that the defendant committed the offense(s) against the peace and dignity of the people of the State of Florida; and that this summons and complaint was signed and served upon the defendant at the location and on the date referenced above

Officer: _James_ _1616_ Served by: _Michael James_ Complaining Witness _____

Figure 6.5 *Front of Misdemeanor Summons and Complaint Form*

Probable Cause Affidavit

On 05-23-2015 I, Officer James 1616, was dispatched to 1890 W. Jackson St. in reference to a theft. Upon arrival I made contact with Nathan Emerson, the victim, who stated that he was having a yard sale in his driveway when an unknown male arrived and began looking at a Pioneer car stereo that he had for sale. This unknown male asked several questions concerning the stereo while looking at it. Mr. Emerson stated that he started helping another visitor and when he turned around he observed the unknown male walking to his car carrying the car stereo. Mr. Emerson called out to the male who quickly entered his car and drove away with the car stereo that Mr. Emerson valued at $250.00

Mr. Emerson described the unknown male as a white male, 6'03-6'05" and approximately 400lbs. with dark hair, wearing a white t-shirt and blue jeans. Mr. Emerson also observed that the male had a Tattoo of an anchor on his left arm. Mr. Emerson stated that the man drove away in a Gray or Silver in color Ford Mustang with a Florida plate number of CHIEF24.

I checked NCIC and discovered that the plate number came back to a Glenn Walter Smith at 119 Beech St.

I drove over to 119 Beech St. and upon arrival I observed a Gray Ford Mustang parked on the street bearing Florida Plate CHIEF24. The Mustang had its passenger door open and when I walked up to it I observed that the dashboard was taken apart with screws and the face plate laying on the passenger seat. I then observed a white male walk out of the garage carrying a car stereo. When the male observed me standing next to the car he dropped his hands to his side and stated "I was just checking to see if the stereo would work in my car and if it did I was going to bring the guy his money."

I asked the man for his identification and he handed me his Florida Driver License at which time I identified him as Glenn Walter Smith. I charged Smith with Misdemeanor theft and released him on summons number 1800900. I then took a photo of the vehicle, the stereo, and placed the photos into evidence at the Police Operations Center on 05-23-2015 at approximately 1830 hours. I also returned the car stereo back to Mr. Emerson.

WEATHER: ☐ CLEAR ☐ CLOUDY ☐ RAIN ☐ SNOW ☐ FOG ☐ DAWN ☐ DUSK   **ATTITUDE:** ☐ EXCELLENT ☐ GOOD ☐ FAIR ☐ POOR

TRAFFIC: ☐ VEHICLE ☐ PED ☐ BICYCLE ☐ ONCOMING ☐ SAME ☐ CROSS   **SURFACE CONDITIONS:** ☐ DRY ☐ WET ☐ SNOWPACKED ☐ ICY

DIRECTION OF TRAVEL: ☐ NORTH ☐ SOUTH ☐ EAST ☐ WEST   ☐ INTERSECTION ☐ CROSSWALK ☐ STOP BAR

RADAR: GUN NUMBER _____ TUNING FORKS _____   ☐ SPEED POSTED ☐ NOT POSTED ☐ SCHOOL ZONE

OFFICER(S) TO BE NOTIFIED FOR TRIAL

OFFICER   *JAMES* _____ BADGE NUMBER *1616*

OFFICER   _____ BADGE NUMBER ____

Victim Name *Nathan Emerson* Contact Phone *850-555-0186* Address: *1890 W. Jackson St. Meresonville, FL 88088*

UNDER PENALTY OF PERJURY, I AFFIRM THAT ALL THE INFORMATION CONTAINED UPON THIS DOCUMENT IS TRUE AND CORRECT TO THE BEST OF MY KNOWLEDGE.

AFFIANT_____ PRINT NAME_____

ADDRESS_____

HOME PHONE_____ WK. PHONE_____
ON THIS DATE, THE AFFIANT SIGNED THIS AFFIDAVIT AND SWORE TO ITS TRUTH

NOTARY PUBLIC_____ MY COMMISSION EXPIRES DATE_____

Figure 6.6 *Back of Misdemeanor Summons and Complaint Form*

4. FELONY CRIMES

Felony crimes are those criminal offenses that typically, upon conviction, impose a sentence of one year or more in the state penitentiary system. Felony crime reports are obviously the most detailed and thorough case reports that a law enforcement professional will be required to complete. These reports must be accurate, thorough, and contain all of the pertinent information involving the case.

As with the summons and complaint forms, the face sheet of the felony case report form will be utilized by the agency's records section to retrieve valuable crime data. The felony case narrative should begin with a description of the person who is writing the report and how he or she became involved.

> *Were they dispatched to a call for service?*
>
> *Were they flagged down by a citizen requesting assistance?*
>
> *In short, how did the case begin?*

This information helps to set the stage of the officer's involvement from beginning to end.

The body of the narrative portion of the felony case report simply contains a chronological record of all of the activities that occurred regarding the incident. Following these guidelines helps to ensure an accurate understanding of the incident and traps, permanently, essential case information. A more detailed accounting of format and content is included in other sections of this textbook.

Figure 6.7 shows an example of a face sheet for a felony report.

5. DOMESTIC VIOLENCE CRIMES (DOMESTIC VIOLENCE FORMS AND ALL REQUIRED ADDITIONAL FORMS)

The violent crime that occurs within a family was once viewed by law enforcement agencies as a family problem rather than a crime. In most cases no report was completed by the responding law enforcement agency. Over time, the seriousness of the offense was recognized, and domestic violence advocates launched a public awareness campaign. Law enforcement officers, prosecutors, and the general public were educated on the severity and the potential for devastating consequences of domestic violence offenses. Many states have enacted mandatory arrest in any domestic violence incident involving an injury. The following is information that is gathered by government agencies, which demonstrates the importance of properly documenting incidents involving domestic violence.

Figures 6.8, 6.9, and 6.10 show examples of domestic violence reports.

6. INCIDENT REPORTS (USUALLY A FACE SHEET)

Incident reports are typically the forms that are utilized for calls for service that do not fit into a clear niche of criminal cases or other types of standard case report forms. They form a catch-all category and are thus applicable in numerous situations.

Incident report forms mirror the format of case reports and domestic violence forms. That is, they are designed as a preprinted form to guide you through obtaining basic information

FAYE CITY POLICE DEPARTMENT COVER SHEET

City of Faye Police Department Cover Sheet	Offense ☒ Supplement ☐ Other ☐		Case Number 13-18901

Offense Title *Second Degree Burglary*	City/State Statute Number 18-4-203	Date of this Report 09/24/2013

Zone 4	Date and Time Reported				Date and Time of Occurrence			
	Month	Day	Year	Time	Month	Day	Year	Time
Sector 2	09	24	2013	1730	On or Between 09 / 09	24 / 24	2013 / 2013	0830 / 1700

Victim's Name (Last, First, Middle) Smith, Steven Michael	Date of Birth 11/05/1976	Age 38	Sex M	Race WHT	Occupation *Driller*

Residential Address 119 Beech St.	City Faye	State LA	Zip Code 88088	Victim's Brochure ☒ Yes ☐ No	Home Phone 225-555-0199
Business Address 3028 N. Lincoln St.	City Faye	State LA	Zip Code 97052	Work Phone 225-555-0186	Cell Phone 225-555-0172
Name of Business if Victim	Address	City	State	Zip Code	Business Phone

Codes RP = Reporting Party AV = Additional Victim W = Witness LO = Law Enforcement Officer A = Arrestee S = Suspect O = Other

Code	Last, First, Middle	Date of Birth	Age	Sex	Race	Occupation
Residential Address	City	State	Zip Code	Home Phone		Other Phone

Clothing Description		Alias	Summons Number

Identifying Marks/Scars/Tattoos/Birthmarks	HGT	WGT	Build	Hair	Eyes

Elements/Narrative

On 09-24-2013, (Officer James, Michael 1616P), was dispatched to 119 Beech St. in reference to a burglary. Upon arrival, I made contact with the victim, Steven Smith. Mr. Smith stated that between 09/24/13 at approximately 0830 hours and 09/24/13 at approximately 1700 hours unknown person(s) unlawfully entered his residence located at 119 Beech St. and stole various items of value kept inside.

See Property Descriptors for more information on stolen items.

Neighborhood Follow-Up – Yes

Witness Information – No

Suspect Information – No

Evidence – No

Photos – Yes

See Supplement For more information

Case Disposition Open ☒ Closed ☐ Cleared by Arrest ☐ Unfounded ☐	Patrol Investigation Continued ☐ Yes ☒ No	Assigned to:

Officer Name/Employee Number James, Michael 1616P	Supervisor Name/Employee Number Jones, Mackenzie 0923	Page 1 of 3

Figure 6.7   *Face Sheet for Felony Report*

Monroe Police Department   ☒ Offense Report   Summons Number

DOMESTIC VIOLENCE COMPLAINT/SUMMONS   **1900034**

THE PEOPLE OF THE STATE OF NORTH CAROLINA

☒ADULT   ☐JUVENILE

Case Number	Call Screen Number	Zone		Sector		Booking Number	
14-23456	123456	4		3		0987-321	

Defendants Name (First)	(Middle)	(Last)	DOB	Age
Glenn	Walter	Smith	11-05-1968	46

Defendants Address	(City)	(State)	Zip Code	Home Telephone
119 Beech St.	Monroe	NC	88088	252-555-0199

Employer Name	Address	(City)	(State)	Zip Code	Other Telephone
Retired					

Place of Birth City/State	Race	Sex	Height	Weight	Hair	Eyes	SSN
Pensacola, FL	WHT	M	6"04"	380	BRO	BRO	123-45-6789

Scars/Marks/Tattoos
Tattoo Left Shoulder of Anchor with USN over it

To Answer Charges of Violation(s) of 1973 North Carolina Revised Statute as Amended   ☒ Misdemeanor   ☐ Felony   ☐ Both

CHARGE #1	Statute Number	Title
	18-3-204	Assault in the Third Degree

Description
Defendant slapped the victim in the face with an open hand causing injury

CHARGE #2	Statute Number	Title
	18-9-111	Harassment

Description
Defendant pushed victim to the ground

CHARGE #3	Statute Number	Title

Description

Approximate Location of Violation	Violation Date	Approximate Time Violation	Companion Summons Number
119 Beech St.	01-23-14	2030	

Custody Location	Custody Date	Custody Time	Cross Complaint Number
119 Beech St.	01-23-14	2130	

☐Weapons Used	☒No Weapons	☐Weapons Displayed, but Not Used	☐Assault With Weapon(s)	☐Edged Weapon	☐ Firearms	☐Blunt Objects	Weapon Description: Open Hand

Circle if Applicable
Drugs   Alcohol   SHO/DI   Reg. Sex Offender Gang ----
Gang Set_____

DVERT Involvement	Parole/Probation Officer
☒Yes ☐No	

EMERGENCY CONTACT INFORMATION (For Defendant)

NAME (Last, First, Middle)	RELATIONSHIP	ADDRESS	TELEPHONE
Smith, Linda	Mother	121 Fort Smith Rd. Monroe, NC	252-555-0197

VICTIM INFORMATION

Victim Name (First)	(Middle)	(Last)	DOB	Age
Smith	Vera	Antoinette	12-01-69	44

Victim Address	(City)	(State)	Zip Code	Home Telephone
119 Beech St.	Monroe	NC	88088	252-555-0199

THE UNDERSIGNED HAS PROBABLE CAUSE TO BELIEVE THAT THE DEFENDANT COMMITTED THE OFFENSE(S) AGAINST THE PEACE AND DIGNITY OF THE PEOPLE OF THE STATE OF NORTH CAROLINA.

OFFICER: _James_   _#1616_ OFFICER_____ #_____

SERVED BY: _James_   _#1616_ COMPLAINING WITNESS: _Vera Smith_   DATE: _10-23-14_

Figure 6.8   Domestic Report: Example 1

PROBABLE CAUSE AFFIDAVIT

On 01-23-2014 I, Officer James 1616, was dispatched to 119 Beech St. in reference to a disturbance. Upon arrival I made contact with Vera Smith, the victim, who stated that her husband Glenn Smith, the suspect, came home intoxicated at approximately 2000 hours and demanded that she make him dinner. Mrs. Smith refused to prepare anything for him because she has been sick and on medication for the flu. Mr. Smith became angry when she would not get out of bed and started calling her a "Lazy Whore." Mrs. Smith stated that she was upset and screamed at Mr. Smith to leave her alone and to fix his own dinner at which time she got out of bed and stood behind him. Mr. Smith then turned toward Mrs. Smith and slapped her across the left side of her face with an open hand causing her visible injury. Mr. Smith then pushed Mrs. Smith backward with both hands causing her to trip over the corner of the bed and fall to the floor. Mrs. Smith stated that Mr. Smith then stood over her and continued to call her names and after a few minutes he walked out of the bedroom into the living room where she heard him turn on the television.

Mrs. Smith took the opportunity to call 911 and explained to the 911 Dispatcher what had occurred.

When I arrived at the residence Mrs. Smith answered the door and informed me that her husband was in the living room watching television. I entered the home and I contacted Mr. Smith sitting in a recliner at which time I smelled a strong odor of an unknown alcoholic beverage. When I spoke to Mr. Smith I noticed that he had slurred speech and blood shot watery eyes.

Mr. Smith declined to make a statement and he was taken into custody at 2130 on 01-23-14 and booked in to the Morris County Criminal Justice Center on the misdemeanor charges of Third Degree Assault and Harassment.

Photos of Mrs. Smith's injuries were taken and those photos were copied and are attached to this report and the originals were placed into evidence at the Police Operations Center.

The DIVERT team responded and assisted the victim and will continue any additional investigation if needed.

UNDER PENALTY OF PERJURY, I AFFIRM THAT ALL THE INFORMATION CONTAINED UPON THIS DOCUMENT IS TRUE AND CORRECT TO THE BEST OF MY KNOWLEDGE.

AFFIANT *Michael James 1616*   PRINT NAME *Michael James*

On this date, The Affiant signed this Affidavit and swore to its truth

01-23-14	*Stefanie Wells* **Stefanie Wells**	01-31-2018
Date	Notary Public	My Commission Expires

Figure 6.9   *Domestic Report: Example 2*

about the case. The real utility of the incident report form is that it can be used when no other type of form fits the specific characteristics of the incident.

Common situations that may need to be documented as an incident report are:

1. Property ownership involving a civil agreement between parties
2. Violation of jail rules by an inmate
3. Child custody issues involving parents in different states who have a court order giving them custody of the child issued by their state of residence

MPD

VICTIM INFORMATION

CASE NUMBER 14-23456

Victim's Name (First) Vera	(Middle) Antoinette	(Last) Smith	DOB 12-01-1969	Age 44

Victim's Address 119 Beech St.	(City) Monroe	(State) NC	Zip Code 88088	HM Telephone 252-555-0199

Employer Name Unemployed	Address	(City)	(State)	Zip Code	Work Phone

Place of Birth City/State Pensacola, FL	Race WHT	Sex F	Height 5"05"	Weight 150	Hair BRO	Eyes BRO	Cross Complaint #

Child Name	DOB	Address (If different from victim)	Did Child Witness Incident ☐Yes ☐No
Child Name	DOB	Address (If different from victim)	Did Child Witness Incident ☐Yes ☐No
Child Name	DOB	Address (If different from victim)	Did Child Witness Incident ☐Yes ☐No

Witness Name	DOB	Address	Home Phone	Other Phone
Witness Name	DOB	Address	Home Phone	Other Phone

Active Restraining Orders	☒*Mandatory (72 hour)*	☐*Temporary*	☐*Permanent*	☐*Domestic Relations*	Case Number

Victim/Suspect status	☒Married	☐Separated/Divorce	☐Cohabitants	☐Dating (not living together)	☐Other

Who called	☒Victim	☐Family Member	☐Neighbor	☐Suspect	☐Other

Check if Applicable	☐Drugs	☒Alcohol	☐Pregnant	☐Child Protective Services Notified	☐Animals in Home	☐Humane Society Notified

Check if Applicable	☐Throwing Things	☒Pushing Shoving	☐Grabbing	☒Slapping Open Hand	☐Kicking	☐Biting	☐Hitting Closed Fist	☐Choking

Weapons Used	☒No Weapons	☐Weapons Displayed, Not Used	☐Assault With Weapon(s)	☐Edged Weapon	☐Firearms	☐Blunt Objects	Weapon Description:

Injuries Noted	☐No Injury	☐Pain, but No Visible Injury	☒Visible Injury	☒Photographs (MANDATORY IF VISIBLE INJURIES) ☒Digital ☐35mm ☐Polaroid ☐Video ☐None

Medical Attention		☐Refused	☒Medical at Scene	☐Hospital or Medical Facility

Victims Emotional State:	☐Calm	☐Angry	☐Withdrawn	☐Apologetic	☒Crying	☒Upset	☐Scared	☐Other

Victim Questions

Has the suspect ever done this before? _Yes_ If so, when? _Vera Smith the victim_

Any previous violence with another person? _No_ If so, whom? _____

Has suspect made threats? _Yes_ If so, What and to whom? _He will kill victim, made to Vera Smith during last incident in 2013_

Were all the injuries to the victim caused by the suspect? _Yes_ If not, by whom?

_____

☒**The above listed victim has requested that he/she be notified of the pending release of the defendant by Morris County Jail Authorities.**

Victim Signature _Vera Smith_ _____ **Victim Notified by:** _____
Date: _____

Victim Statement: _My husband came home drunk and wanted me to make dinner and when I refused he slapped me and pushed me down. He has done this before and I think this is the second time that I have had him arrested._ _____

Victim Name (Print) _Vera Smith_ _____ **Victim Signature** _Vera Smith_ _____

Figure 6.10 *Domestic Report: Example 3*

These are just a few examples of the many incidents you will come across while on duty, and Figure 6.11 provides an example of an incident report.

7. SUSPICIOUS CIRCUMSTANCES (USUALLY A FACE SHEET)

A suspicious circumstances report is similar to an incident report. The only difference between the two reports is that an incident report is normally noncriminal and a suspicious circumstances report could lead to a criminal investigation at a later time. A suspicious circumstances report can be completed on a simple department face sheet or on a form specifically designed for circumstances where intelligence on suspicious activity is documented and followed up by detectives who require more information before initiating a criminal report.

Common situations that may need to be documented and titled suspicious circumstances are:

1. Suspicious vehicles in a neighborhood late at night
2. Unknown people loitering near an abandoned building
3. Adults or young adults contacting high school students near the school
4. People passing unknown items from a car to pedestrians on the sidewalk
5. Many visitors to a residence late at night

These are just a few examples of the many different situations you may encounter that would not, at the time of documentation, be identified as a crime. Figure 6.12 provides an example of a suspicious circumstances report.

THE *RIGHT* WAY TO *WRITE*

The various types of reports you may encounter often require a different style of writing depending upon the use and application of the report or form. Many common forms and reports are completed by simply checking boxes and sometimes writing a brief narrative. Often, abbreviations and symbols are acceptable in some types of forms (such as a traffic citation or summons). The narrative style of report writing does not always apply. Nor is it appropriate in some types of reports. However, for items such as correctional incident reports (on major incidents such as escapes, inmate deaths, major assaults/murders, etc.), the narrative case report format is appropriate.

The methods for writing the miscellaneous forms described in this chapter will vary greatly between jurisdictions and also within specific agencies. For example, in a traffic summons or complaint, the bulk of the writing will be simply filling in boxes, followed by an abbreviated probable cause affidavit (see the Lynn City Police Department Summons and Complaint Penalty Assessment Form found earlier in this chapter). Most jurisdictions will allow you to abbreviate and use improper English grammar on these types of forms. Again, it is important to recognize that various departments will require different techniques for completing these forms. The Lynn City Police Department document is representative of a typical traffic citation.

The writing style of the various forms listed in this chapter will be driven by jurisdictional and departmental directives. This chapter presents several of the more common forms that a criminal justice professional may encounter. This is not meant to be an all-inclusive list, as

MCSO FACE SHEET

Mills County Sheriff's Office Face Sheet	Offense ☐ Supplement ☐ Other ☒	Case Number 13-12890

Offense Title *Incident Report*	City/State Statute Number	Date of this Report *09/01/2013*

Zone 5	Date and time Reported				Date and Time of Occurrence			
Sector 2	Month	Day	Year	Time	Month	Day	Year	Time
	09	*01*	*2013*	*1330*	On or Between	*09* *09*	*01* *01*	*2013* *2013*

(Date and Time of Occurrence: On or Between — 09 01 2013 1230 / 09 01 2013 1315)

Victim's Name (Last, First, Middle)		Date of Birth	Age	Sex	Race	Occupation	
Residential Address	City	State	Zip Code	Victim's Brochure ☐ Yes ☐ No		Home Phone	
Business Address	City	State	Zip Code	Work Phone		Cell Phone	
Name of Business if Victim	Address	City	State	Zip Code		Business Phone	

Codes RP = Reporting Party   AV = Additional Victim   W = Witness   P = Police Officer   A = Arrestee   S = Suspect   O = Other

Code RP	Last, First, Middle *David, Nathan, Robert*	Date of Birth *03/18/1980*	Age *33*	Sex *M*	Race *WHT*	Occupation *store manager*	
Residential Address *640 Oak Dr.*		City *Mills*	State *AZ*	Zip Code *88088*	Home Phone *520-555-0176*	Other Phone *520-555-0182*	
Clothing Description				Alias		Summons Number	
Identifying Marks/Scars/Tattoos			HGT	WGT	Build	Hair	Eyes

Elements/Narrative

On 09/01/2013 at approximately 1335 I, (Deputy James, Michael 1616D), was dispatched to 640 Oak Dr. in reference to a disturbance between neighbors. Upon arrival, I made contact with the Reporting Party, Nathan David, who stated that at approximately 1230 he heard noises coming from his backyard and when he went to see what it was he discovered his neighbor Paul Sims painting the privacy fence that separated their property. When he asked Mr. Sims what he was doing Mr. Sims told him that one side of the fence belonged to him and that he was going to paint it to help accent his yard.

Mr. David stated that Mr. Sims never mentioned that he was going to paint the fence and that he should have discussed it with him before damaging it. Mr. David explained that the paint was now showing through the cracks between the slats thus making his side of the fence unattractive. Mr. David stated that he wanted Mr. Sims to stop the painting as it was ruining his side of the fence.

I spoke to Paul Travis Sims DOB 02-23-78 at his residence at 644 Oak Dr. with a contact number of 520-555-0167. Mr. Sims stated that he was not going to stop painting the fence and that the Ridgeline Homeowners Association for their neighborhood told him that there were no rules stopping him from painting the fence as long as he chose a color from their rulebook, which he said he had done.

Mr. Sims also stated that there were no rules in the Association's rulebook about discussing it with his neighbor before painting the fence. Mr. Sims provided me with a copy of the Ridgeline Homeowners Association Rulebook. I could not locate any information that would stop Mr. Sims from painting the fence. I checked the rulebook and discovered he was in compliance with the color he had selected as well.

I then spoke to Mr. David once more and advised him that this was a situation where he needed to contact the Ridgeway Homeowners Association and try to find how he should file a grievance with them regarding the fence being painted. According to the rulebook it appears that both individuals own and share the fence that sits on the property line between their homes. According to the association rules Mr. Sims appears to be in compliance. No further information.

Case Disposition Open ☒ Closed ☒ Cleared by Arrest ☐ Unfounded ☐	Patrol Investigation Continued ☐ Yes ☒ No	Assigned to:
Deputy Name/Employee Number *James, Michael 1616D*	Supervisor Badge Number *Jones, Mackenzie 0923D*	Page 1 of 1

Figure 6.11   Incident Report

MEEKER POLICE DEPARTMENT

City of Meeker Police Department Face Sheet	Offense ☐ Supplement ☐ Other ☒	Case Number 13-12890

Offense Title *Suspicious Circumstances*	City/State Statute Number	Date of this Report 07/25/2013

Zone 5	Date and time Reported				Date and Time of Occurrence			
	Month	Day	Year	Time	Month	Day	Year	Time
Sector 2	07	25	2013	0930	On or Between	07 07	24 24	2013 2013	2315 2345

Victim's Name (Last, First, Middle)		Date of Birth	Age	Sex	Race	Occupation

Residential Address	City	State	Zip Code	Victim's Brochure ☐ Yes ☐ No	Home Phone

Business Address	City	State	Zip Code	Work Phone	Cell Phone

Name of Business if Victim	Address	City	State	Zip Code	Business Phone

Codes   RP=Reporting Party   AV=Additional Victim   W=Witness   P=Police Officer   A=Arrestee   S= Suspect   O=Other

Code RP	Last, First, Middle Emerson, Linda, Faye	Date of Birth 08/21/1938	Age 72	Sex F	Race BLK	Occupation Retired

Residential Address 119 Elm St.	City Meeker	State AZ	Zip Code 88088	Home Phone 520-555-0197	Other Phone

Clothing Description		Alias	Summons Number

Identifying Marks/Scars/Tattoos/Birthmarks	HGT	WGT	Build	Hair	Eyes

Elements/Narrative

On 07/25/2013 at approximately 0940 I, (Officer James, Michael 1616P), was dispatched to 119 Elm St. in reference to a suspicious vehicle that the reporting party observed the previous night. Upon arrival I made contact with Linda Emerson who told me that on 07/24/2013 at approximately 2100 hours she went to bed, but was awakened at approximately 2315 by the sound of people yelling behind her residence in the alley.

Mrs. Emerson stated that she got up and looked out her back bedroom window and saw the figure of a man standing next to the passenger side of a dark in color, four door sedan. She stated that she knew it was a man because she could hear his voice as he shouted at the people inside the car. She did not know what he was saying but believed he was angry because she observed him slam his hands on the hood of the car.

Mrs. Emerson stated that she watched this man for about 10 minutes before the driver in the car honked his or her horn and sped out of the alley spinning the wheels loudly. The man who was next to the car ran out of the alley in the opposite direction.

Mrs. Emerson stated that she did not know what kind of car it was but knew it was dark in color and had four doors, she also did not know the year of the car nor could she describe the driver. Mrs. Emerson said that she did not recognize the man next to the car nor could she describe him.

I spoke to the individuals living on both sides of Mrs. Emerson and both told me that they were home last night but did not hear or see anything like Mrs. Emerson had described. No further information.

Case Disposition Open ☒ Closed ☒ Cleared by Arrest ☐ Unfounded ☐	Patrol Investigation Continued ☐ Yes ☒ No	Assigned to:

Officer Name/Employee Number James, Michael 1616P	Supervisor Name/Employee Number Jones, Mackenzie 0923	Page 1 of 1

Figure 6.12   *Suspicious Circumstances Report*

many jurisdictions utilize different forms and reports. Most of these forms will have some type of "fill-in" cover sheet followed by a very short or abbreviated narrative. To cover every jurisdictional or agency requirement would be too daunting a task to attempt in this textbook. What is presented in this textbook are some generic or common forms to give the reader a broad view of the typical types of reports. Study the style and format of the examples given and apply whatever is appropriate to your jurisdiction.

TIPS FOR TYPES OF REPORTS

- First and foremost, acquaint yourself on what types of forms are available and appropriate to use in the various types of incidents that may occur.
  - These types of reports are typically given in your agency policy and procedure manual or may be found in the agency's standard operating procedures (SOP).
  - If your agency has developed a specific report or form for a specific type of incident, use it.
  - Ask for examples of well-written, completed reports to use as guides to help educate you on each type of report.
  - As always, be accurate, be brief, be complete, and be understandable.

SUMMARY

All law enforcement agencies have various types of reports to be utilized in specific situations. There is no "one size fits all" type of report that covers every situation. Thus, specialized forms are designed to help guide the officer through specific types of incidents, thereby minimizing needless verbiage and maximizing efficiency. These forms trap critical information and help to guide you through the documentation process.

Specific types of reports create a workable format for the officer to input critical information regarding an incident. Simply put, these reports trap the critical elements of the incident, the players involved, and the actions you took to resolve the situation. These types of reports document the who, what, when, where, and how of an incident. Normally, using these types of reports will help to shorten the amount of time the officer spends on the incident. Remember that your agency has spent numerous hours developing and refining these specialized types of reports to help you focus on the essential information that must be captured regarding the incident.

EXERCISES

1. In this exercise you will watch a video scenario of an incident involving a disagreement between neighbors over the ownership of a lawnmower. While watching the video scenario, you will be required to take notes and then complete an incident report documenting this particular call for service. *(Video Scenario of an Incident 6.1)* Use the interview sheets, face sheet or cover sheet, and supplement or continuation report

forms that can be found in the "Appendix: Sample Forms" of this book to complete this exercise.

Additional Information:

Zone: 4

Sector: 4

Date: Your Current date

Time: The time announced in the video

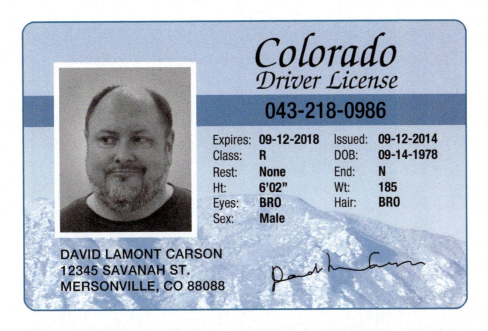

2. In this next exercise, you will watch a video scenario involving suspicious circumstances that is being reported to the police by a concerned citizen. While watching the video scenario, you will be required to take notes and then complete a suspicious circumstance report documenting this particular call for service. *(Video Scenario of Suspicious Circumstances 6.2)* Use the interview sheets, face sheet or cover sheet, and supplement or continuation report forms that can be found in the "Appendix: Sample Forms" to complete this exercise.

Additional Information:

Zone: 4

Sector: 5

Date: Your Current date

Time: The time announced in the video

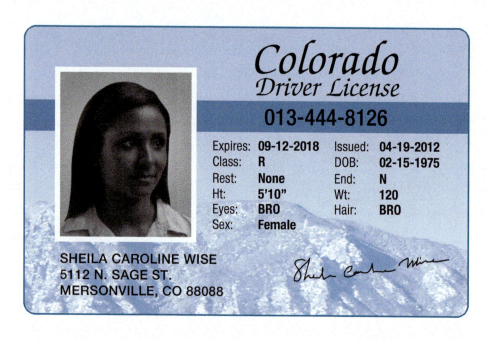

7

TRAFFIC SUMMONS/ TICKETS AND CRASH REPORTS

LEARNING OBJECTIVES

- Understand the importance of traffic enforcement within a community.

- Understand that, although each state may present driver and vehicle information differently, there are numerous commonalities in completing the bulk of the information required in completing the traffic report.

- Be familiar with some of the additional questions that may need to be answered by the operator of a motor vehicle to ensure the traffic summons or traffic crash report is completed correctly.

- Understand the use of shorthand on the backside or probable cause section of a traffic summons/ticket.

- Apply your knowledge to practical examples by successfully completing the chapter exercises.

INTRODUCTION

Community-oriented policing dictates that positive community relations are a cornerstone of law enforcement. Every action by law enforcement affects the relationship between your agency and the community. A major source of contacts with law enforcement officers and citizens are traffic stops. Law enforcement officers should use this opportunity to build understanding and trust with the citizens of their community.

As a law enforcement officer you have an opportunity to positively impact a citizen's attitude toward traffic safety in the future. The dialog between the officer and the citizen at a traffic stop should be polite, factual, and based on the understanding that traffic safety is the goal of the encounter. Citizens are more willing to change their improper driving practices if they are treated with respect and professionalism.

The old adage "There is no such thing as a routine traffic stop" should not be taken lightly. Statistically, traffic stops are dangerous. Traffic stops contribute to numerous officer line-of-duty deaths every year. Traffic enforcement is also an effective way to reduce criminal activity. Another adage appears to be appropriate: "Bad guys are bad drivers." This is true. Officers conducting traffic stops often encounter impaired drivers, drugs, illegal weapons, wanted fugitives, and other criminal circumstances.

A good rule of thumb is to always practice officer safety and assume a defensive posture when conducting any traffic stop. It is important to always look for something other than the traffic citation when stopping motorists.

THE TRAFFIC SUMMONS/TICKET

One of the many responsibilities of law enforcement professionals will usually involve the enforcement of traffic laws within an assigned patrol area during one's shift. Therefore, knowing how to complete a traffic summons or crash report is essential to the successful performance of one's assigned duties. The primary traffic objective of any law enforcement agency is the safe and orderly flow of traffic through their respective jurisdiction. An agency can achieve this traffic objective by:

1. Regulating the flow of traffic in diverse ways, which may include:

    Restricting commercial vehicles to certain streets

    Reducing or increasing the speed limits on specific streets

2. Traffic law enforcement, which may include:

    Traffic stops

3. Educating drivers, which may include:

    Penalty assessments for specific violations that could or do jeopardize community safety

    Monitoring traffic saturation points (in school zones, high-collision areas, driver license checkpoints and DUI checkpoints)

4. Investigating automobile crashes, which may include:

    Designating specific traffic units in multiple divisions or precincts (crash car, DUI car, red light or intersection enforcement officers, and school speed zone officers)

    Creating felony or fatal crash investigation teams

TRAFFIC ENFORCEMENT AND THE COMMUNITY

Traffic stops account for more than half of all the contacts between citizens and law enforcement professionals across the nation each year. The goal for each traffic stop should be to make the violator aware of the violation either through education or enforcement. The education aspect can be achieved by simply using officer discretion and advising the violator about the violation without the issuance of a traffic summons.

The issuance of a traffic summons to a driver who violates a jurisdiction's traffic statute/law should be made with the goal of either specific or general deterrence in mind. The "specific deterrence" aspect is for the violator in the belief that the issuance of the traffic summons, along with a punishment assessment attached to it, will prevent him or her from committing the same traffic violation in the future. The "general deterrence" aspect of issuing a traffic summons is for the benefit of the rest of society who may become aware of the punishment associated with a violation to a specific traffic violation. Thus, the intended result is that other citizens will understand the consequences of committing a similar offense and will refrain from violating the traffic statute/law.

COMPLETING THE TRAFFIC SUMMONS/TICKET

Once you have stopped a motorist for a traffic violation, it is time to complete the traffic summons/ticket.

Best Practices: Before you stop a motorist for a traffic violation, you should already know what you are going to do before the stop. Either you should be prepared to write the traffic summons/ticket or be prepared to give a verbal warning.

The following pages will cover how to complete a traffic summons/ticket proceeding from the driver's license to the registration and finally proof of insurance. Each state is different in regard to the requirements for each section, but the concepts of completing the traffic summons/ticket remains the same.

Figure 7.1 contains four different state driver's licenses for the same individual. Each one of the state license identification cards is unique in its shape, design, and the way information is formatted on it. As a law enforcement professional, you will come into contact with many different variations of state licenses, but the one thing that remains the same is that each one contains the same or some of the same basic information for the subject of that driver license. Collecting the correct information is extremely important in case the driver does not pay the violation or does not appear in court. The following list illustrates the basic information you may find on a driver's license that is needed to complete a traffic summons/ticket followed by questions that should be asked to ensure the driver can be located in the future.

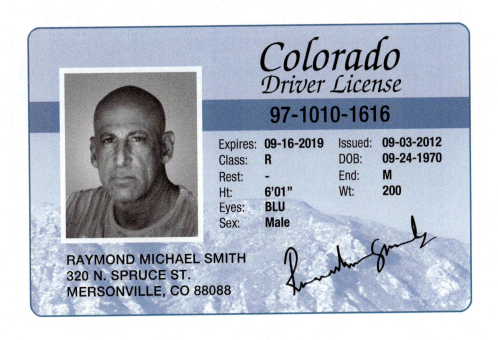

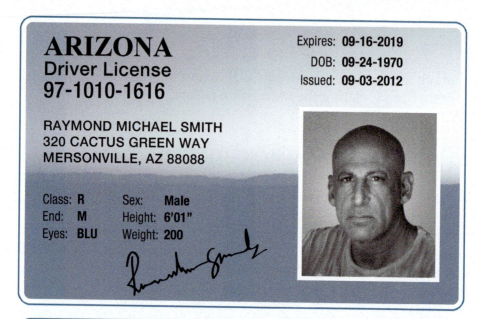

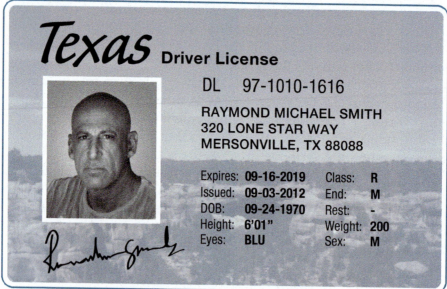

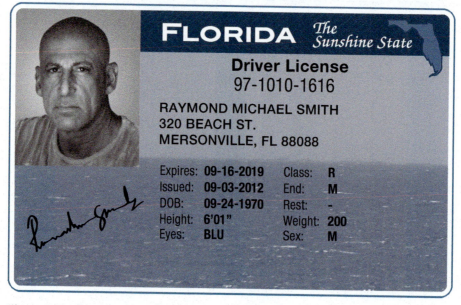

Figure 7.1(a–d) *Variation in Driver's License Formats*

Best Practices: Once you have the driver's license in hand, make sure you look at the photo to ensure you have the correct person driving the vehicle. Also make sure that, if there are restrictions on the license, such as wearing glasses, the driver is in compliance.

State issuing the license: *Texas*

License Number: *97-1010-1616*

Date the license was issued: *09-03-2012*

Date the license expires: *09-16-2019*

Class (regular license, commercial license, etc.): *R*

Endorsements or "End": *Driving a motorcycle* (example)

Restrictions or "Rest": *Must wear glasses at night* (example)

Name: *Raymond Michael Smith*

Date of Birth: *09-24-1970*

Address: *320 Lone Star Way Mersonville, TX 88088*

Height (Ht): *6'01"*

Weight (Wt): *200 lbs*

Eyes (Color): *BLU*

Sex (Male or Female): *M*

The previous information is only part of what you need to complete a traffic summons/ticket in regard to the operator/driver. You must ask the driver additional questions to ensure you are completing the traffic summons/ticket thoroughly. These questions should be asked before you start completing the traffic summons/ticket information.

1. *Is the address and the other information on your license correct?*
2. *What is your home phone number or the best number to contact you?*
3. *Are you currently employed? (If the answer is yes, the next question should be "where?".)*
4. *What is the phone number for your place of employment?*

The registration is the second form of information that you will need to complete the traffic summons/ticket. The registration for the vehicle should be requested along with the driver's license upon first contacting the driver and advising him or her of the traffic violation.

Best Practices: Some type of proof of insurance for motor vehicles is mandatory. Therefore, you should ask for proof of insurance along with the driver's license and vehicle registration. Drivers who cannot provide proof of insurance can be charged for this additional violation as well.

The vehicle registration is required in most states to be in the vehicle at all times, and failure to do so may leave the operator in a situation where they can be issued a violation for this infraction as well. The vehicle registration, like the state driver's license, can be unique in its shape, design, and information formatting, but once again, it will usually contain all of the needed information to complete the traffic summons/ticket. On the following pages are examples of four different state registrations (Figures 7.2 through 7.5).

COLORADO REGISTRATION/OWNERSHIP TAX RECEIPT

TYPE	PLATE	TAB/VAL	VIN		EXPIRE
PAS-REG	1BADGUY	A711111	1234567891P0LCVB7		12/2015

TITLE	YEAR	MAKE	BODY	CWT/PAS	T/C	FLEET	FUEL	PREV EXP
Y231	2012	ACURA	SD	35	C		G	

PUR DATE	PUR PRICE	ORIGINAL TAXABLE VALUE	BUS DATE	CO#	UR/CODE
11/15/2014	45,000	43,000	12/30/2014	11U	0001

EM FEE	TITLE FEE	PRIOR O.T.	OWN TAX	LIC FEE	ROAD FEE	BRIDGE FEE
0.00	0.00	0.00	850.00	120.00	23.00	13.50

RTD TAX	COUNTY TAX	CITY/DIS TAX	STATE TAX	SPECIAL FEE	OTHER FEE
0.00	50.00	30.00	25.00	0.00	0.00

UNIT	GVW	MILES	HT GVW	HC DATE

OWNER MAILING ADDRESS   FEES IN BOLD INCLUDED IN UC FEE

                                                E09933456   4356

SMITH RAYMOND M

320 N. SPRUCE ST.   SIGNATURE REQUIRED ON REVERSE SIDE
MERSONVILLE, CO 88088

VALIDATION	LN		TOTAL
PAID TELLER	24	09/10/2012	

MOTOR VEHICLE INSURANCE IS COMPULSORY IN COLORADO, NON-COMPLIANCE IS A IS A MISDEMEANOR TRAFFIC OFFENSE

Figure 7.2   *State Registration: Example 1*

ARIZONA VEHICLE REGISTRATION

MOTOR VEHICLE *ADOT* **DIVISION**

Print Date/time
12/30/2014/13:05

Expiration Date
12/30/2015

Carry In Vehicle At All Times

	Vehicle Identification Number		Veh. Lic. Tax	$250.00
	1234567891P0LCVB7		Registration	$8.25

RAYMOND M SMITH
320 Cactus Green Way
Mersonville, AZ 88088

Air Quality $3.00
Postage/Handling $0.45

Record Number	01234567
Plate Number	1BADGUY
Unit Number	
Year/Make	2012 ACURA
Body Style	4DSD
First Registered	12/2014
List Price	042500
Fuel Type	G
Category	A
Weight (GVW)	
County	MORRIS
Registration Type	FUL

TOTAL $261.70

Figure 7.3   *State Registration: Example 2*

TEXAS
TITLE APPLICATION RECEIPT

COUNTY: MORRIS

TAC NAME: MICHAEL J. GARCIA
DATE: 12/30/2014   EFEECTIVE DATE: 12/30/2014

PLATE NO: 1BADGUY   TIME: 01:05 PM   EXPIRATION DATE: 12/2015
DOCUMENT NO: 1234567891012131415   EMPLOYEE ID: 1234567   TRANSACTION ID: 12309876456
PREV DOC NO: 123409657809847362   P
OWNER NAME AND ADDRESS
RAYMOND SMITH
320 LONE STAR WAY
MERSONVILLE, TX 88088

REGISTRATION CLASS: PASSENGER-LESS/EQL 6000
PLATE TYPE: PASS CAR PLT
ORGANIZATION:
STICKER TYPE WS

VEHICLE IDENTIFICATION NO: 1234567891P0LCVB7   VEHICLE CLASSIFACTION: PASS
YR/MAKE: 2012/ACURA   MODEL: TL   BODY STYLE 4D   UNIT NO:
EMPTY WT: 2800   CARRYING CAPACITY: 0   GROSS WT: 2800   TONNAGE: 0.00 TRAILER TYPE:
BODY VEHICLE IDENTIFICATION NO: TRAVEL TRLR LNG/WDTH: 0
PREV OWNER NAME: GLENN ROBERTS   PREV CITY/STATE: MERSONVILLE, TX.

	FEES ASSESSED		
	TITLE APPLICATION FEE	$	13.00
VEHICLE RECORDS APPLICATION	TEXAS MOBILITY FUND FEE	$	15.00
PAPER TITLE	SALES TAX FEE	$	10.00
MAJOR COLOR: BLACK	TRANSFER	$	2.50
	TOTAL	$	40.50

ODOMOTER READING: 15990   BRAND:
OWNERSHIP EVIDENCE: CERTIFIED COPY TEXAS TITLE   SALES TAX CATEGORY: USED

1ST LIEN   Date of Assignment/Sales Tax Date: 12/30/2014

	Sales Price	$	42500.00
	Less Trade in Allowance	$	0.00
	Taxable Amount	$	0.00
	Sales Tax Paid	$	150.00
2nd LIEN	Less Other State Tax Paid	$	0.00
	Tax Penalty	$	0.00
	TOTAL TAX PAID	$	150.00

3RD LIEN   Batch no: 0000008970   Batch Count: 1

THIS RECEIPT TO BE CARRIED IN ALL COMMERCIAL VEHICLES

Figure 7.4   *State Registration: Example 3*

FLORIDA VEHICLE REGISTRATION

CO/AGY 9 /5   T#   012345678

B#   135792

| PLATE | **1BADGUY** | DECAL | 01234567 | | Expires **Midnight Thur. 12/31/2015** |

YR/MK   **2012/ACURA**   BODY   **SD**   COLOR **BLK**   Reg. Tax   65.00   Class Code 31
VIN   **1234567891P0LCVB7**   TITLE **12345678**   Init. Reg.   Tax Months 12
Plate Type **RGR**   NET WT **2800**   County Fee   3.00   Back Tax Months
                                                                         Mail Fee   Credit Class
DL/FEID **V40076856781616**   Sales Tax   Credit Months
Date Issued **12/18/2014**   Plate Issued **12/22/2014**   Voluntary Fees
                                                                         Grand Total 68.00

IMPORTANT INFORMATION

RAYMOND M SMITH   1. The Florida License Plate must remain with the registrant upon sale of the vehicle.
320 Beach   2. The registration must be delivered to a Tax Collector or Tag Agent for transfer to a replacement vehicle.
St.Mersonville,   3. Your registration must be updated to your new address within 20 days of moving.
FL 88088   4. Registration renewals are the responsibility of the registrant and shall occur during the 30-day period
                           prior to the expiration date shown on this registration. Renewal notices are provided as a courtesy and
                           are not required for renewal purposes

RGR-FLORIDA REGULAR

THIS RECEIPT IS YOUR PROOF OF APPLICATION FOR CERTIFICATE OF TITLE AND REGISTRATION

Figure 7.5   *State Registration: Example 4*

Best Practices: Always compare the registration handed to you with the vehicle that has been stopped for the violation to ensure that they are one and the same. This can easily be accomplished by comparing the VIN on the registration to the VIN on the vehicle.

On the following pages, you will view an example of a traffic summons/ticket along with the information that was needed to complete the form (Figure 7.6 and Figure 7.7). Remember that, when you examine the traffic summons/ticket, it contains information that can also be used for additional criminal charges, if necessary.

QUESTIONS AND RESPONSES

1. *Is the address and the other information on your license correct?* **Yes**
2. *What is your home phone number or the best number to contact you?* **719- 555-0199**
3. *Where are you currently employed?* **I am retired, I no longer work.**
4. *Is there another number you can be reached at besides your home?* **Yes my cell phone, and that number is 719-555-0187**
5. *What is your place of birth?* **Pensacola, FL.**

Now you may have noticed that the last question is not: *What is the phone number for your place of employment?* Sometimes you will not get some information for the traffic summons/ticket because the operator of the vehicle simply does not have it or it does not apply to them because:

They may not be employed.

They do not have a home phone.

They do not have a cell phone.

Mersonville Police Department Summons and Complaint Penalty Assessment	MPD	☒ Mersonville Municipal Court ☐ Morris County Court ☒ Traffic ☐ Non-Traffic ☐ Other	Summons 1800900 Case Number

The People of Colorado, City of Mersonville vs

First	Middle	Last	DOB
Glenn	Walter	Smith	11/05/68

Residential Address			City	State	Zip Code
320 N. Spruce St.			Mersonville	CO	88088

Drivers' License Number Presented ☒ Yes ☐ No	State	Race	Sex	HGT	WGT	Hair	Eyes	Alias
99-1100-1600	CO	WHT	M	6'04"	280	BRO	BRO	

Home Phone	Cell Phone	Work Phone	Occupation	Employer
719-555-0199	719-555-0187		Retired	U.S. Navy

Identifying Marks/Scars/Tattoos	Place of Birth
Tattoo Left Shoulder of Anchor with USN over it	Pensacola, FL

Vehicle Information

License Plate Number	Vehicle Year	State	License Year	Last Four of Vehicle Identification Number	Evidence
CHIEF241	2009	CO	15	BLER	☐ Yes ☒ No

Make	Model	Body Style	Damage	Color(s)	Traffic Crash	Photos
FORD	Mustang	CP	N/A	GRY	☐ Yes ☒ No	☐ Yes ☒ No

Towed	Towed	Towed By:	Towed To:
☐ Yes	☒ No		

Charges

City/State Statute Number	Title	Fine	Surcharge	Points
9-34-5234	SPEEDING 10-15 over	$100.00	$20.00	4

Description		☐ Felony
Defendant drove 65MPH in a posted 50MPH zone		☐ Misdemeanor

City/State Statute Number	Title	Fine	Surcharge	Points
		$	$	

Description		☐ Felony
		☐ Misdemeanor

Approximate Location of Violation	Violation Date	Violation Time
2300 N. Washington Ave.	01-01-2014	1250

Custody/Service Location	Service Date	Service Time
2300 N. Washington Ave.	01-01-2014	1300

You are hereby directed to appear as indicated

☐ Morris County Court located at 3030 Pembrook Blvd. Ste. 13, Mersonville, CO 88888

☒ Mersonville Municipal Court located at 640 Smith Rd. Ste. 303 Mersonville, CO 88888

On the _03_ day of _____ January _____ 2014 at _13.00_ AM/PM

To answer charges of violations of the ☐1970 CRS as Amended ☐ California Children's Code ☒The Code of Mersonville 2014

☐ Non Payable Summons ☐ Traffic ☐ Criminal	☒ Payable Summons ☒ Traffic ☐ Criminal
Without admitting guilt, I hereby promise to appear at the time and place indicated. Failure to appear constitutes a separate offense and will result in a warrant being issued.	Upon signing below I promise to pay the assessed fine within 20 days to the County Treasurer's Office per the instructions on the reverse side. Further, upon payment of this Penalty Assessment I acknowledge guilt of all charges. I am aware that the Penalty Assessment must be paid within 20 days or it becomes by law a Summons and Complaint and REQUIRES my appearance before the court at the time and place indicated above.
X _____	X _Glenn Smith_____

☐ Defendant Held in Custody ☐ Morris County Justice Center ☐ Defendant Released

The undersigned have probable cause to believe that the defendant committed the offense(s) against the peace and dignity of the people of the State of Colorado; and that this summons and complaint was signed and served upon the defendant at the location and on the date referenced above

Officer: _James_ _1616_ Served by: _Michael James_ Complaining Witness _____

Figure 7.6 *Traffic Summons/Ticket*

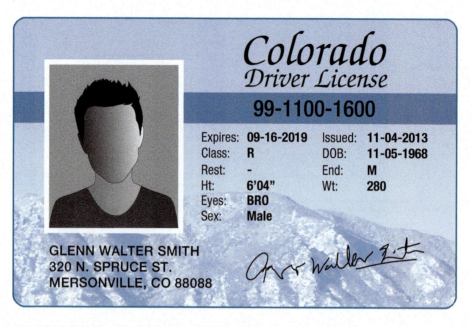

Figure 7.7   *Information Needed to Complete Traffic Summons/Ticket*

You may have also noticed that the color of the vehicle has been identified on the traffic summons/ticket, along with the model of the vehicle, although this information was not on the registration. This may occur during the traffic stop, and when it does, you will simply have to look at the vehicle and determine the color and model, or you can ask the operator.

You should have also noticed that the operator's hair color was not identified on the license, but it was on the traffic summons/ticket. Once again, this is just another feature you may have to simply observe yourself or ask the operator.

Best Practices: Licenses and registrations can be unique to each state, but you must adapt; if there is a box on the traffic summons/ticket that you cannot find the corresponding information for among the information given to you at the time of the stop, then you must simply use your observation skills or simply ask the operator for it.

Figure 7.8 shows the reverse side of the previous traffic summons/ticket written to Glenn Walter Smith.

When you look at the reverse side of the provided traffic summons/ticket, you will discover that the officer's probable cause affidavit supports the charge on the front side of

---

On 01-01-2014 at approx 1250 I, Officer James 1616, observed the defendant, Smith, NB in the LL of the 2300 block of N. Washington Ave. Vis: 65 Radar Conf. 65 Posted 50MPH No other veh. No obstr.

Mr. Smith Stated that he was late for a party and did not notice that he was that much over the speed limit

Radar Calib. B and A each stop. No further information

WEATHER: ☒ CLEAR ☐ CLOUDY ☐ RAIN ☐ SNOW ☐ FOG ☐ DAWN ☐ DUSK

TRAFFIC: ☒ VEHICLE ☐ PED ☐ BICYCLE ☐ ONCOMING ☐ SAME ☐ CROSS

DIRECTION OF TRAVEL: ☒ NORTH ☐ SOUTH ☐ EAST ☐ WEST

RADAR: GUN NUMBER _890_ TUNING FORKS _128-50MPH/128-35MPH_

ATTITUDE: ☒ EXCELLENT ☐ GOOD ☐ FAIR ☐ POOR

SURFACE CONDITIONS: ☒ DRY ☐ WET ☐ SNOWPACKED ☐ ICY

☐ INTERSECTION ☐ CROSSWALK ☐ STOP BAR

☒ SPEED POSTED ☐ NOT POSTED ☐ SCHOOL ZONE

OFFICER(S) TO BE NOTIFIED FOR TRIAL

OFFICER   _JAMES_   BADGE NUMBER _1616_

OFFICER   _____   BADGE NUMBER ____

UNDER PENALTY OF PERJURY, I AFFIRM THAT ALL THE INFORMATION CONTAINED UPON THIS DOCUMENT IS TRUE AND CORRECT TO THE BEST OF MY KNOWLEDGE.

AFFIANT_____   PRINT NAME_____

ADDRESS_____

HOME PHONE_____ WORK PHONE_____

ON THIS DATE, THE AFFIANT SIGNED THIS AFFIDAVIT AND SWORE TO ITS TRUTH

NOTARY PUBLIC_____ MY COMMISSION EXPIRES DATE_____

Figure 7.8 *Back of Traffic Summons/Ticket*

the traffic summons/ticket for a speeding violation. The violation occurred in the city of Mersonville, which has a city statute for speeding 10 to 15 miles over the posted speed limit (9-34-5234).

You may have also noticed that the officer used shorthand in the probable cause affidavit, which is acceptable in most jurisdictions due to the limited amount of space found on the back of the traffic summons/ticket. If you refer back to Chapter 2 concerning notes, then you may understand some of the shorthand.

On 01-01-2014 at approx 1250 I, Officer James 1616, observed the defendant, Smith, NB in the LL of the 2300 block of N. Washington Ave.

Vis: 65 Radar Conf. 65 Posted 50MPH No other veh. No obstr.

Mr. Smith Stated that he was late for a party and did not notice that he was that much over the speed limit.

Radar Calib. B and A each stop. No further information.

Translated it may be written as:

On 01-01-2014 at approximately 1250, I, Officer James, 1616, observed the defendant, Mr. Smith, northbound in the left lane of the 2300 block of N. Washington Ave. My visual estimate of the vehicle's speed was 65 mph, my radar confirmed 65 mph, and the posted speed limit for that section of roadway was 50 mph. There were no other vehicles and no obstructions in my view or driving in the direction of the radar unit. Mr. Smith stated that he was late for a party and did not notice that he was driving that much over the speed limit.

My radar unit was calibrated before and after the traffic stop. No further information.

Officer James has included the most important information so that he may recall the circumstances and testify in court. This court appearance may be months from the date the traffic summons/ticket was issued to Mr. Smith. The important information in this traffic summons/ticket probable cause affidavit is:

Direction of travel

Lane of travel

Location

Visual speed estimate, radar speed confirmation, and the posted speed limit

Lack of obstructions that would interfere with observing the violation or with the use of the radar

Driver statement that he was running late for a party and possibly distracted because of this fact

Radar calibration and proper functioning before and after the stop

We also know the following information from Officer James completing the bottom section as well:

It was a clear day.

Mr. Smith's attitude was excellent.

Traffic conditions involved only Mr. Smith's vehicle.

The surface or road conditions were dry.

The direction of travel was north.

The radar gun number was 890.

The tuning forks for radar 890 are 123 for 50 mph and 128 for 35 mph (used to calibrate the radar). The officer to be notified for any questions regarding this violation or to appear in court is Officer James 1616.

In the next section, we will cover traffic crashes and the report form needed to complete the investigation, as well as the issuance of the traffic summons/ticket for any traffic violation that may have occurred during the crash. Some law enforcement agencies across the nation may have specific units designated for investigating traffic crashes within their jurisdiction. However, there may be times when you will find that, if that traffic unit is not available, you will be conducting the investigation and completing the report and any other additional paperwork that may accompany it.

In Figures 7.9 through 7.13, you will find an example of a traffic crash report, operator/driver information, registration, and the traffic summons/ticket that was issued to the operator/driver who caused the crash.

Best Practices: Vehicle 1 should be completed for the driver most responsible for the crash, unless told otherwise.

The provided crash report is a representation of a common report that law enforcement professionals across the nation complete in their routine duties. Writing the crash or accident report is similar to a traffic summons/ticket in regard to collecting information that will be needed to complete the report accurately. You may find that many of the reports that you complete routinely as a law enforcement professional are simply accomplished by filling in the appropriate boxes with the correct information, but understand that, as simple as this sounds, many people do not do it correctly. This can lead to confusion and, in some situations, a criminal case or charges being dropped against a defendant.

The front of the crash report can be viewed section by section:

☐ Amended/ Supplement ☐ Under 1,000 ☐ Private Property ☐ Counter Report				Page 1 of 1	
DOT CODE	DOR CODE	☐ Interstate HWY HWY Number ___ ___ ___ ☐ State HWY MILE Point ___ ___ ___.___ ___ ☒ City State County Road		Case Number 14-02456	
Date of Accident 01-26-14	City Mersonville	State CO	Agency Mersonville Police Dept.	County Morris	County # 3
Time (24 Hour) 1500	Officer Number 1616	Officer Name James	Officer Signature *Michael James*	Zone Sector/Detail 4-3	
Date of This Report 01-26-14		Agency Code 3		Number Killed 0	Number Injured 0
Location Street, Road, Route ____Miles ____ Feet ☐ North ☐ South ☐ East ☐ West of: North Rd. _____ ☒ At Jackon St. _____ Latitude ___ ___ ___ Longitude ___ ___ ___					
Investigated at Scene ☒ Yes ☐ No	Total Vehicles 2	District Number 4-3	Bridge Related ☐ Yes ☒ No	Public Property or Employee ☐ Yes ☒ No	Railroad Crossing ☐ Yes ☒ No

	Const. Zone	HWY Interchange	Photos
	☐ Yes ☒ No	☐ Yes ☒ No	☒ Yes ☐ No

Any State Department of Revenue Traffic Accident Report

☐ Amended/ Supplement ☐ Under 1,000 ☐ Private Property ☐ Counter Report	Page 1 of 1

DOT CODE	DOR CODE	☐ Interstate HWY HWY Number ___ ___ ___ ☐ State HWY MILE Point ___ ___ ___.___ ___ ☒ City State County Road	Case Number 14-02456

Date of Accident 01-26-14	City Mersonville	State CO	Agency Mersonville Police Dept.	County Morris	County # 3

Time (24 Hour) 1500	Officer Number 1616	Officer Name James	Officer Signature	Zone Sector/Detail 4-3

Date of This Report 01-26-14	Agency Code 3	Number Killed 0	Number Injured 0

Location Street, Road, Route _____ Miles ____ Feet ☐ North ☐ South ☐ East ☐ West of:
North Rd.   ☒ At Jackon St.
Latitude _____ _____ _____   Longitude _____ _____ _____

Investigated at Scene ☒ Yes ☐ No	Total Vehicles 2	District Number 4-3	Bridge Related ☐ Yes ☒ No	Public Property or Employee ☐ Yes ☒ No	Railroad Crossing ☐ Yes ☒ No	Const. Zone ☐ Yes ☒ No	HWY Interchange ☐ Yes ☒ No	Photos ☒ Yes ☐ No

Vehicle 1 or ____ ☒ Vehicle ☐ Parked ☐ Bicycle ☐ Pedestrian ☐ Non-Vehicle ☐ Non-Contact Vehicle	Vehicle 2 or ____ ☒ Vehicle ☐ Parked ☐ Bicycle ☐ Pedestrian ☐ Non-Vehicle ☐ Non-Contact Vehicle

Last Name Smith	First Name Glenn	MI W	Last Name Emerson	First Name Steven	MI M

Street Address 320 N. Spruce Sr.	Home Phone 719-555-0199	Street Address 8150 Fort Smith Rd.	Home Phone 719-555-0188

City Mersonville	State CO	Zip 88088	Other Phone 719-555-0187	City Mersonville	State CO	Zip 88088	Other Phone 719-555-0193

Driver License Number 99-1100-1600	CDL	State CO	Sex M	DOB 11-05-68	Driver License Number 98-7608-5432	CDL	State CO	Sex M	DOB 09-13-76

Primary Violation ☐ DUI Careless Driving	Primary Violation ☐ DUI None

Violation Code 42-4-1402	Citation Number 18009001	Common Code	Violation Code	Citation Number	Common Code

Year 2009	Make Ford	Model Mustang	Body Type CP	Year 2010	Make Ford	Model F150	Body Type TRK

License Plate Number CHIEF241	State or County CO	Color Gray	License Plate Number RGHNEK12	State or County CO	Color Red

Vehicle Identification Number 1234567891P12BLER	Vehicle Identification Number 4567FT98765432ZYK

Vehicle Owner Last Name ☒ Same	First	MI	Vehicle Owner Last Name ☒ Same	First	MI

Address	City	State	Zip	Address	City	State	Zip

Towed due to damage ☐ By: To:	Towed due to damage ☐ By: To:

_2 ☒ (Vehicle 1 damage diagram)   ☒_2 (Vehicle 2 damage diagram)
_2 ☒   ☒_2
_2 ☒   ☒_2
_2 ☒   ☒_2
_2 ☒   ☒_2

Slight = 1 Moderate = 2 Severe = 3 / Shade in areas of Damage	Slight = 1 Moderate = 2 Severe = 3 / Shade in areas of Damage

Insurance Company ☐ None ☐ No Proof All Right Insurance Policy # 945098-ARI-01	Exp. Date 01-31-2015	Insurance Company ☐ None ☐ No Proof Colorado Best Ins. Grp. Policy # ADI 31-039-090	Exp. Date 09-30-15

Owner Damage Property Last Name	First	MI	Address	City	State	Zip

TU #	Pos	Rest	Endo	Saf Eqp	Air Bag	Eject.	Susp Imp	Inj Sev	Age	Sex	Name/Address
1	1	Y	N	N	N	N	N	N	38	M	Same as Driver #1
2	1	Y	N	N	N	N	N	N	46	M	Same as Driver #2

Approved BY: Sgt. Davis	ID. # 2345	Date 01-26-2014

Figure 7.9   *Traffic Crash Report*

Case # 14-02456	DOR CODE	Accident Date 01-26-2014	Agency Mersonville Police Dept

Describe Accident

Vehicle # 2 was northbound on North Rd. stopped at the intersection of Jackson St. at the stop sign.

Vehicle # 1 was also northbound on North Rd. approaching the intersection of Jackson St. behind Vehicle # 2.

Vehicle # 1 failed to stop and struck the rear end of Vehicle #2 with its front end causing moderate damage to both vehicles.

Details

Driver Vehicle #2 Statement:

Vehicle #2, Driver Emerson, said that he was northbound on North Rd. and had stopped at the intersection of Jackson St. at the stop sign waiting for traffic to clear so that he could turn left onto Jackson St. when he was hit from behind by vehicle #1.

Driver Vehicle #1 Statement:

Vehicle #1, Driver Smith said that he was northbound on North Rd. approaching Jackson St. when he dropped his cell phone into the passenger floorboard. Mr. Smith said that he reached down to retrieve the cell phone and took his eyes off the road for only a second not knowing that he was that close to the intersection. Mr. Smith said that when he looked back at the road he saw the truck and he tried to stop but could not and struck the rear end of the truck with the front end of his car.

Officer Statement:

The intersection of Jackson St. and North Rd. is controlled by a traffic sign for traffic moving north and south on North Rd.

Traffic moving east and west on Jackson St. is not required to stop at the intersection and all vehicles moving north and south on North St. must stop before entering the intersection as directed by a visible stop sign.

Both drivers stated that they did not have any injuries and that they were wearing their seatbelts.

Both drivers exchanged information.

Neither vehicle involved in the crash needed to be towed.

No photos were taken.

Damage to Vehicle #1 estimated to be over $1,000.

Damage to Vehicle #2 estimated to be over $1,000.

Driver #1 Mr. Glenn Walter Smith was issued traffic summons #18009001 for Careless Driving.

No further information

Carrier Name	☐ US DOT ☐ ICC ☐ State DOT
Address	Carrier Identification #
Carrier Name	☐ US DOT ☐ ICC ☐ State DOT
Address	Carrier Identification #

Figure 7.10   *Driver Statements*

The above information from the crash report that you need to be concerned about covers the following:

Type of roadway location: City State County Road (This is used for jurisdiction.)

Case number: 14-02456

Date of the crash: 01-26-14

The city the crash occurred in: Mersonville

The agency completing the crash report: Mersonville Police Department

The county where the city is located: Morris

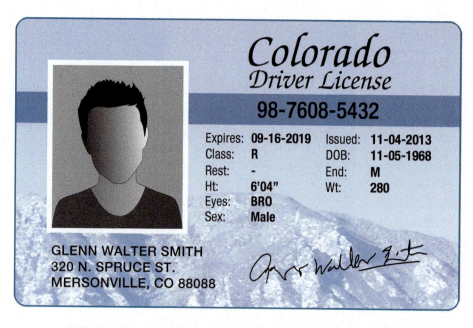

All Right Insurance INC.
Policy Number 945098-ARI-01
Insured: 2009 Ford CP VIN: 1234567891P12BLER
Dates: 01-01-14 thru 01-31-15
Insured Drivers: Glenn W. Smith 320 N. Spruce St. Mersonville, CO 88088
Agent: David Roberts 3030 Snow Pass Dr. Mersonville, CO 88088 Office Phone: 719-555-0157 24 Hour Service 719-555-0158 Fax: 719-555-0159

COLORADO REGISTRATION/OWNERSHIP TAX RECEIPT

TYPE	PLATE		TAB/VAL	VIN		EXPIRE
PAS-REG	CHIEF241		A711111	1234567891P12BLER		12/2015

TITLE	YEAR	MAKE	BODY	CWT/PAS	T/C	FLEET	FUEL	PREV EXP
Y231	2009	FORD	CP	35	C		G	

PUR DATE	PUR PRICE	ORIGINAL TAXABLE VALUE		BUS DATE	CO#	UR/CODE
11/15/2009	40,000	42,000		12/30/2014	11U	0001

EM FEE	TITLE FEE	PRIOR O.T.	OWN TAX	LIC FEE	ROAD FEE	BRIDGE FEE
0.00	0.00	0.00	850.00	120.00	23.00	13.50

RTD TAX	COUNTY TAX	CITY/DIS TAX	STATE TAX	SPECIAL FEE	OTHER FEE
0.00	50.00	30.00	25.00	0.00	0.00

UNIT	GVW	MILES	HT GVW	HC DATE

OWNER MAILING ADDRESS

SMITH GLENN WALTER

320 N. SPRUCE ST.
MERSONVILLE, CO 88088

FEES IN BOLD INCLUDED IN UC FEE
E09933456   4356

SIGNATURE REQUIRED ON REVERSE SIDE

VALIDATION PAID TELLER	LN 24	12/30/2014	TOTAL

MOTOR VEHICLE INSURANCE IS COMPULSORY IN COLORADO, NON-COMPLIANCE IS A IS A MISDEMEANOR TRAFFIC OFFENSE

Figure 7.11   *Vehicle/Driver Number 1 Information*

County number: 3 (Usually, this is just a sector within the county for collecting and documenting information in relationship to that area of the county and what happens there.)

Time the crash: 1500 or 3:00 PM

Officer number: 1616 (This can be the deputy or officer's badge number or employee ID number.)

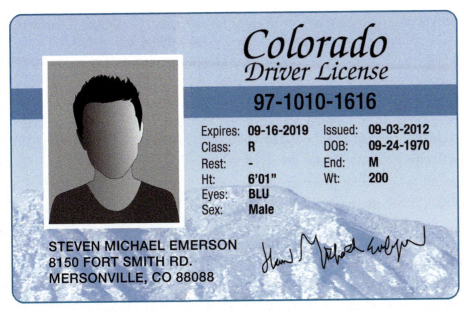

Colorado's Best Insurance Group
Policy Number ADI 31-039-090
Insured: 2010 Ford F150 VIN:4567FT98765432ZYK
Dates: 09-01-14 thru 09-30-15
Insured Driver: Steven Emerson 8150 Fort Smith Rd. Mersonville, CO 88088
ADI Office Branch: 5678 Hidden Springs Rd. Mersonville, CO 88088 Office Phone: 719-555-0166 24 Hour Service 719-555-0188 Fax: 719-555-0176

Figure 7.12   *Vehicle/Driver Number 2 Information*

COLORADO REGISTRATION/OWNERSHIP TAX RECEIPT

TYPE PAS-REG		PLATE RGHNEK12	TAB/VAL A711111		VIN 4567FT98765432ZYK		EXPIRE 11/2015
TITLE Y231	YEAR 2010	MAKE FORD	BODY TRK	CWT/PAS 40	T/C C	FLEET	FUEL G	PREV EXP
PUR DATE 10/15/2009	PUR PRICE 40,000	ORIGINAL TAXABLE VALUE 42,000		BUS DATE 11/30/2014	CO# 11U	UR/CODE 0001
EM FEE 0.00	TITLE FEE 0.00	PRIOR O.T. 0.00	OWN TAX 850.00	LIC FEE 120.00	ROAD FEE 23.00	BRIDGE FEE 13.50
RTD TAX 0.00	COUNTY TAX 50.00	CITY/DIS TAX 30.00	STATE TAX 25.00	SPECIAL FEE 0.00	OTHER FEE 0.00
UNIT	GVW	MILES	HT GVW	HC DATE

OWNER MAILING ADDRESS

EMERSON STEVEN MICHAEL

8150 FORT SMITH RD.
MERSONVILLE, CO 88088

FEES IN BOLD INCLUDED IN UC FEE
E09933456 4356

SIGNATURE REQUIRED ON REVERSE SIDE

VALIDATION   LN   TOTAL
PAID MORRIS   24   11/30/2014

MOTOR VEHICLE INSURANCE IS COMPULSORY IN COLORADO, NON-COMPLIANCE IS A IS A MISDEMEANOR TRAFFIC OFFENSE

Figure 7.13   *Registration*

Officer name = James (This is the law enforcement professional who is completing the crash report.)

Officer signature = Handwritten name (This section is for the signature of the officer or deputy who completed the crash report.)

Date of this report: 01-26-14 (This is the date the crash was reported to the law enforcement agency at which time the crash report started.)

Sector or detail: 4-3 (This is the reporting officer or deputy's sector of assignment for that day. Note that you may be called in from a different sector to take the case.)

Location: North Rd. at Jackson St. (This section is for the exact point of impact that the crash occurred at or as close as possible.)

Investigated at scene: Investigation conducted where the crash occurred, if applicable. (Remember some people drive to an agency to report crashes if there are no injuries or severe damage to the vehicles, or they simply call from home.)

Total vehicle: 2 (This is the number of vehicles involved in the crash.)

District number: The sector area for that precinct or division

Bridge related: Yes or No (Either the bridge was the location or it was part of the crash in another way.)

Public property or employee: Yes or No (This is for information that relates to government agencies that are involved in crashes.)

Railroad crossing: Yes or No (Either the railroad crossings was the location or it was part of the crash in another way.)

Construction Zone: Yes or No (Either a construction zone was the location or it was part of the crash in another way.)

Highway Interchange: Yes or No (Either a highway interchange was the location or it was part of the crash in another way).

Photos: Yes or No in regard to whether or not you took photos of the crash.

The next section of the crash report is concerned with the drivers and vehicles involved and are similar to the traffic summons/ticket and the information can be found either on the driver's license or his or her registration.

Vehicle 1 or _____	☒ Vehicle ☐ Parked ☐ Bicycle ☐ Pedestrian ☐ Non-Vehicle ☐ Non-Contact Vehicle			Vehicle 2 or _____	☒ Vehicle ☐ Parked ☐ Bicycle ☐ Pedestrian ☐ Non-Vehicle ☐ Non-Contact Vehicle		
Last Name Smith	First Name Glenn		MI W	Last Name Emerson	First Name Steven		MI M
Street Address 320 N. Spruce Sr.		Home Phone 719-555-0199		Street Address 8150 Fort Smith Rd.		Home Phone 719-555-0188	
City Mersonville	State CO	Zip 88088	Other Phone 719-555-0187	City Mersonville	State CO	Zip 88088	Other Phone 719-555-0193
Driver License Number 99-1100-1600	CDL	State CO	Sex M / DOB 11-05-68	Driver License Number 98-7608-5432	CDL	State CO	Sex M / DOB 09-13-76
Primary Violation ☐ DUI Careless Driving				Primary Violation ☐ DUI None			
Violation Code 42-4-1402	Citation Number 18009001	Common Code		Violation Code	Citation Number	Common Code	
Year 2009	Make Ford	Model Mustang	Body Type CP	Year 2010	Make Ford	Model F150	Body Type TRK
License Plate Number CHIEF241	State or County CO	Color Gray		License Plate Number RGHNEK12	State or County CO	Color Red	
Vehicle Identification Number 1234567891P12BLER				Vehicle Identification Number 4567FT98765432ZYK			
Vehicle Owner Last Name ☒ Same	First	MI		Vehicle Owner Last Name ☒ Same	First	MI	
Address	City	State	Zip	Address	City	State	Zip

The next section is for the damage the vehicles in the crash sustained. The diagram should be used in relationship to the following numbers to indicate the severity of the damage.

1 = for minor or no damage

2 = for moderate damage

3 = for severe damage (which usually requires the vehicle to be towed)

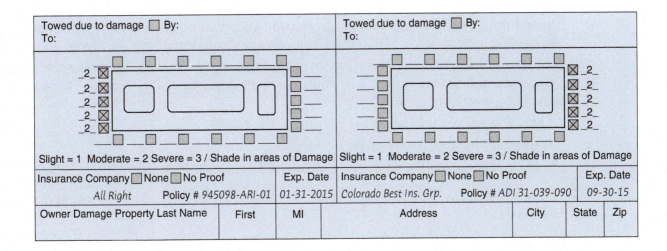

From our crash report, we know that the damage is moderate as well as who the insurance carrier is for both vehicles. In the crash report there are boxes at the end of the form that you may not be familiar with, but you should understand that these state forms are usually accompanied by a cover page or a template. This template requires you to place it over your report and to add additional information. This information will be submitted and eventually reported to the federal government for data collection. The following is that portion of the crash report from the previous page.

TU #	Pos	Rest	Endo	Saf Eqp	Air Bag	Eject.	Susp Imp	Inj Sev	Age	Sex	Name/Address
1	1	Y	N	N	N	N	N	N	38	M	Same as Driver #1
2	1	Y	N	N	N	N	N	N	46	M	Same as Driver #2

The boxes above indicate:

TU # = Unit or vehicle 1 or 2.

POS = Position of the occupant. 1 would represent the driver, 2 would be the front center passenger, 3 the front right side passenger, 4 the rear left passenger, 5 the rear center passenger, and 6 the rear right passenger.

Rest = Y for Yes or a N for No, in regard to whether or not the occupant wore a **seatbelt/restraint** at the time of the crash. The injuries inflicted on the occupants of the vehicle as a result of the impact may help answer this question.

Endo = Y for Yes or a N for No, in regard to whether or not the driver had some type of **endorsement** for the vehicle driven.

Saf Eqp = Y for Yes or a N for No, in regard to whether or not any additional **safety equipment** was used in the crash. This could be a car seat or booster seat for a child.

Air Bag = Y for Yes or a N for No, in regard to whether or not the vehicles **air bags** deployed.

Eject = Y for Yes or a N for No, in regard to whether or not the occupant was **ejected** during the crash.

Susp Imp = Y for Yes or a N for No, in regard to whether or not some type of **impairment is suspected** to be involved. This could be alcohol or drugs impairing the driver.

Inj Sev = Y for Yes or a N for No, in regard to whether or not the **injury the occupant sustained was severe** or not. Use your own state's guidelines in regard to felony charges involving injuries in a crash.

Age = The **age** of the occupant at the time of the crash.

Sex = M for Male or F for Female.

Name and address = The **name and address** for that particular occupant sitting in that position.

Finally, we know who the supervisor was that reviewed the crash report and signed it on 01-26-2014.

Approved BY:	ID. #	Date
Sgt. Davis	*2345*	*01-26-2014*

The back of the crash report is where you, the investigating law enforcement professional, will document the circumstance that led to the crash, as explained to you by the drivers and occupants involved, as well as witnesses who may have observed the crash.

The first section we will discuss covers the case number and agency reporting the crash. This is nothing that was not covered on the front side of the form, but it should be completed on the back side as well, in case this report is a supplement to another officer's crash investigation.

Case #	DOR CODE	Accident Date	Agency
14-02456		01-26-2014	*Mersonville Police Dept*

The next section is how you, as an investigator, will present the circumstance of the crash to the reader. It must be written in a way that the reader will understand without the need for any additional explanation from you if you are not available. It should also be written in a way that helps you recall the circumstances of the crash if you are required to testify in a criminal or civil trial at a later time.

Describe Accident
Vehicle # 2 was northbound on North Rd. stopped at the intersection of Jackson St. at the stop sign.
Vehicle # 1 was also northbound on North Rd. approaching the intersection of Jackson St. behind Vehicle # 2.
Vehicle # 1 failed to stop and struck the rear end of Vehicle #2 with its front end causing moderate damage to both vehicles.

From the description, we understand that this was a rear end collision between two vehicles at an intersection where a stop sign controlled traffic.

The next section is completed in regard to the statements that were made by the drivers of the vehicles and the investigating officers' actions concerning the crash. When you read the statements, remember that the drivers are referred to as Mr. Smith and Mr. Emerson, after being identified as Driver 1 and Driver 2.

Details

Driver Vehicle #2 Statement:
Vehicle #2, Driver Emerson, said that he was northbound on North Rd. and had stopped at the intersection of Jackson St. at the stop sign waiting for traffic to clear so that he could turn left onto Jackson St. when he was hit from behind by vehicle #1.

Driver Vehicle #1 Statement:
Vehicle #1. Driver Smith said that he was northbound on North Rd. approaching Jackson St. when he dropped his cell phone into the passenger floorboard. Mr. Smith said that he reached down to retrieve the cell phone and took his eyes off the road for only a second not knowing that he was that close to the intersection. Mr. Smith said that when he looked back at the road he saw the truck and he tried to stop but could not and struck the rear end of the truck with the front end of his car.

Officer Statement:
The intersection of Jackson St. and North Rd. is controlled by a traffic sign for traffic moving north and south on North Rd.

Traffic moving east and west on Jackson St. is not required to stop at the intersection and all vehicles moving north and south on North St. must stop before entering the intersection as directed by a visible stop sign.

Both drivers stated that they did not have any injuries and that they were wearing their seatbelts.
Both drivers exchanged information.
Neither vehicle involved in the crash needed to be towed.
No photos were taken.
Damage to Vehicle #1 estimated to be over $1,000.
Damage to Vehicle #2 estimated to be over $1,000.
Driver #1 Mr. Glenn Walter Smith was issued traffic summons #18009001 for Careless Driving.
No further information

The following information is specifically used for commercial vehicles that may be involved in a traffic crash. The section will usually be completed by a Department of Transportation certified inspector or a law enforcement professional in your agency who is certified to document these crashes. If none of these people are available, then follow your agency's guidelines for completing the information.

Carrier Name	☐ US DOT ☐ ICC ☐ State DOT
Address	Carrier Identification #
Carrier Name	☐ US DOT ☐ ICC ☐ State DOT
Address	Carrier Identification #

From the details section, the reader understands the circumstances that led up to this crash at the intersection of Jackson St. and North Rd. Some of the information is just a recap of what the front page had already identified in regard to towing, damage, photos, and the traffic summons/ticket that was issued to Mr. Smith for careless driving.

THE *RIGHT* WAY TO *WRITE*

In this chapter, both traffic citations/summons and traffic crashes were presented. As previously discussed in Chapter 6, the writing style of the basic traffic citation/summons in most jurisdictions can be accomplished by simply filling in boxes and providing a very short written synopsis on the traffic violation. Abbreviations and symbols in most jurisdictions are perfectly acceptable when writing the synopsis (usually termed a "probable cause affidavit"). Again, the specifics on how to complete this type of form will usually be driven by jurisdictional and departmental guidelines.

Traffic crashes (i.e., vehicle accidents) require a little different approach to complete their documentation. Traffic crash documentation typically requires the following information:

- Traffic summons/citation for the offending subject
- Driver statements
- Witness statements (if available)
- Officer statements
- Listing of injuries (Medical assistance requested? / Transportation to hospital?)
- Photos/diagrams
- Vehicle damage estimate(s)
- Towing by a commercial carrier (tow slip documentation)

As with the simple traffic summons/citations, the specifics of completing the documentation on a traffic crash will vary by agency. Most agencies will allow one form with all of the described documentation. Typically, though not always, abbreviations and symbols are perfectly acceptable. Should the traffic crash result in a serious injury or death, obviously, the report style typically becomes much more formalized and detailed, and many agencies (although not all) require a shift into the narrative style of report writing for these type of major traffic incidents. Your department policy and procedure manual or standard operating procedure manual will give specific agency guidelines regarding the format of these reports.

TIPS FOR TRAFFIC SUMMONS/TICKETS AND CRASH REPORTS

- Determine if medical assistance is needed.
- Interview all drivers at the crash scene if possible before determining fault.
- Ensure that drivers are not under the influence.
  - Do you smell alcohol?
  - Do you observe any other behavior that would lead you to believe they are under some other type of influence other than alcohol?
- Check that the crash scene reflects what was explained to you by the drivers during the interview.
- Make sure that drivers are current on insurance, registration, and that their license is valid.
- Document injuries.
  - This includes photos, treating medical personnel, or hospitals where occupants were transported to for treatment.

SUMMARY

One of the most basic tenets in law enforcement is that police activity should be guided by the citizens that they serve. Traffic safety is a high priority in every jurisdiction. Citizens want safe streets. A visible police traffic stop at a roadside has an immediate effect on other traffic and motorists' perception of effective enforcement of traffic laws in their community. Visible police presence sends a powerful message to the community, way beyond the single traffic stop itself.

A traffic stop serves as an opening in community dialogue. Law enforcement officers should look at this traffic stop as an opportunity to communicate with the citizen the importance of driving safety. It need not be an adversarial relationship. This is why professionalism is so essential in the traffic stop.

Making a professional traffic stop entails a skill set that has been developed during the officer's training and past experiences. The traffic stop can serve a myriad of purposes, including the following: reduce speed violations, educate the public, and save lives. The bottom line is the traffic stop offers an opportunity to increase citizen safety, improve the citizens' view of the law enforcement agency, and affect crime.

EXERCISES

1. **Refresh Your Note-Taking Skills.** The completion of the report in this chapter was accomplished with the assistance of the officer's notes. The "Appendix: Sample Forms" contains blank interview sheets. Try to complete the blank interview sheets with the use of the information found in the provided crash report. We will help with the dispatch time by telling you that you were dispatched to this crash at 1445 or 2:45 PM.

2. **Traffic Summons/Ticket.** After reviewing the information below, complete a traffic summons that can be found in the back of this book.

   You are northbound on N. Academy Blvd. in the 4000 block, when you observed a coupe that is red in color make a lane change without signaling from the right lane into the center lane of this three lane highway.

   You are traveling in the left lane, and when you observe this lane change, you notice that the red coupe cut off another driver occupying the center lane, forcing this other driver to unexpectedly brake, which nearly caused a rear end collision with the vehicle directly behind him.

   You decide to conduct a traffic stop and pull the vehicle over in the parking lot of Franks Deli located at 4125 N. Academy Blvd. You contact the driver who says that he was unaware of the unsafe lane change, and he was in a hurry to get to work at Big Mikes Movie Mart.

   The traffic summons/ticket should be written for the charge of "unsafe lane change." So use your states' statute for this violation as well as the fines. If you do not know the statute for the violation then use the following:

   Unsafe lane change city statute is 9-34-0990.

   The fine is $100.00 with a $20.00 surcharge and a 3 point violation.

The red coupe and the drivers' information are listed below, as well as the traffic summons/ticket you need to complete.

The driver's phone number is 719- 555-0189.

The driver's work number is 719- 555-0199.

The driver's work address is Big Mikes Movie Mart at 5555 N. Academy Blvd. The driver is a clerk.

The driver's cell phone number is 719-555-0163.

The driver's hair color is brown, and the driver is a white male.

The driver does not have an alias.

The driver has no tattoos or birth marks.

All the information the driver gave you is correct.

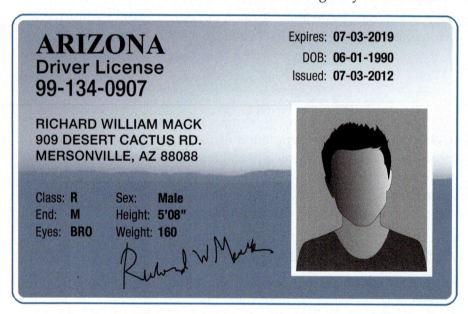

ARIZONA
Driver License
99-134-0907

Expires: **07-03-2019**
DOB: **06-01-1990**
Issued: **07-03-2012**

RICHARD WILLIAM MACK
909 DESERT CACTUS RD.
MERSONVILLE, AZ 88088

Class: **R**   Sex: **Male**
End: **M**   Height: **5'08"**
Eyes: **BRO**   Weight: **160**

Better Than Them Ins.Co.
Policy Number 000987-ARI-05
Insured: 1990 Honda 2DR HB VIN: 9876543211P0LPKNH
Dates: 01-01-14 thru 01-31-15
Insured Drivers: Richard Mack 909 Desert Cactus Rd. Mersonville, AZ 88088
Agent: Carlos Sanchez 4568 N. Canyon Rd. Mersonville, AZ 88088 Office Phone: 719-555-0158 24 Hour Service 719-555-0157 Fax: 719-555-0160

MOTOR VEHICLE *ADOT* DIVISION	ARIZONA VEHICLE REGISTRATION		Expiration Date
	Print Date/time	Carry In Vehicle At All Times	11/28/2015
	11/28/2014/15:05		
	Vehicle Identification Number 9876543211P0LPKNH	Veh. Lic. Tax	$80.00
		Registration	$8.25
		Air Quality	$3.00
Richard William Mack 909 Desert Cactus Rd. Mersonville, AZ 88088	**Record Number** 98765432	Postage/Handling	$0.45
	Plate Number MYLANE1		
	Unit Number		
	Year/Make 1990 HONDA		
	Body Style 2DR HB		
	First Registered 12/1991		
	List Price 020000		
	Fuel Type G		
	Category A		
	Weight (GVW)		
	County MORRIS	TOTAL	$86.70
	Registration Type FUL		

3. **Crash Report.** In this practical exercise, you will have an opportunity to complete a traffic crash report involving two vehicles. A "not to scale" diagram has been provided for you, along with the information concerning each driver and vehicle. Review the information below and then complete a crash report and a traffic summons/ticket that can be found in the "Appendix: Sample Forms".

Additional Information:

Zone: 3

Sector: 2

Date: Your current date

Time: The time announced in the video

Below is the information for driver and vehicle 1.

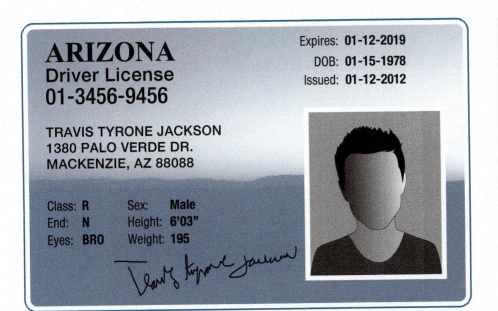

The following information is for driver and vehicle 2.

FLORIDA VEHICLE REGISTRATION

CO/AGY 9 /5   T#   012345678
B#   135792

PLATE	**SUNNY1**	DECAL	**87654321**	

Expires **Midnight Thur. 11/30/2015**

YR/MK	**2010 NISSAN**	BODY	**CP**
VIN	**9215569892INCMNOU**		
Plate Type	**RGR**	NET WT	**2800**

COLOR **WHT**
TITLE **12345678**

Reg. Tax	45.00	Class Code	31
Init. Reg.		Tax Months	12
County Fee	3.00	Back Tax Months	
Mail Fee		Credit Class	
Sales Tax		Credit Months	
Voluntary Fees			
Grand Total	48.00		

DL/FEID   **V40076856781970**
Date Issued **11/28/2014**   Plate Issued **11/28/2014**

IMPORTANT INFORMATION

Mary Ann Hill
620 Sandy Island Way
Morrisville, FL 88086

1. The Florida License Plate must remain with the registrant upon sale of the vehicle.
2. The registration must be delivered to a Tax Collector or Tag Agent for transfer to a replacement vehicle.
3. Your registration must be updated to your new address within 20 days of moving.
4. Registration renewals are the responsibility of the registrant and shall occur during the 30-day period prior to the expiration date shown on this registration. Renewal notices are provided as a courtesy and are not required for renewal purposes

RGR-FLORIDA REGULAR

Case #: 15-039873   Title: Crash
Dispatch: 1330   Arrival: 1340   Cleared: 1430
Date: 06/05/2014   Time: 1325   Offense Location: Washington/Main
Suspect/Victim/Witness/Other: D2 White Nissan Altima
Name: Hill
DOB: Race: W   HGT: WGT: Hair: BRO   Eyes: GRN
POB:
Clothing Description:
Address: City: State: Zip Code:
Contact Numbers: Home: 850-555-0199   Cell: 850-555-0196   WK: 850-555-0193
Employer: Pirates Inn   Occupation: Waitress
Business Address: 908 Seaside Dr.   City: Morrisville   State: FL   Zip Code: 88086
Business Phone: Business Victim: Yes   No

I was going to work and was NB on Main when the other driver just pulled out of side street (Washington) and hit the front side of my car.
I honked my horn but he just kept coming out and I could not stop in time
All information handed over is correct.
Not injured/ had seatbelt on
Estimated speed 25 Mph
No impairment suspected

D2 was clear and valid through NCIC.

Case #:   Title:
Dispatch: Arrival: Cleared:
Date: Time: Offense Location:
Suspect/Victim/Witness/Other: D1 Red Acura MDX
Name:
DOB: Race: B   HGT: WGT: Hair: BRO   Eyes: BRO
POB:
Clothing Description:
Address: 3030 Blue Sail Cir.   City: Morrisville   State: FL   Zip Code: 88086
Contact Numbers: Home: None   Cell: 850-555-0177   WK: 850-555-0178
Employer: US Navy   Occupation: Sonar specialist
Business Address: 1313 Navy Point Rd   City: Morrisville   State: FL   Zip Code: 88086
Business Phone: Business Victim: Yes   No

I don't really know what happened. I stopped at the stop sign and thought it was clear and suddenly there she was and I could not stop in time.
Maybe she was speeding because I did not see her.
Information handed over is not correct. Address change see above, Insurance is correct.
Driver is new resident of Florida as of 20 days ago. Military transfer.
Not injured/ had seatbelt on
Estimated speed 10 Mph
No impairment suspected

D1 was clear and valid through NCIC.

Case #:   Title:
Dispatch: Arrival: Cleared:
Date: Time: Offense Location:
Suspect/Victim/Witness/Other: Witness
Name: Sharon Michelle Taylor
DOB: Race: W   HGT: 5'08"   WGT: 130   Hair: BRO   Eyes: BLU
POB:
Clothing Description:
Address: 1590 Main St.   City: Morrisville   State: FL   Zip Code: 88086
Contact Numbers: Home: 850-555-1056   Cell: 850-555-0159   WK: 850-555-0157
Employer: Self   Occupation: Artist
Business Address: Same as Above   City: State: FL   Zip Code:
Business Phone: Business Victim: Yes   No

I was out for a run and came to the intersection (Main and Washington) SB
Stopped to check for traffic before running across Washington when I observed Red Acura stopped at the sign.
I waited until he crossed intersection before I ran across.
I saw the white Nissan coming and then I heard the Acura accelerate and pull forward.
The Nissan honked its horn but it was too late and the two hit.
I don't think anyone was hurt.

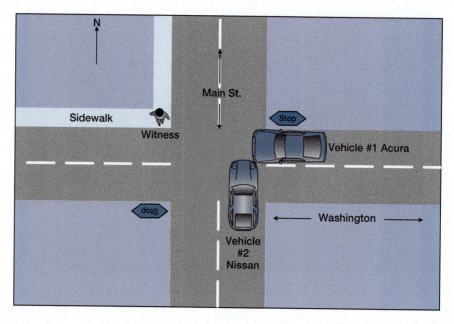

4. **Traffic Violation.** In this exercise, you watch a video scenario involving a law enforcement professional and a motorist who has committed a traffic violation *(Video Scenario Traffic Violation 7.1)*. You must take notes while watching the video scenario and then complete the traffic summons for the violation the motorist committed. Use the interview sheets and a traffic summons form that can be found in the Appendix.

Below you will find the driver license, registration, and insurance card for the motorist who was stopped in the video scenario for the traffic violation.

Additional Information:

Zone: 3

Sector: 6

Date: Your Current date

Time: The time announced in the video

Colorado	
Driver License	
416-423-0021	

Expires:	08-20-2018	Issued:	08-20-2012
Class:	R	DOB:	09-24-1971
Rest:	None	End:	N
Ht:	5'06"	Wt:	120
Eyes:	GRN	Wt:	BLO
Sex:	Female		

CARLA JO TANNER
3912 MOUNTAIN TOP WAY
MERSONVILLE, CO 88088

All Right Insurance INC.
Policy Number 65489PBU-RT
Insured: 2012 BMW SD VIN: 9876543211L0KCVB4
Dates: 01-01-14 thru 01-31-15
Insured Drivers: Carla Jo Tanner 3912 Mountain Top Way Mersonville, CO 88088
Agent: David Roberts 3030 Snow Pass Dr. Mersonville, CO 88088 Office Phone: 719-555-0157 24 Hour Service 719-555-0158 Fax: 719-555-0159

COLORADO REGISTRATION/OWNERSHIP TAX RECEIPT

TYPE	PLATE	TAB/VAL	VIN	EXPIRE
PAS-REG	2FST4U	A711111	9876543211L0KCVB4	12/2015

TITLE	YEAR	MAKE	BODY	CWT/PAS	T/C	FLEET	FUEL	PREV EXP
Y231	2012	BMW	SD	35	C		G	

PUR DATE	PUR PRICE	ORIGINAL TAXABLE VALUE	BUS DATE	CO#	UR/CODE
11/15/2014	45,000	43,000	12/30/2014	11U	0001

EM FEE	TITLE FEE	PRIOR O.T.	OWN TAX	LIC FEE	ROAD FEE	BRIDGE FEE
0.00	0.00	0.00	850.00	120.00	23.00	13.50

RTD TAX	COUNTY TAX	CITY/DIS TAX	STATE TAX	SPECIAL FEE	OTHER FEE
0.00	50.00	30.00	25.00	0.00	0.00

UNIT	GVW	MILES	HT GVW	HC DATE

OWNER MAILING ADDRESS	FEES IN BOLD INCLUDED IN UC FEE
	E09933456 4356
TANNER, CARLA JO	
3912 MOUNTAIN TOP WAY	SIGNATURE REQUIRED ON REVERSE SIDE
MERSONVILLE, CO 88088	

VALIDATION	LN		TOTAL
PAID TELLER	24	09/10/2012	

MOTOR VEHICLE INSURANCE IS COMPULSORY IN COLORADO, NON-COMPLIANCE IS A IS A MISDEMEANOR TRAFFIC OFFENSE

5. **Traffic Crash and Traffic Violation.** In this exercise you watch a video scenario involving a law enforcement professional and two motorists who were involved in a traffic crash (*Video Scenario Traffic Crash 7.2*). You must take notes while watching the video scenario and then complete the traffic crash report and complete a summons for the violation for the motorist who was at fault for the crash. Review the information that follows and then complete a crash report and a traffic summons/ticket that can be found in the "Appendix: Sample Forms".

Colorado Driver License

023-161-1711

Expires: 05-05-2018	Issued: 05-05-2013
Class: R	DOB: 05-05-1975
Rest: -	End: M
Ht: 5'04"	Wt: 120
Eyes: GRN	
Sex: Female	

STEFANIE LYNN JOHNSON
2020 WILDFLOWER RD.
MERSONVILLE, CO 88088

All Right Insurance INC.
Policy Number PAE4590-2347
Insured: 2012 Lexus GX 460 VIN: 1234567891S12EXEP
Dates: 02-04-14 thru 02-04-15
Insured Drivers: Stefanie Johnson 2020 Wildflower Rd. Mersonville, CO 88088
Agent: David Roberts 3030 Snow Pass Dr. Mersonville, CO 88088 Office Phone: 719-555-0157 24 Hour Service 719-555-0158 Fax: 719-555-0159

COLORADO REGISTRATION/OWNERSHIP TAX RECEIPT

TYPE	PLATE	TAB/VAL	VIN		EXPIRE
PAS-REG	1WILD1	A711111	1234567891S12EXEP		12/2015

TITLE	YEAR	MAKE	BODY	CWT/PAS	T/C	FLEET	FUEL	PREV EXP
Y231	2012	LEXUS	SUV	35	C		G	

PUR DATE	PUR PRICE	ORIGINAL TAXABLE VALUE	BUS DATE	CO#	UR/CODE
11/15/2009	40,000	42,000	12/30/2014	11U	0001

EM FEE	TITLE FEE	PRIOR O.T.	OWN TAX	LIC FEE	ROAD FEE	BRIDGE FEE
0.00	0.00	0.00	850.00	120.00	23.00	13.50

RTD TAX	COUNTY TAX	CITY/DIS TAX	STATE TAX	SPECIAL FEE	OTHER FEE
0.00	50.00	30.00	25.00	0.00	0.00

UNIT	GVW	MILES	HT GVW	HC DATE

OWNER MAILING ADDRESS	FEES IN BOLD INCLUDED IN UC FEE
	E09933456 4356
JOHNSON STEFANIE LYNN	
2020 WILDFLOWER RD. MERSONVILLE, CO 88088	SIGNATURE REQUIRED ON REVERSE SIDE

VALIDATION PAID TELLER	LN 24 12/30/2014	TOTAL

MOTOR VEHICLE INSURANCE IS COMPULSORY IN COLORADO, NON-COMPLIANCE IS A IS A MISDEMEANOR TRAFFIC OFFENSE

Additional Information:

Zone: 3

Sector: 1

Date: Your Current date

Time: The time announced in the video

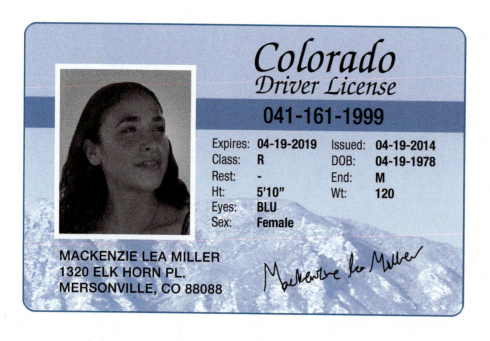

Colorado's Best Insurance Group
Policy Number 78POL09-345-987
Insured: 1999 FORD PICK-UP VIN:03765EKNU987NER10
Dates: 11-01-14 thru 11-30-15
Insured: Mackenzie Miller 1320 ELK HORN PL. Mersonville, CO 88088
ADI Office Branch: 5678 Hidden Springs Rd. Mersonville, CO 88088 Office Phone: 719-555-0166 24 Hour Service 719-555-0188 Fax: 719-555-0176

COLORADO REGISTRATION/OWNERSHIP TAX RECEIPT

TYPE	PLATE	TAB/VAL	VIN	EXPIRE
PAS-REG	CHEERLDR	A711111	03765EKNU987NER10	11/2015

TITLE	YEAR	MAKE	BODY	CWT/PAS	T/C	FLEET	FUEL	PREV EXP
Y231	1999	FORD	TRK	40	C		G	

PUR DATE	PUR PRICE	ORIGINAL TAXABLE VALUE	BUS DATE	CO#	UR/CODE
11/15/2012	4,000	4,000	11/15/2014	11U	0001

EM FEE	TITLE FEE	PRIOR O.T.	OWN TAX	LIC FEE	ROAD FEE	BRIDGE FEE
0.00	0.00	0.00	850.00	120.00	23.00	13.50

RTD TAX	COUNTY TAX	CITY/DIS TAX	STATE TAX	SPECIAL FEE	OTHER FEE
0.00	50.00	30.00	25.00	0.00	0.00

UNIT	GVW	MILES	HT GVW	HC DATE

OWNER MAILING ADDRESS

FEES IN BOLD INCLUDED IN UC FEE
E09933456   4356

MILLER MACKENZIE LEA

8150 FORT SMITH RD.
MERSONVILLE, CO 88088

SIGNATURE REQUIRED ON REVERSE SIDE

VALIDATION	LN		TOTAL
PAID TELLER	24	11/30/2014	

MOTOR VEHICLE INSURANCE IS COMPULSORY IN COLORADO, NON-COMPLIANCE IS A IS A MISDEMEANOR TRAFFIC OFFENSE

8

TYPES OF STATEMENTS

LEARNING OBJECTIVES

- Understand the differences between the reporting party, victim, witness, and suspect.
- Understand the importance of identifying each person on scene and his or her role in regard to being a victim, a witness, or a suspect.
- Understand the importance of translating interview notes into a clear and concise report that others will be able to read and understand.
- Understand how to clarify what an interviewee is telling you during the interview and how you may need to ask follow-up questions to obtain vital information.
- Apply your knowledge to practical examples by successfully completing the chapter exercises.

INTRODUCTION

The law enforcement professional will spend much of his or her time speaking to victims, suspects, and witnesses. The information collected from all three of these sources is important and must be documented correctly in the case report to ensure nothing is misunderstood or missing. Conducting a law enforcement interview can be a challenging and daunting task. This task can be simplified by following some of the basic interviewing guidelines presented in this chapter. As with all aspects of law enforcement, practice makes perfect. Your training has provided you some of the basic skills in the interview process. Applying these basic concepts, coupled with experience and supervisory input, will help hone your interviewing skills.

THE REPORTING PARTY

The reporting party (RP) is the individual who contacted the law enforcement agency to report a crime or some other situation that they believe needs the involvement of a law enforcement professional. In the majority of these situations, the reporting party is either the victim or the witness to a crime. It is important for you to identify the individual reporting the criminal activity upon your arrival, while ensuring officer safety.

Upon your arrival, and after you have secured the scene, you need to identify the reporting party and determine whether or not that person is a victim, witness, or other involved individual.

Best Practices: It's important to remember that the reporting party may first start out as a victim or witness and then turn into a suspect as additional information is collected.

VICTIM AND WITNESS STATEMENTS

The victim is the individual who has been wronged in a criminal manner by another. The wrong committed is defined as a crime by statutory law. The statutory law stipulates the elements of each crime. These statutory elements must be present to arrest or charge an individual for a violation of a particular crime. When you interview the victim or witness allow the person to first explain what happened so that you may determine what type of crime you are investigating. Once you make the determination that a crime has been committed, ask the victim to repeat what he or she has just told you while you take notes.

It is important to develop a rapport with the victim or witness before attempting to record any of the information. Remember, you have contacted a citizen on probably one of the worst days of his or her life. Emotions and the enormity of the incident have to be neutralized. The interview process entails separating critical information from irrelevant, unimportant, and useless information. Your task is to document descriptive words that accurately present the facts of the case in a clear and concise manner. Your ultimate goal is to gather the facts of the incident for future criminal prosecution.

Prior to the interview process, make sure that the scene is safe. Do what you can to make the victim feel safe and comfortable. Once the scene is secure and the victim is able to respond, begin the interview. Probably, the best way to start any interview is to simply begin by asking an open-ended question. Simply state, "Tell me what happened." This will start the communication process flowing. During this initial interviewing stage, be a good listener and use your nonverbal skills to keep the interview going. Typically you are not taking notes at this point.

The next phase of the interview is commonly called the recording or documentation phase. Ask the victim to repeat the story while you take notes. If the victim or witness tells the same story twice, in the same manner, he is probably telling the truth. Keep the victim on track and focused. This is not the time for side-bar conversations.

The final phase is the clarification phase. This is the time to mentally review what has been said and ask follow-up questions. The focus here is on asking specific questions. You need to communicate to the individual what exactly you are looking for to bring closure to your interview.

Best Practices: Allow the victim to explain the reported crime first. This affords you the opportunity to determine if a crime has been committed before you start taking lengthy notes. Next, have the victim repeat the statement a second time. This gives you the opportunity to ensure that there are no discrepancies between the first explanation and the second explanation. It is during the second explanation that you should begin taking notes, which will be used to complete your report.

Figure 8.1 shows sample notes and a completed case report for a hypothetical harassment complaint.

Case #: *14-33456*   Title: *Harassment 13-2921*

Dispatch: *1430*   Arrival: *1440*   Cleared: *1530*

Date: *01-28-14*   Time: Offense Location: *5344 Winter St.*

~~Suspect/Victim/Witness/Other:~~

Name: *Michelle Marie Jackson*   Male   Female

DOB: *09/09/86*   Race: *W*   HGT: *5'04"*   WGT: *120*   Hair: *BLON*   Eyes: *GRN*   POB: *Hobbs, NM*

Clothing Description: *Blue jeans, white t-shirt, white tennis shoes*

Address: *5344 Winter St.*   City: *Mersonville*   State: *AZ*   Zip Code: *88088*

Contact Numbers: Home: *602-555-0183*   Cell: *602-555-0199*   WK: *602-555-0183*

Employer: *Three Rivers*   Occupation: *Waitress*

Business Address: *45678 N. Chase St.*   City: *Mersonville*   State: *AZ*   Zip Code: *88088*

Business Phone: *602-555-0183*   Business Victim: ~~Yes~~   No

When I got home from work this afternoon at approximately 2:25 there were 3 male teenagers sitting in my driveway. I honked the horn for them to move so I could park. One got up walked over to my car and spit on my vehicle hood and then yelled "I will end you" while he held up his skateboard with both hands over his right shoulder like a bat as if he was going to hit my car with it. Then all of them ran away down the street.

Q-Have you ever seen any of them before?

A-No I don't think there from around here.

Q-How many were there?

A-Just three.

Q-Do know what they're wearing?

A-I really only saw what the kid who spit on my car was wearing. He had on black baseball style hat with a flat brim. He was wearing long board shorts that were black and he had on a white long sleeved shirt with a black design of a skateboarder on the front. And Black shoes.

Q-Do you know if he was black, white or Hispanic? And, do you know how tall he was or how much he weighed? Or anything else about him like a tattoo or a scar. Maybe his eye or hair color. Or even how old he might have been.

A-I think he was a white male maybe 5'8" to 5'10" and around 140 to 155 pounds. I did not notice any scars or tattoos on him. And he had a hat on covering his hair and I could not really see his eyes. I think he was 15-17 Years old.

Q-When this individual walked up to your car what did you think was going to happen?

A-I thought he was going to hit my car with the skateboard and then me. I mean it was scary he looked angry and said he would end me. I mean I just wanted to park my car in my driveway.

Q-Can you describe the skateboard? And how were you able to hear what he said?

A-No not really, I mean it was black on top and white on the bottom with a design painted in multiple colors. I think the design could've been a dragon or snake. I had my window down and could hear everything.

Q-Which direction did they run?

A-North on Winter Street toward the skate park.

Q-Would you recognize this individual if you saw him again?

A-Yes, probably.

Neighborhood follow-up/witnesses-I knocked on the doors of the homes directly north and south from the victim's home and across the street but was unable to contact anyone who might have seen the incident.

I then drove to the skate park but was unable to locate any individuals matching the victim's description.
Evidence-none and Photos-none

Figure 8.1   *Sample Notes and Case Report for Harassment Complaint*

Figure 8.1 shows the notes completed by a law enforcement professional that were taken from an individual who is the apparent victim of the crime of harassment, as it is defined by the Arizona Revised Statutes. When you look at the notes, you will notice that the victim was allowed to explain the incident and then was asked specific follow-up questions by the investigating officer.

The follow-up questions clarify missing information that was unintentionally left out by the victim during her explanation of the crime. These follow-up questions were also open ended, which allowed the victim to answer them in her own words. It is important to allow the victim to tell you the facts of the crime as he or she recalls it.

Best Practices: Don't lead or give the impression that you led the victim into saying something that did not happen. This can be achieved by using open-ended questions during the interview.

Figure 8.2 shows the completed harassment report by the investigating officer.

In the report (Figures 8.1 and 8.2) you will notice that the face sheet was completed and that the synopsis supports the elements to the crime of harassment. The synopsis also communicates to anyone who reads it that a neighborhood follow-up was completed, there were no witnesses to the crime, there is suspect information, no arrest was made, and that no photos or any other type of evidence was collected.

In the supplement section, you will notice that it begins with the victim's statement. When you compare the notes the investigating officer took during the interview, you will see that the information is communicated in a reader-friendly format in the supplement. In the interview with the victim, eight follow-up questions were asked, and the answers to those eight follow-up questions are accurately expressed under the heading *Victim Statement*.

A law enforcement professional must be able to translate his or her interview notes into an understandable and accurate case report. When transcribing your notes into the report, it is extremely important to be accurate in what was said by the person being interviewed. This does not mean you must write exactly what the person says verbatim throughout the entire report. However, there will be times when it is important for you to write exactly what was said during an interview. This is explained, in detail, later in this chapter.

During an interview, the victim or witness may leave important information out of their explanation of the incident. This missing information may be discovered later in the interview or during the investigator's follow-up questions. This missing information may belong at the beginning of the victim's explanation of the incident, but he or she may not reveal it to you until the end of the interview. When you write the report and begin to transcribe your notes from the interview, you will include this information where it belongs, at the beginning of the victim or witness statement. Keep things in chronological order.

You may also collect confusing or lengthy information from a victim or witness during the interview. For the purpose of clarity, you may express it more clearly, but accurately, in the report.

Mersonville Police Department Cover Sheet	☒ Offense ☐ Supplement ☐ Other	Case Number 14-33456

Offense Title Harassment	City/State Statute Number 13-2921	Date of this Report 01/28/2014

Zone 5	Date and time Reported				Date and Time of Occurrence			
Sector 4	Month	Day	Year	Time	Month	Day	Year	Time
	01	28	2014	1440	On or Between	01 / 01	28 / 28	2014 / 2014	1425 / 1430

Victim's Name Last, First, Middle Jackson, Michelle Marie	Date of Birth 09/09/1986	Age 27	Sex F	Race W	Occupation Waitress

Residential Address 5344 Winter St.	City Mersonville	State AZ	Zip Code 88088	Home Phone 602-555-0183	Victims ☒ Yes Brochure ☐ No

Business Address 45678 N. Chase St.	City Mersonville	State AZ	Zip Code 88088	Home Phone 602-555-0183	Cell Phone 602-555-0199

Business Name Three Rivers	Business Address 45678 N. Chase St.	City Mersonville	State AZ	Zip Code 88088	Business Phone 602-555-0183

Codes RP = Reporting Party AV = Additional Victim W = Witness LO = Law Enforcement Officer A = Arrestee S = Suspect O = Other

Code S	Last, First, Middle Unknown	Date of Birth	Age 15-17	Sex M	Race W	Occupation
Residential Address	City	State	Zip Code	Home Phone	Other Phone	

Clothing Description Black hat and shorts, white shirt with black unknown design and black shoes.	Alias	Summons Number

Identifying Marks/Scars/Tattoos	Height 5'8"-5'10"	Weight 140-155	Build M	Hair UNK	Eyes UNK

Elements/Narrative

On 01-28-2014 at approximately 1430 I, Officer Smith 1616, was dispatched to 5344 Winter St. in reference to a Harassment complaint. Upon arrival I made contact with Michelle Jackson, the victim, who stated that she returned home from work at approximately 1425 on 01-28-2014 at which time she discovered three male teenagers sitting in her driveway. Mrs. Jackson honked her horn for the teenagers to move so she could park in her driveway. One of the teenagers walked over to Mrs. Jackson's car and spit on her car hood and then held a skateboard up in a threatening manner while saying "I will end you" after which the three teenagers ran north on Winter Street.

Neighborhood Follow-Up/YES

Witness Information/NO

Suspect Information/YES

Arrest/NO

Evidence/NO

Photos/NO

See Supplement for more information.

Case Disposition ☒ Open ☐ Closed ☐ Cleared by Arrest ☐ Unfounded	Patrol Investigation Continued ☐ Yes ☒ No	Assigned to:

Officer Name/Employee Number Smith 1616	Supervisor Name/Employee Number Carter 090	Page 1 of 2

Figure 8.2   Completed Harassment Report (*continued on next page*)

Mersonville Police Department Continuation/Supplement		Case Number 14-33456		
Offense Title *Harassment*		City/State Statute Number *13-2921*	Date of this Report *01/28/2014*	

Codes RP=Reporting Party   AV= Additional Victim   W=Witness   LO= Law Enforcement Officer   A=Arrestee   S=Suspect   O=Other

Code	Last, First, Middle	Date of Birth	Age	Sex	Race	Occupation
RP	*Jackson, Michelle Marie*	*09/09/1986*	*27*	*F*	*W*	*Waitress*

Residential Address *5344 Winter St.*	City *Mersonville*	State *AZ*	Zip Code *88088*	Home Phone *602-555-0183*	Other Phone *602-555-0199*
Clothing Description				Alias	Summons Number

Identifying Marks/Scars/Tattoos	Height *5'04"*	Weight *120*	Build *S*	Hair *BLO*	Eyes *GRN*

Elements/Narrative

Victim Statement:

Mrs. Jackson stated that on 01/28/2014 at approximately 1425 she returned home to her residence at 5344 Winter St. at which time she discovered three unknown male teenagers sitting in her driveway. Mrs. Jackson wanted to park her vehicle in her driveway so she honked her horn for the three male teenagers to move.

After honking her horn one of the male teenagers walked over to her car and spit on the car hood and then held his skateboard up over his right shoulder as if he was going to hit her car with it and said "I will end you" he then along with the other two male teenagers ran north on Winter Street.

Mrs. Jackson said she was able to hear the male because she had her window down.

Mrs. Jackson described the male teenager who threatened her as a white male, 15 to 17 years of age, approximately 5'8" to 5'10" and 140-155 lbs. wearing black in color "board shorts," a black in color "baseball style hat" with a flat bill, a white in color long sleeved shirt with a design of a skateboard on the front, and black in color shoes.

Mrs. Jackson believed the skateboard was black in color on the top and white in color on the bottom with the design of a dragon or snake on the bottom painted in multiple colors.

Mrs. Jackson said that she thought the male teenager was going to hit her car and then her with his skateboard based on his comment "I will end you" and said that the incident was scary. Mrs. Jackson could not describe what the other two male teenagers looked like or what they were wearing but could probably identify the one who spit on the car and threatened her if she saw him again.

Neighborhood Follow-up

I attempted to contact the residents located to the north and south of the victim's home as well as across the street but discovered that no one was home.

Witnesses

No witnesses could be located.

Evidence/Photos

None Discovered/ None Taken

Officer Statement

I drove north on Winter St. to the skate park but could not locate the suspect or anyone fitting his description. No further information

Officer Name/Employee Number *Smith 1616*	Supervisor Name/Employee Number *Carter 090*	Page **2** of **2**

Figure 8.2   *Completed Harassment Report*

For example:

The interviewer may ask the victim:

"Mr. Jones what type of shirt was the man who stole your wallet wearing?"

Mr. Jones may answer:

"The guy was wearing a black and white sweater."

The interviewer may ask this follow-up question:

"Did the sweater have black and white stripes or was it some type of black and white design?"

Mr. Jones may answer:

"The left side of the sweater was white and the right side of the sweater was black."

In the report the description of the sweater given to the investigator by Mr. Jones may be expressed in the following manner:

Mr. Jones stated that the unknown male who stole his wallet was wearing a sweater that was white on the left side and black on the right side.

As mentioned, when completing the victim and witness statements in your report, it can be important to write exactly what they say when you need to express to the reader the emotions of an individual (as is demonstrated in the harassment example on the previous pages). If this is the case, use quotation marks to document their statements.

"After honking her horn, one of the male teenagers walked over to her car and spit on the car hood and then held his skateboard up over his right shoulder as if he was going to hit her car with it and said, 'I will end you' he then along with the other two male teenagers ran north on Winter Street."

In this passage, taken from Figure 8.2, the phrase *"I will end you"* by the possible suspect in this case, can be taken as a threat to the victim. Therefore, it is important that you quote this statement correctly in the victim's statement.

As a law enforcement professional, you will have the opportunity to interview suspects involved in various crimes. It is important to remember that there is a difference between an interview and an interrogation. The basic distinction is that during an interview the individual is free to leave if he or she so chooses. During an interrogation, the individual is NOT free to leave. An interview can quickly turn into interrogation based on what is revealed during the interview process. You need to be able to recognize when an interviewee reveals something to you that may incriminate this individual. Upon receiving this incriminating information, you should stop the interview and advise the person of his or her Miranda rights. This is especially important if you plan on questioning the individual any further.

Many law enforcement agencies have requirements that their officers must adhere to when advising an individual of Miranda rights. It is your responsibility to ensure you follow the requirements your agency has put in place.

One such requirement may be to have the investigating officer complete a Miranda Rights/Warning Interview form. This form is signed by both the person being advised of her Miranda rights and the officer who is advising the individual about Miranda rights. Figure 8.3 is an example of a Miranda Rights/Warning Interview form.

Miranda Interview Report			
Offense	Victim	Date of This Report	Case Report Number
Date	Time	Day	Officer (s)
Location of Interview (Address, City, State, Zip)		Officer/Detective Uniform Non Uniform Credential Shown	
Name of Person Being Interviewed (Last, First, Middle)			
Address (City, State, Zip)			
DOB	Age	Sex	Race
HGT	WGT	Hair	Eyes
Physical Description (Birth Marks, Tattoos, Scars)			
Clothing Description			

Miranda Warning (Must initial after each comment below. Parent and Child for Juveniles)
1. You have the right to remain silent. ____　　____
2. Anything you say can and will be used against you in a court of law. ____　　____
3. You have the right to talk to a lawyer and have him present with you while you are being questioned. ____　　____
4. If you cannot afford to hire a lawyer, one will be appointed to represent you before any questioning, if you wish. ____　　____

Waiver
1. Do you understand each of these rights I have explained to you? ____　　____
2. Having these rights in mind, do you wish to talk to me now? ____　　____

Notes

Officer Signature	Supervisors Signature and Date	Page _____ of _____

Figure 8.3 *Miranda Rights/Warning Interview Form*

SUSPECT STATEMENTS

In dealing with a potential suspect, the same basic interview principles apply. The one major difference in interviewing a suspect is ALWAYS interview a suspect from a position that ensures officer safety. As with any interview, try to establish a rapport with the individual. Suspects typically don't want to tell law enforcement officials anything—break down these barriers as quickly as possible. There are various techniques and strategies to use when interviewing potential suspects. As this textbook is focused on case report writing, not interview and interrogation techniques, it provides only general guidelines for questioning suspects.

Probably the biggest variable when interviewing a suspect is determining when to provide the Miranda warning. There is no specific time when the warning works best.

It varies from interrogation to interrogation. If the suspect incriminates himself or herself, the time is now! The two critical elements in any Miranda warning are:

1. Was it properly given?
2. Are they willing to give a statement having understood the warning?

To ensure the Miranda warning will stand the test of case law, most agencies require you read the Miranda warning, verbatim, from their agency's printed Miranda card. It will be easier to defend in court if you read it word-for-word from the agency's card rather than trying to recollect the exact verbiage you used regarding this specific interrogation. Document in your case report that he or she understood the Miranda warning and was willing to talk to you. Document the exact responses to both parts of the Miranda warning (Do you understand your rights? Are you willing to talk to us?). Never let the suspect simply nod affirmatively. Ask him or her, "Do you understand?" Then document his or her verbal response (use quotes).

Sometimes an effective way to establish a rapport is to downplay the crime. Remember that empathy often works as well with suspects as it does with victims. It is OK to offer the suspect a face-saving scenario. Normally, a nonthreatening approach is the best way to begin the interrogation. Give him or her a cup of coffee or a soft drink; make the suspect feel comfortable. Let the suspect know that you have some critical information and you want to hear his or her side of the story. Be aware of your body language and do not be judgmental. Your goal is to get the individual comfortable and talkative. If this strategy fails, you can always shift into a more confrontational or aggressive approach.

Listen carefully to everything the suspect says. Minimize your time recording your notes. Your focus should be on the suspect's statements and his nonverbal demeanor. Paying attention to the suspect could also put additional stress on the suspect, which may help gain a confession. Be a good listener and let the suspect lay out his or her version of the events. There should be no interruption by the interviewer. Listen carefully to all of the information that is given by the suspect. Try to lock the suspect into a lie and then pick the lie apart, giving the suspect no way out.

Always be in control of the interrogation. The suspect must be aware of who is in charge, what the issue is before him or her, and what is at stake. Find out what the suspect fears most and then exploit this weakness. For example, if the suspect's greatest fear is being arrested and going to jail, let the suspect know that telling the truth is in his best interest. Don't make deals but let him know that honesty and cooperation are the best alternative given the circumstances.

Once you have all of the information you need (or if the suspect invokes his or her Constitutional Rights), conclude the interview. If the suspect confessed, thank the individual for cooperating. If the suspect was evasive, assure him or her that the investigation will continue. Leave the suspect with the final thought that cooperation is the best course of action.

THE *RIGHT* WAY TO *WRITE*

Probably one of the most important strategies in writing statements from the various actors involved in an incident is to always be cognizant of getting direct quotes of anything regarding an element of a crime, incriminating statement, admission of guilt, waiver of medical attention, and so on. As mentioned previously, record these statements exactly, in quotes, in your case report. If the Miranda warning was given, record this fact in your notes, stating the time/date given and the individual's response to the Miranda warning (in quotes).

Another great "how" or "what" to include in your narrative report is to have the individual write a statement. These statements should be referenced and attached to your original case report. Ask the individual to simply "write the story" in his or her own words. Guide the individual through the process, but do not dictate any portion of the statement. This can be achieved by asking open-ended questions prior to the individual starting to write the statement. A good request may be something like "Please write down all of the objective facts and observations regarding this incident." Your role is to keep them on track with the events of the crime and not have the interviewee focus on irrelevant material. The actual words of the suspect are especially compelling evidence in court.

TIPS FOR GATHERING STATEMENTS

- Place yourself in a position of safety.
- Always separate witnesses ASAP; do not allow them to talk to each other.
- Always attempt to develop a rapport with the individual prior to documenting any information.
- Ask open-ended questions; get the person to tell the story.
- During the question-and-answer phase, clarify the interviewee's statements and review the significant facts or elements of the crime
- Listen well and observe nonverbal communication.
- Have the individual write out a statement.

SUMMARY

Obtaining statements from the various actors at a crime scene is a critical part of any thorough investigation. Conducting a law enforcement interview can be a challenging task. This task can be achieved by following some of the basic guidelines presented in this chapter. The good news is that interviewing is an acquired skill, and your interview techniques and skills will improve with practice. Law enforcement officers are in a people business; we deal with various types of people and circumstances every day. By honing your communication skills as your law enforcement career continues, you will find that conducting a successful interview becomes second nature.

This chapter contains various forms and interview or interrogation strategies, which you will utilize throughout your law enforcement career. As you begin your law enforcement career, observe the nuances that "seasoned" officers use in obtaining statements from individuals. Pay attention during your field-training period and ask questions—learn what types of techniques and strategies work best for you when obtaining statements. As always, read professional journals and articles on the topic to improve your techniques.

EXERCISES

1. Figures 8.1 and 8.2 gave you the opportunity to view different reports of a harassment complaint. In this exercise, you will watch a video involving a harassment complaint. You must complete your notes and the report. *(Harassment Complaint Video 8.1)* Use the interview sheets, face sheet or cover sheet, and supplement/continuation report forms that can be found in the "Appendix: Sample Forms" of this book to complete this exercise.

   Additional Information:

   Case Number: 14-00003

   Zone: 4

Sector: 2

Date: Your current date

Time: The time announced in the video

Wendy Benson additional information:

Home phone number: 719-555-0999

Cell phone number: 719-555-0178

Work phone number: 719-555-0188

Place of employment: Wendy's Boutique

Address: 4132 East Beech St.

Mersonville, CO 88088

Occupation: Hair Stylist

Social Security number: 111-22-8888

2. Officer E. Literate has completed a report for a theft that has occurred, and, as usual, it is filled with errors. This report is worse than his other reports, and errors can be found everywhere. Look for them by paying attention to the details!

List the mistakes here:

1. _____

2. _____

3. _____

4. _____

5. _____

6. _____

MERSONVILLE POLICE DEPARTMENT COVER SHEET

Offense ☒	Supplement ☐	Other ☐	Case Number 12-35780

Offense Title	City/State Statute Number	Date of this Report
Theft	637:3	12-14-14

Zone/Sector		Date and time Reported				Date and Approximate Time of Occurrence			
		Month	Day	Year	Time	Month	Day	Year	Time
4	3	12	14	2014	1330	12	14	2014	1245

Victim's Name: Last, First, Middle	Date of Birth	Age	Sex	Height	Weight	Build	Hair	Eyes	Race
Jackson, Glenn, Walter	11/05/1968	46	M	6'04"	350	L	BRO	BRO	W

Residential Address	City	State	Zip Code	Home Phone	Cell Phone
119 Beech St.	Ladybird	NH	88088	603-555-1345	603-555-8090

Business Address	City	State	Zip Code	Business Phone	Occupation
2034 White Birch Lane	Ladybird	NH	88088	603-555-1567	Construction

Location of Offense	City	State	Zip Code
40225 Purple Finch Way	Ladybird	NH	88088

If a business is the victim complete the information below

Name of Business	Business Address	City	State	Zip Code	Business Phone
Big Boy Construction	119 Beech St.	Ladybird	NH	88088	603-555-1345

Codes RP = Reporting Party AV = Additional Victim W = Witness LO = Law Enforcement Officer A = Arrestee S = Suspect O = Other

Code	Name: Last, First, Middle	Date of Birth	Age	Sex	Height	Weight	Build	Hair	Eyes	Race

Residential Address	City	State	Zip Code	Home Phone	Cell Phone

Business Address	City	State	Zip Code	Business Phone	Occupation

Clothing Description	Alias

Identifying Marks	Summons Number

Narrative

On 12-14-2014 at approximately 1340 I, Officer Literate 1617P, was dispatched to 40325 Purple Finch Way in reference to a theft. Upon arrival I made contact with the victim, Glen Jackson, who told me that between 1130 and 1245 on 12-14-15 unknown person(s) unlawfully removed his Super Cut 12' table saw from the front porch of 40325 Purple Finch Way. Mr. Jackson said that she was installing a new hardwood floor in the residence an using the saw on the porch. Mr. Jackson had decided to go to lunch at approximately 1130 with his coworker and when they retuned at 1245 the discovered his saw had ben stolen.

Suspect(s): No
Witness(es): No
Photos: No
Evidence: No
Neighborhood Follow-p: Yes
See Supplement for more information.

Report Completed by:	Signature:	
E. Literate 1617P	E. Literate 1617P	Page 1 of 3 Page
Report Reviewed by:	Signature:	
David Carter 0987	David Carter 0987	

Mersonville Property Supplement

Offense Title	State/City Statute	Date of this Report	Case Number
Theft	*637:3*	*12-14-14*	*12-35780*

Victim's Name: Last, First, Middle	Date of Birth	Age	Sex	Height	Weight	Build	Hair	Eyes	Race
Jackson, Glenn, Walter	*11/05/1968*	*46*	*M*	*6'04"*	*350*	*L*	*BRO*	*BRO*	*W*

Residential Address	City	State	Zip Code	Home Phone	Cell Phone
2034 White Birch Lane	*Ladybird*	*NH*	*88088*	*603-555-8090*	*603-555-1345*

Suspect's Name: Last, First, Middle	Date of Birth	Age	Sex	Height	Weight	Build	Hair	Eyes	Race

Residential Address	City	State	Zip Code	Home Phone	Cell Phone

Vehicle Property Information

Stolen _____ Victim_____ Suspect_____ Local Recovery_____ Outside Recovery_____ Owner Notified_____

Vehicle Status

Returned to Owner_____ Impounded_____ Placed into Evidence_____ Towed by:

_____

Vehicle Year	Vehicle Color	Vehicle Make	Vehicle Model	Vehicle Style

License Plate Number	License Plate Type	License Plate Year	License Plate State	License Plate Color

Vehicle Identification Number	Insured by:

Vehicle Owner's Name: Last, First, Middle	Owner Notified of Recovery Yes_____ No_____ Date:_____

Vehicle Owner's Residential Address	City	State	Zip Code	Home Phone	Cell Phone

Pick-up Issued into NCIC for Above Vehicle Yes_____ No_____	Pick-up Cancelled in NCIC for Above Vehicle Yes_____ No_____

Firearm Property Information

Stolen _____ Victim_____ Suspect_____ Local Recovery_____ Outside Recovery_____ Owner Notified_____

Firearm Status

Returned to Owner_____ Placed into Evidence_____

Firearm Make	Firearm Model	Firearm Caliber	Firearm Serial Number	Firearm Color

Pick-up Issued into NCIC for Above Firearm Yes_____ No_____	Pick-up Cancelled in NCIC for Above Firearm Yes_____ No_____

Other Property Information

Stolen __✗__ Victim _✗_ Suspect_____ Local Recovery_____ Outside Recovery_____ Owner Notified_____

Property Status

Returned to Owner_____ Impounded_____ Placed into Evidence_____ Towed by:

_____

Pick-up Issued into NCIC for Above Other Property Yes_____ No_____	Pick-up Cancelled in NCIC for Above Other Property Yes_____ No_____

Item #	Quantity #	Brand	Model	Serial #	Damaged	Value
1	*1*	*Super Cut 13" Table Saw*	*Unknown*	*45-349087*	Yes_____ No_____	*850.00*
Description *Red in color 13" Table Saw with visible wear/use*						
Item #	Quantity #	Brand	Model	Serial #	Damaged Yes_____ No_____	Value
Description						
Item #	Quantity #	Brand	Model	Serial #	Damaged Yes_____ No_____	Value
Description						

Any other Description Not Covered Above Vehicle_____ Firearm_____ Other property_____	Total Loss of All Property Listed: *$850.00*

Officer Completing Property Report and ID # *E. Literate 1617P*	Supervisor Name and ID# *David Carter 0987*	Page __*2*___ of __*3*___

Mersonville Police Department Supplement Report										
Offense Title	City/State Statute		Date of this Report			Case Number				
Theft	*637:3*		*12-14-14*			*12-35780*				

Codes RP = Reporting Party AV = Additional Victim W = Witness LO = Law Enforcement Officer A = Arrestee S = Suspect O = Other										
Code	Name: Last, First, Middle	Date of Birth	Age	Sex	Height	Weight	Build	Hair	Eyes	Race

Residential Address	City	State	Zip Code	Home Phone	Other Phone
Business Address	City	State	Zip Code	Home Phone	Occupation

Clothing Description	Alias
Identifying Marks	Summons Number

Narrative

Victim Statement:

Mr. Jackson stated that he did not see anyone around the residence prior to leaving for lunch with his coworker Mr. Baker. Mr. Jackson described his table saw as an Super Cutter 12" table saw that was red in color with visible wear/use. Mr. Jackson stated that he purchased the saw in January of 2009 from The Big Box Store an that he paid $1400.00 for it. Mr. Jackson deneid owing any money on the saw or having a loan against it. Mr. Jackson could not provide a photo or a reciept for the saw but valued it at $850.00.

Neighborhood Follow-up

Daryn Rogers
40328 Purple Finch Way Ladybird, NH. 88088
603-555-5690 HM
603-555-9878 Cell
Mr. Rogers resides directly across form the location of the theft but was on the backyard during the time of the offense and did not see anything or anyone unusual.
No other neighbors could be located.

Officer Statement:

The location of the theft is within a new residential neighborhood and many homes are complete but not occupied. The front of the home faces north. The only other occupied home is located at 40328 Purple Finch Way and I contacted that resident, Darin Rogers, who could not provide any information regarding the theft.

The front of the home faces west and the fornt entrance, where the saw was located, is visible form the street.

Photos:
None were taken

Evidence:
Nothing found
No further information.

Report Completed by: *E. Literate 1617P*	Signature: *E. Literate 1617P*	Page 3 of 3 Pages
Report Reviewed by: *David Carter 0987*	Signature: *David Carter 0987*	

9

MISDEMEANOR CRIMES INVOLVING PEOPLE AND PROPERTY

LEARNING OBJECTIVES

- Identify some of the different misdemeanor crimes against people and property that you may encounter during your career as a law enforcement professional.

- Recognize that each state is different in how crimes are defined, and you must ensure you document the crime in your report in accordance with the appropriate state statute for where the crime was committed.

- Apply your knowledge to practical examples by successfully completing the chapter exercises.

INTRODUCTION

Although misdemeanor crimes involving people and property may seem like minor types of case reports, these types of crimes are commonplace and need to be properly documented to facilitate potential future prosecution and closure of the incident. Remember, a minor theft of property may seem insignificant to you, the officer, but it may become a major event in the life of the victim. Do not take these types of cases lightly. The old adage "if you do the little things correctly, the big things will follow" applies here. Take the time to do it right. Most law enforcement agencies will have preprinted forms for these types of cases to help guide you through the process.

There are numerous other applications of the concepts presented in this chapter with regard to misdemeanor crimes involving people and property. Some typical minor cases you will encounter are minor assaults, trespassing, harassment, drug possession, and numerous other misdemeanor crimes.

For the sake of simplicity, this chapter will focus primarily on the misdemeanor crime of theft. The definition of the crime of theft is given, and the chapter exercises are focused exclusively on this type of offense. This theft case is representative of other types of misdemeanor offenses, and as such, it shares many commonalities with the preparation of other types of misdemeanor property crimes.

The following is part of Colorado's definition of the crime of theft.

18-4-401. Theft

(1) A person commits theft when he or she knowingly obtains, retains, or exercises control over anything of value of another without authorization or by threat or deception; or receives, loans money by pawn or pledge on, or disposes of anything of value or belonging to another that he or she knows or believes to have been stolen, and:

   (a) Intends to deprive the other person permanently of the use or benefit of the thing of value;

   (b) Knowingly uses, conceals, or abandons the thing of value in such manner as to deprive the other person permanently of its use or benefit;

   (c) Uses, conceals, or abandons the thing of value intending that such use, concealment, or abandonment will deprive the other person permanently of its use or benefit;

   (d) Demands any consideration to which he or she is not legally entitled as a condition of restoring the thing of value to the other person; or

   (e) Knowingly retains the thing of value more than seventy-two hours after the agreed-upon time of return in any lease or hire agreement.

(1.5) For the purposes of this section, a thing of value is that of "another" if anyone other than the defendant has a possessory or proprietary interest therein.

(2) Theft is:

   (a) (Deleted by amendment, L. 2007, p. 1690, § 3, effective July 1, 2007.)

   (b) A class 1 petty offense if the value of the thing involved is less than fifty dollars;

   (b.5) Repealed.

   (c) A class 3 misdemeanor if the value of the thing involved is fifty dollars or more but less than three hundred dollars;

   (d) A class 2 misdemeanor if the value of the thing involved is three hundred dollars or more but less than seven hundred fifty dollars;

   (e) A class 1 misdemeanor if the value of the thing involved is seven hundred fifty dollars or more but less than two thousand dollars;

   (f) A class 6 felony if the value of the thing involved is two thousand dollars or more but less than five thousand dollars;

   (g) A class 5 felony if the value of the thing involved is five thousand dollars or more but less than twenty thousand dollars;

   (h) A class 4 felony if the value of the thing involved is twenty thousand dollars or more but less than one hundred thousand dollars;

   (i) A class 3 felony if the value of the thing involved is one hundred thousand dollars or more but less than one million dollars; and

   (j) A class 2 felony if the value of the thing involved is one million dollars or more.

(3) and (3.1) Repealed.

(Source: Colorado Legal Resources, Provided by Lexis Nexis, Official Publisher of the Colorado Revised Statutes, http://www.lexisnexis.com/hottopics/Colorado/)

The following is part of Arizona's definition of the crime of theft

13-1802 Theft

(A)   *A person commits theft if, without lawful authority, the person knowingly:*

1.   *Controls property of another with the intent to deprive the other person of such property; or*

2.   *Converts for an unauthorized term or use services or property of another entrusted to the defendant or placed in the defendant's possession for a limited, authorized term or use; or*

3.   *Obtains services or property of another by means of any material misrepresentation with intent to deprive the other person of such property or services; or*

4.   *Comes into control of lost, mislaid or misdelivered property of another under circumstances providing means of inquiry as to the true owner and appropriates such property to the person's own or another's use without reasonable efforts to notify the true owner; or*

5.   *Controls property of another knowing or having reason to know that the property was stolen; or*

6.   *Obtains services known to the defendant to be available only for compensation without paying or an agreement to pay the compensation or diverts another's services to the person's own or another's benefit without authority to do so; or*

7.   *Controls the ferrous metal or nonferrous metal of another with the intent to deprive the other person of the metal; or*

8.   *Controls the ferrous metal or nonferrous metal of another knowing or having reason to know that the metal was stolen; or*

9.   *Purchases within the scope of the ordinary course of business the ferrous metal or nonferrous metal of another person knowing that the metal was stolen.*

(G)   *Theft of property or services with a value of twenty-five thousand dollars or more is a class 2 felony. Theft of property or services with a value of four thousand dollars or more but less than twenty-five thousand dollars is a class 3 felony. Theft of property or services with a value of three thousand dollars or more but less than four thousand dollars is a class 4 felony, except that theft of any vehicle engine or transmission is a class 4 felony regardless of value. Theft of property or services with a value of two thousand dollars or more but less than three thousand dollars is a class 5 felony. Theft of property or services with a value of one thousand dollars or more but less than two thousand dollars is a class 6 felony. Theft of any property or services valued at less than one thousand dollars is a class 1 misdemeanor, unless the property is taken from the person of another, is a firearm or is an animal taken for the purpose of animal fighting in violation of section 13-2910.01, in which case the theft is a class 6 felony.*

Source: Arizona State Legislature: (http://www.azleg.gov/FormatDocument
.asp?inDoc=/ars/13/01802.htm&Title=13&DocType=ARS)

A misdemeanor crime against property is usually one that is associated with a financial loss to the victim. Both Colorado and Arizona separate misdemeanor and felony property crimes by the amount of the financial loss to the victim. The amount of the financial loss can be found in each state's statutory law defining a specific property crime. The following are examples of different types of property crimes that you may experience during your routine duties as a law enforcement professional.

Theft

Criminal mischief

Vandalism

Damage to private property

Best Practices: When the situation allows, you should ask the victim if he or she has documentation that supports the value amount being reported. The documentation provided by the victim should be identified in your theft report, as it will help support the charge of theft as either a petty offense, a misdemeanor, or a felony.

PROPERTY FORMS

Crimes involving property will require an additional page in the case report; this is usually referred to as a property continuation/supplement or inventory sheet. This form identifies each stolen, damaged, or missing item. The information for each item listed on the property continuation/supplement may include:

Item number

Quantity

Brand

Model

Description

Serial number

Damage

Value

Pictures, if available, of the stolen, missing, or damaged property

The property continuation/supplement may include additional areas for specific property that could include:

Automobiles

Firearms

THE *RIGHT* WAY TO *WRITE*

The best way to write a report of a misdemeanor crime involving a person or property is simply using all of the tools that have been presented thus far for the narrative case report. Tell the story of the incident, in chorological order, in simple, understandable words. Every law enforcement agency will have its own agency-specific cover or face sheet, which you will have to complete. The next stage involves transposing your field notes into a comprehensive narrative case report. Remember, when writing the report, that proper information and evidence collection is crucial in order to support a subsequent legal proceeding.

What do you need to focus on when writing these types of reports? First, let us examine crimes against property. Your report should provide a description of the criminal incident. Was property destroyed or taken? How did this occur? Your report should contain a description of items and estimated values of the property (Ask for receipts of property, if appropriate, and attach these to the case report.). Ask the victim for any serial numbers, special markings, or other things that may help in the recovery of the items. Always review the proper state statute that applies to the criminal episode and list these elements of the offense in your case report.

Regarding misdemeanor crimes against persons, you once again need to detail in your report a description of the incident. Were there any injuries? How did they occur? Is the suspect known? Describe the injuries in detail and take photos. If possible, ask all involved parties to complete written statements. Review the proper state statutes regarding this crime and incorporate those elements into the case report. If the suspect is known, be sure to list all of the elements of the crime, along with the suspect's information in your probable cause affidavit.

TIPS FOR MISDEMEANOR CRIMES INVOLVING PEOPLE AND PROPERTY REPORTS

- Review your state statutes regarding the elements of the crime.
  - Always have a state statute book available in your vehicle for reference.

- Regarding crimes against persons, if there are observable injuries:
  - Document and take photos.
  - Have the victim contact you a few days after the incident and take additional photos.
    - Note that injuries are often more visible a day or two after the assault.
  - Was medical attention required? If so, describe in detail.
  - ALWAYS have the victim contact you if his or her incident-related injuries require additional treatment or hospitalization in the future (you may need to increase the severity of the charges).

- Regarding crimes against property, take the time to accurately document the property items:
  - Serial numbers (if available)
  - Receipts (if available), attached to the report
  - Distinguishing characteristics (if any)
    - For example:
      - The TV set had broken a volume control knob, and the attached TV stand had a large crack (approximately three inches in length) in the center of the base of the stand.
      - The suspect vehicle observed leaving the scene was described as a late model Ford Mustang, with a dented rear fender on the driver's side, driven by an unknown white male wearing a blue baseball cap and dark sunglasses.

SUMMARY

Misdemeanor crimes involving people and property entail two different types of offenses. Misdemeanor crimes against people are typically designated by the nature and the degree of injury, as defined by state statutes. The term misdemeanor implies that the injuries were not of a life-threatening nature. Crimes against property are typically defined by the dollar amount of the item involved. The appropriate state statutes will describe, in detail, both of these types of crimes. Most law enforcement agencies will have preprinted report forms to help guide you through the process. Additionally, agency policy and procedure manuals, or standard operating procedures, will have specific guidance on completing these types of reports.

Although this chapter considers relatively minor crimes (i.e., misdemeanors), never forget that they are violations of the law. The documentation that you generate could possibly be subpoenaed into a court of law. These types of offenses should never be taken lightly. Remember that the victim you contact regarding these incidents may look upon this incident as one of the worst days of their lives—be empathetic and professional. Take the time to obtain essential information that will, hopefully, bring some type of closure to the event. Your professional bearing and demeanor will have a lasting effect upon the citizens that you encounter.

EXERCISES

1. In this section, you are going to watch a video of a law enforcement professional responding to a report of a theft/shoplifting at a department store. *(Theft/Shoplifting Video 9.1)* Use the interview sheets, face sheet/cover sheet, supplement/continuation, and summons/ticket report forms that can be found in the "Appendix: Sample Forms" to complete this exercise.

   Additional Information:

   Case Number: 14-0008

   Zone: 4

   Sector: 3

   Date: Your current date

   Time: The time announced in the video

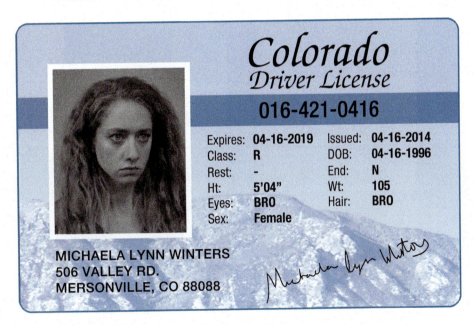

   Suspect's Additional Information

   Home phone: 719-555-0199

   Cell phone: 719-555-0188

   Identifying marks: None visible

   Occupation: None

Information for Witness\Victim

    Witness/victim: John Smith

    Date of birth: 10-24-68

    Height: 6'01"

    Weight: 200 lbs.

    Build: Medium

    Hair: Brown

    Eyes: Brown

    Race: White

    Employer: Emerson Department Store

    Job title: Store security manager

    Work address: 3840 Lincoln Ave. Mersonville, CO 88088

    Contact phone: 719-555-0183

2. In many crimes involving theft, the suspect may not be identified; therefore, you must complete a theft report and not a summons and complaint form, as you have done previously. In this exercise, you will watch a video involving a theft scenario, and you must record your notes and then complete the theft report. *(Theft Video 9.2)* Use the interview sheets, face sheet/cover sheet, supplement/continuation, and property supplement report forms that can be found in the "Appendix: Sample Forms" to complete this exercise.

    Additional Information:

    Case Number: 14-20001

    Zone: 3

    Sector: 2

    Date: Your current date

    Time: The time announced in the video

10

FELONY CRIMES INVOLVING PROPERTY

LEARNING OBJECTIVES

- Identify some of the different felony crimes involving property that you may encounter during your career as a law enforcement professional.

- Understand that each state defines felony property crimes differently, and you must ensure you document the crime in your report in accordance with the state statute for where the crime was committed.

- Apply your knowledge to practical examples by successfully completing the chapter exercises.

INTRODUCTION

A felony crime against property is usually an offense that is associated with a financial loss to the victim. Below are possible examples of different types of felony property crimes that you may experience during your day-to-day duties as a law enforcement professional.

Theft

Criminal mischief

Vandalism

Damage to private property

Motor vehicle theft

Burglary

Below is part of Colorado's definition of the crime of criminal mischief.

18-4-501. Criminal Mischief

(1) A person who knowingly damages the real or personal property of one or more other persons, including property owned by the person jointly with another person or property owned by the person in which another person has a possessory or proprietary interest, in the course of a single

criminal episode commits a class 2 misdemeanor where the aggregate damage to the real or personal property is less than five hundred dollars. Where the aggregate damage to the real or personal property is five hundred dollars or more but less than one thousand dollars, the person commits a class 1 misdemeanor. Where the aggregate damage to the real or personal property is one thousand dollars or more but less than twenty thousand dollars, the person commits a class 4 felony. Where the aggregate damage to the real or personal property is twenty thousand dollars or more, the person commits a class 3 felony.

Source: Colorado Legal Resources, provided by Lexis Nexis, Official Publisher of the Colorado Revised Statutes, lexisnexis.com/hottopics/Colorado

Below is part of Arizona's definition of the crime of criminal damage.

13-1602. *Criminal Damage*

A. A person commits criminal damage by:

1. Recklessly defacing or damaging property of another person.

2. Recklessly tampering with property of another person so as substantially to impair its function or value.

3. Recklessly damaging property of a utility.

4. Recklessly parking any vehicle in such a manner as to deprive livestock of access to the only reasonably available water.

5. Recklessly drawing or inscribing a message, slogan, sign or symbol that is made on any public or private building, structure or surface, except the ground, and that is made without permission of the owner.

6. Intentionally tampering with utility property.

B. Criminal damage is punished as follows:

1. Criminal damage is a class 4 felony if the person recklessly damages property of another in an amount of ten thousand dollars or more.

2. Criminal damage is a class 4 felony if the person recklessly damages the property of a utility in an amount of five thousand dollars or more or if the person intentionally tampers with utility property and the damage causes an imminent safety hazard to any person.

3. Criminal damage is a class 5 felony if the person recklessly damages property of another in an amount of two thousand dollars or more but less than ten thousand dollars.

4. Criminal damage is a class 6 felony if the person recklessly damages property of another in an amount of one thousand dollars or more but less than two thousand dollars.

5. Criminal damage is a class 1 misdemeanor if the person recklessly damages property of another in an amount of more than two hundred fifty dollars but less than one thousand dollars.

6. In all other cases criminal damage is a class 2 misdemeanor.

C. For a violation of subsection A, paragraph 5 of this section, in determining the amount of damage to property, damages include reasonable labor costs of any kind, reasonable material costs of any kind and any reasonable costs that are attributed to equipment that is used to abate or repair the damage to the property.

Source: Arizona State Legislature: http://www.azleg.gov/FormatDocument .asp?inDoc=/ars/13/01802.htm&Title=13&DocType=ARS

In both Colorado and Arizona, criminal mischief and criminal damage are similar in definition, and each state associates the severity of the crime with the financial loss to the victim.

Best Practices: Ensure that the elements of the crime you are investigating coincide with your jurisdiction's statutory definitions.

THE *RIGHT* WAY TO *WRITE*

The writing style of felony crimes involving property is basically the same as the style for misdemeanor crimes involving property. There is one exception, however: the monetary value of the property taken. Your state statutes will describe, in detail, the thresholds of property value that elevate the crime into a felony offense. Additionally, because of the increased property value of the offense, these types of reports will probably entail more follow-up. Thus, they are more prone to require supplemental reports. Aside from these minor distinctions, the same principles apply to both misdemeanor and felony crimes against property reports.

TIPS FOR FELONY CRIMES INVOLVING PROPERTY

- Always consult your appropriate state statute book for specific charging information.
- Often the dollar amount designates which crimes are misdemeanors and which are felonies.
- Get specifics from the victim on the missing property (property continuation/supplement or inventory sheet).
  - Do they have serial numbers?
  - Are there identifying marks on the property?
  - Any distinguishing features of the missing items?
  - Are there photos of the missing items?
  - Do they have receipts?

SUMMARY

Crimes against property are common occurrences in the world of criminal justice. The more you can establish some uniqueness about the missing items, the better your chances of recovery. Take the time to ask the victim follow-up questions that may help identify the missing items. If the victim has no specifics, now is the time to educate the victim on the importance of recording serial numbers, keeping receipts, and photographing their high-dollar property items. Remember that community-oriented policing does not simply respond to a crime. It helps to prevent future victimization.

Example 1

1. In this example you're going to watch a video of a law enforcement professional responding to a motor vehicle theft *(Motor Vehicle Theft Video 10.1)*. Review the following notes that a law enforcement professional completed during his investigation of the reported crime you just watched, as well as the case report that was completed.

Colorado
Driver License
957-456-8567

Expires:	**03-06-2019**	Issued:	**03-06-2013**
Class:	**R**	DOB:	**03-08-1981**
Rest:	**-**	End:	**N**
Ht:	**6'03"**	Wt:	**220**
Eyes:	**BLU**	Hair:	**BRO**
Sex:	**Male**		

HENRY ROBERT DRUM
640 FRONT RANGE DR.
MERSONVILLE, CO 88088

All Right Insurance INC.
Policy Number 097456-234-ADF
Insured: 2000 Ford F350   VIN: 6578YT12345679GKL
Dates: 08-01-14 thru 08-31-15
Insured Drivers: Henry Drum   640 Front Range Dr.   Mersonville, CO 88088
Agent: David Roberts   3030 Snow Pass Dr.   Mersonville, CO 88088   Office Phone: 719-555-0157   24 Hour Service 719-555-0158   Fax: 719-555-0159

COLORADO REGISTRATION/OWNERSHIP TAX RECEIPT

TYPE		PLATE	TAB/VAL		VIN		EXPIRE
PAS-REG		1UPSET	A711111		6578YT12345679GKL		11/2015

TITLE	YEAR	MAKE	BODY	CWT/PAS	T/C	FLEET	FUEL	PREV EXP
Y231	2000	FORD	TRK	40	C		G	

PUR DATE	PUR PRICE	ORIGINAL TAXABLE VALUE	BUS DATE	CO#	UR/CODE
08/11/2008	6,000	7,000	08/12/2014	11U	0001

EM FEE	TITLE FEE	PRIOR O.T.	OWN TAX	LIC FEE	ROAD FEE	BRIDGE FEE
0.00	0.00	0.00	850.00	120.00	23.00	13.50

RTD TAX	COUNTY TAX	CITY/DIS TAX	STATE TAX	SPECIAL FEE	OTHER FEE
0.00	50.00	30.00	25.00	0.00	0.00

UNIT	GVW	MILES	HT GVW	HC DATE

OWNER MAILING ADDRESS

DRUM ROBERT HENRY

640 FRONT RANGE DR.

MERSONVILLE, CO 88088

FEES IN BOLD INCLUDED IN UC FEE

E09933456   4356

SIGNATURE REQUIRED ON REVERSE SIDE

VALIDATION PAID MORRIS	LN 24	11/30/2014	TOTAL

MOTOR VEHICLE INSURANCE IS COMPULSORY IN COLORADO, NON-COMPLIANCE IS A IS A MISDEMEANOR TRAFFIC OFFENSE

Case #: 14-01987   **Title:** *Aggravated Motor Vehicle Theft*

Dispatch: *0930*   **Arrival:** *0945*   **Cleared:** *1015*

Date: *01-15-2015*   **Time:** *0815*   **Offense Location:** *640 Front Range Dr.*

~~Suspect~~/(Victim)/~~Witness/Other~~:

Name: *Drum, Henry, Robert*

DOB: *03-08-81*   **Race:** W   **HGT:** *6'03"*   **WGT:** 220   **Hair:** BRO   **Eyes:** BLU

POB: **SEX:** *Male*   ~~Female~~

Clothing Description:

Address: *640 Front Range Dr.*   **City:** *Mersonville*   **State:** *CO*   **Zip Code:** *88088*

Contact Numbers: Home: *719-555-0134*   **Cell:** *719-555-0156*   **WK:** *719-555-0177*

Employer: *H&H Construction*   **Occupation:** *Frontend loader*

Business Address: *47890 Black Diamond WY.* **City:** *Mersonville*   **State:** *CO*   **Zip Code:** *88088*

Business Phone: **Business Victim:** Yes (No)

Vi = I went out and started truck at approx. 0815 and then went inside and got coffee and to turn everything off before leaving for work.

Did not hear anything nor did he observe anyone unusual around the house.

After turning things off and going back outside to go to work he discovered his truck missing.

V = describes truck as a 2000 Drk blu in color Ford F350 Crew Cab with a dent in the ®) front fender.

V = value is 6,000.

V = advised no one had permission to drive vehicle.

V = vehicle is paid off and he does not have a loan on it.

V = no one had keys to it. Only 1 set of keys. Lost the spare a couple of years ago.

V = thinks his neighbor Bill Jackson may have been home during the theft.

Case #: 14-01987   **Title:**

Dispatch: **Arrival:**   **Cleared:**

Date: **Time:**   **Offense Location:**

~~Suspect/Victim/Witness~~/(Other:)

Name: *William (Bill) Jackson*

DOB: **Race:**   **HGT:**   **WGT:**   **Hair:**   **Eyes:**

POB: **SEX:** *Male*   *Female*

Clothing Description:

Address: *638 Front Range Dr.*   **City:** *Mersonville*   **State:** *CO*   **Zip Code:** *88088*

Contact Numbers: Home: *719-555-0191*   **Cell:**   **WK:**

Employer: **Occupation:**

Business Address: **City:**   **State:**   **Zip Code:**

Business Phone: **Business Victim:** Yes No

Jackson = did not see anyone unusual.

Jackson = heard the truck start up @ about 0810-0815 and then pull out. Thought it was Henry.

MERSONVILLE POLICE DEPARTMENT COVER SHEET

Offense ☒	Supplement ☐	Other ☐	Case Number 14-01987

Offense Title	State/City Statute Number	Date of this Report
Aggravated Motor Vehicle Theft	18-4-409	01/15/2015

Zone/Sector		Date and time Reported				Date and Approximate Time of Occurrence			
		Month	Day	Year	Time	Month	Day	Year	Time
4	3	01	15	2015	0915	01	15	2015	0815

Victim's Name Last, First, Middle	Date of Birth	Age	Sex	Height	Weight	Build	Hair	Eyes	Race
Drum, Henry, Robert	03/08/1981	34	M	6'03"	220	L	BRO	BLU	W

Residential Address	City	State	Zip Code	Home Phone	Cell Phone
640 Front Range Dr.	Mersonville	CO	88088	719-555-0134	719-555-0156

Business Address	City	State	Zip Code	Business Phone	Occupation
47890 Black Diamond WY.	Mersonville	CO	88088	719-555-0177	Frontend Loader

Location of Offense	City	State	Zip Code
640 Front Range Dr.	Mersonville	CO	88088

If a business is the victim complete the information below

Name of Business	Business Address	City	State	Zip Code	Business Phone

Codes RP = Reporting Party AV = Additional Victim LO = Law Enforcement Officer W = Witness S = Suspect A = Arrestee O = Other

Code	Last, First, Middle	Date of Birth	Age	Sex	Height	Weight	Build	Hair	Eyes	Race
O	Jackson, William									

Residential Address	City	State	Zip Code	Home Phone	Cell Phone
638 Front Range Dr.	Mersonville	CO	88088	719-555-0191	

Business Address	City	State	Zip Code	Business Phone	Occupation

Clothing Description	Alias

Identifying Marks	Summons Number

Narrative

Officer Statement:

On 01-15-2015 at approximately 0930 I, Officer Smith 1616P, was dispatched to 640 Front Range Dr. In reference to a reported Aggravated Motor Vehicle Theft. Upon arrival I made contact with Henry Drum, the victim, who told me that at approximately 0810 hours on 01-15-15 an unknown person(s) unlawfully took his 2000 Ford F350 Crew Cab from the front of his home without his permission. Mr. Drum did not see anyone or hear anyone driving away in his truck during the commission of the theft.

Witness = No
Suspect = No
Evidence = No
Photos = No
Neighborhood Follow-up = Yes

Report Completed by:	Signature:	
Officer Smith 1616P	*Michael Smith 1616P*	Page 1 of 3 Pages
Report Completed by:	Signature:	
Sgt. Lynn 0123S	*David Lynn 0123S*	

Mersonville Police Department Supplement Report										
Offense Title		State/City Statute		Date of this Report			Case Number			
Aggravated Motor Vehicle Theft		18-4-409		01-15-2015			15-01987			

Codes   RP=Reporting Party   AV= Additional Victim   LO= Law Enforcement Officer   V=Victim   W=Witness   S=Suspect   A=Arrestee   O=Other

Code	Name: Last, First, Middle	Date of Birth	Age	Sex	Height	Weight	Build	Hair	Eyes	Race
V	Drum, Henry, Robert	03-08-81	34	M	6'03"	220	L	BRO	BLU	W

Residential Address	City	State	Zip Code	Home Phone	Other Phone
640 Front Range Dr.	Mersonville	CO	88088	719-555-0134	719-555-0156
Business Address	City	State	Zip Code	Home Phone	Other Phone
47890 Black Diamond WY.	Mersonville	CO	88088	719-555-0177	Frontend Loader
Clothing Description			**Alias**		
Identifying Marks			**Summons Number**		

Narrative

Victim Statement:

Mr. Drum stated that he started up his 2000 Ford Truck to allow it to warmup before driving to work. After starting the truck Mr. Drum went back inside his home to retrieve his coffee cup and to secure the house. When Mr. Drum went back outside he discovered his truck missing. Mr. Drum did not see anyone outside when he first started the truck up nor did he hear anyone drive away with it.

Mr. Drum said that he did not give anyone permission to drive his truck nor did anyone else have a key to the truck. Mr. Drum denied having a loan on the truck and stated that he paid it off about three years ago. Mr. Drum valued his truck at $6,000.

Mr. Drum described his truck as a dark blue 2000 Ford F350 Crew Cab with a dent in the right front fender.

Neighborhood Follow-up

William Jackson (Bill)
638 Front Range Dr. Mersonville, CO 88088
Contact Phone: 719-555-0191

Mr. Jackson stated that he was at home and heard Mr. Drum's truck start up and drive away but thought it was Henry, the owner of the truck, leaving for work.

Mr. Jackson did not see anyone or anything unusual before the truck was stolen.

Officer Statement:

No witnesses could be located.
No evidence was discovered.
No photos were taken.
A Pick-up was completed and the information was entered into NCIC for the stolen truck on 01-15-15.
No further information.

Report Completed by:	Signature:	Page 2 of 3 Pages
Officer Smith 1616P	*Michael Smith 1616P*	
Report Reviewed by:	**Signature:**	
Sgt. Lynn 0123S	*David Lynn 0123S*	

Mersonville Property Supplement

Offense Title	State/City Statute	Date of this Report	Case Number
Aggravated Motor Vehicle Theft	18-4-409	01-15-2015	15-01987

Victim's Name: Last, First, Middle	Date of Birth	Age	Sex	Height	Weight	Build	Hair	Eyes	Race
Drum, Henry, Robert	03-08-81	34	M	6'03"	220	L	BRO	BLU	W

Residential Address	City	State	Zip Code	Home Phone	Cell Phone
640 Front Range Dr.	Mersonville	CO	88088	719-555-0134	719-555-0156

Suspect's Name: Last, First, Middle	Date of Birth	Age	Sex	Height	Weight	Build	Hair	Eyes	Race
Unknown									

Residential Address	City	State	Zip Code	Home Phone	Cell Phone

Vehicle Property Information:

Stolen __X__ Victim __X__ Suspect_____ Local Recovery_____ Outside Recovery_____ Owner Notified_____

Vehicle Status:

Returned to Owner_____   Impounded_____   Placed into Evidence_____   Towed by:_____

Vehicle Year	Vehicle Color	Vehicle Make	Vehicle Model	Vehicle Style
2000	Dark Blue	Ford	F350	Crew Cab

License Plate Number	License Plate Type	License Plate Year	License Plate State	License Plate Color
1UPSET	PAS REG	2015	CO	GRN WHT

Vehicle Identification Number	Insured by:
6578YT12345679GKL	All Right Insurance

Vehicle Owner's Name: Last, First, Middle	Owner Notified of Recovery Yes_____ No_____
Drum, Henry, Robert	Date:_____

Vehicle Owner's Residential Address	City	State	Zip Code	Home Phone	Cell Phone
640 Front Range Dr.	Mersonville	CO	88088	719-555-0134	719-555-0156

Pick-up Issued into NCIC for Above Vehicle Yes_____ No_____	Pick-up Cancelled in NCIC for Above Vehicle Yes_____ No_____

Firearm Property Information:

Stolen _____ Victim_____ Suspect_____ Local Recovery_____ Outside Recovery_____ Owner Notified_____

Firearm Status

Returned to Owner_____   Placed into Evidence_____

Firearm Make	Firearm Model	Firearm Caliber	Firearm Serial Number	Firearm Color

Pick-up Issued into NCIC for Above Firearm Yes_____ No_____	Pick-up Cancelled in NCIC for Above Firearm Yes_____ No_____

Other Property Information

Stolen _____ Victim_____ Suspect_____ Local Recovery_____ Outside Recovery_____ Owner Notified_____

Property Status

Returned to Owner_____   Impounded_____   Placed into Evidence_____   Towed by:_____

Pick-up Issued into NCIC for Above Other Property Yes_____ No_____	Pick-up Cancelled in NCIC for Above Other Property Yes_____ No_____

Item #	Quantity #	Brand	Model	Serial #	Damaged Yes_____ No_____	Value
Description						

Item #	Quantity #	Brand	Model	Serial #	Damaged Yes_____ No_____	Value
Description						

Item #	Quantity #	Brand	Model	Serial #	Damaged Yes_____ No_____	Value
Description						

Any other Description Not Covered Above Vehicle _X_ Firearm_____ Other property_____ **Stolen F350 has a dent in the right front fender.**	Total Loss of All Property Listed:

Officer Completing Property Report and ID #	Supervisor Name and ID#	Page 3 of 3 Pages
Officer Smith 1616P	Sgt. Lynn 0123S	

EXERCISE

1. In this case exercise, you will watch a video involving a theft *(Theft Video 10.2)*. Then you must complete your notes and the case report. Use the interview sheets, face sheet or cover sheet, and supplement/continuation report forms that can be found in the back of this book to complete this exercise.

   Additional information:

   Case number: 14-45090

   Zone: 3

   Sector: 2

   Date: Your current date

   Time: The time announced in the video

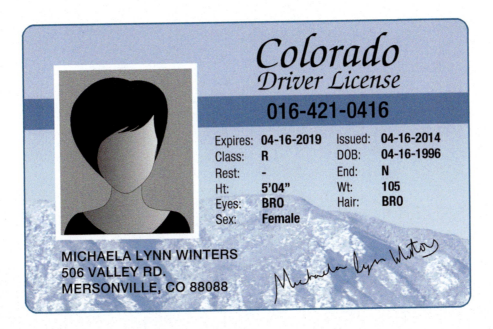

   Suspect's additional information:

   Home phone: 719-555-0199

   Cell phone: 719-555-0188

   Identifying marks: None visible

   Occupation: None

   Custody time: 1305 hours

   Miranda warning: 1400 hours

   Information for witness/victim: John Smith

   Date of birth: 10-24-68

   Height: 6'01"

Weight: 200 lbs

Build: Medium

Hair: Brown

Eyes: Brown

Race: White

Employer: Emerson Department Store

Job title: Store security manager

Work address: 3840 Lincoln Ave., Mersonville, CO 88088

Contact phone: 719-555-0183

11

FELONY CRIMES AGAINST PEOPLE

LEARNING OBJECTIVES

- Identify some of the different felony crimes involving people who you may encounter during your career as a law enforcement professional.

- Understand that each state is different in how felony crimes against people are defined and that you must ensure you document the crime in your report in accordance with the state statute in the appropriate jurisdiction where the felony crime was committed.

- Apply your knowledge to practical examples by successfully completing the chapter exercises.

INTRODUCTION

Felony crimes are more serious offenses, and care should be taken to process these crimes in a professional manner. With regard to felony crimes against people, this chapter will focus on the crime of felony assault. Beware that there are numerous other types of crimes against people defined by your appropriate state statutes. The statute names and definitions of the various offenses against people will vary from state to state. For the sake of simplicity and comprehension, felony assaults were selected for examination and practical exercises in this chapter. Assaults are typically very common events, and the principles involved in completing these types of reports are applicable in most other "crimes against people" incidents.

Each state has its own specific definition of what elements constitute the crime of assault. One of the more accepted definitions of assault is simply an intentional act, using force or the threat of force, to injure or harm another individual. The offense classification of the charge of assault is determined by the severity of the incident. In this chapter we will be presenting the felony classification of the crime of assault. Typically, state statutes define a felony violation as a serious offense that is punishable by more than a year in prison. Obviously, felony assaults are very serious events.

Below are parts of Colorado's definition of Assault in the first degree and assault in the second degree:

18-3-202. Assault in the first degree

(1) A person commits the crime of assault in the first degree if:

    (a) With intent to cause <u>serious bodily injury to another person</u>, he causes serious bodily injury to any person by means of a deadly weapon; or

(b) *With intent to disfigure another person seriously and permanently, or to destroy, amputate, or disable permanently a member or organ of his body, he causes such an injury to any person; or*

(c) *Under circumstances manifesting extreme indifference to the value of human life, he knowingly engages in conduct which creates a grave risk of death to another person, and thereby causes serious bodily injury to any person*

(Source: Colorado Legal Resources, Provided by Lexis Nexis, Official Publisher of the Colorado Revised Statutes, http://www.lexisnexis.com/hottopics/Colorado/)

18-3-203. Assault in the second degree

(1) *A person commits the crime of assault in the second degree if:*

(a) *Repealed.*

(b) *With intent to cause* <u>*bodily injury to another person*</u>*, he or she causes such injury to any person by means of a deadly weapon; or*

(c) *With intent to prevent one whom he or she knows, or should know, to be a peace officer or firefighter from performing a lawful duty, he or she intentionally causes bodily injury to any person; or*

(d) *He recklessly causes serious bodily injury to another person by means of a deadly weapon.*

(Source: Colorado Legal Resources, Provided by Lexis Nexis, Official Publisher of the Colorado Revised Statutes, http://www.lexisnexis.com/hottopics/Colorado/)

Below are parts of Arizona's definition of Aggravated Assault.

13-1204. Aggravated Assault

A. *A person commits aggravated assault if the person commits assault as prescribed by section 13-1203 under any of the following circumstances:*

1. *If the person causes serious physical injury to another.*

2. *If the person uses a deadly weapon or dangerous instrument.*

3. *If the person commits the assault by any means of force that causes temporary but substantial disfigurement, temporary but substantial loss or impairment of any body organ or part or a fracture of any body part.*

4. *If the person commits the assault while the victim is bound or otherwise physically restrained or while the victim's capacity to resist is substantially impaired.*

5. *If the person commits the assault after entering the private home of another with the intent to commit the assault.*

(Source: Arizona State Legislature, http://www.azleg.gov/FormatDocument .asp?inDoc=/ars/13/01802.htm&Title=13&DocType=ARS)

In the statutory elements of both states, you will notice that each one differentiates assault by the severity of the injury inflicted upon the victim by the offender or if a weapon was used.

Best Practices: As a law enforcement professional, it is your responsibility to ensure that you document the severity of the injury in your case report correctly and in accordance with the state statute of where the crime occurred.

On the following pages you can review the notes that a law enforcement professional completed during his investigation of the reported crime you just watched, as well as the report that was completed.

THE *RIGHT* WAY TO *WRITE*

Felony crimes against people are often high-profile cases. Your case report will probably be more scrutinized when these types of cases are submitted for review. The good news is that the same basic principles of a narrative report apply to these cases. As the saying goes, do the little things right, and the big things will follow. All types of case reports should be well documented and prepared. Major cases should not intimidate the law enforcement professional. Practice and feedback will be your best tools to accomplishing these types of reports. Follow the guidelines of the narrative report given in the previous chapters, and you will do fine. Get feedback and don't be afraid to ask questions from more experienced officers.

TIPS FOR FELONY CRIMES AGAINST PEOPLE

- Felony crimes are serious events. Take the time to do things right.
  - These types of cases can be prosecuted in both criminal and civil courts.
  - Your supervisor will be closely reviewing these types of case reports.

- Research your state statute book to determine the specific elements of the crime.
  - Document what actions of this incident constituted a violation of the state statute.
  - Take the time to document the severity of the offense.

- Be sure to describe any injury in detail.
  - Take photos of injuries.
    - Photograph at the time of the incident.
    - Contact victim after a couple of days after the incident for follow-up photos (often injuries appear worse than when first photographed).
  - Obtain doctor's/emergency services reports (if applicable).

- ALWAYS have the victim contact you if their injuries due to this incident require additional treatment or hospitalization in the future. You may need to increase the severity of the charges.

SUMMARY

Felony crimes against people are probably the most serious cases you will encounter as a law enforcement professional. Careful attention must be given and documented to the extent and seriousness of any and all injuries regarding these types of incidents. The seriousness of the injury will dictate the appropriate charge(s), as defined by your state statutes. The body of the report should contain the explanation of the crime and the extent of the injuries, and it should recount the investigation. The elements of the crime, as defined by state statues, must be clearly stated and understandable in the case report.

Crimes against people are high-profile types of incidents. The public expects professionalism and closure to these types of incidents. Probably more than any other type of incident, these cases will be closely scrutinized by prosecutors, defense lawyers, judges, and your supervisors. Remember that the case is not resolved upon the completion of the case report. The culmination of any criminal incident is the successful prosecution of the perpetrator. Cutting corners when completing your case report will result in dire consequences. As always, take the time to do it right!

Examples

1. In this example, you're going to watch a video of a law enforcement professional responding to a report of an assault (**Assault Video 11.1**). The notes and the report that the officer completed are as follows.

Case #: 13-28331   Title: *Assault in the Second Degree*

Dispatch: *1730*   Arrival: *1740*   Cleared: *2000*

Date: *11-21-2013*   Time: *1710*   Offense Location: *2376 15th St.*

Suspect/(Victim)/Witness/Other:

Name: *Clark, Barry, Robert*

DOB: *06-15-71*   Race: *W*   HGT: *6'*   WGT: *190*   Hair: *BRO*   Eyes: *BRO*

POB: Sex: (*Male*) *Female*

Clothing Description:

Address: *4320 Forks Rd.*   City: *Mersonville*   State: *CO*   Zip Code: *88088*

Contact Numbers: Home: *None*   Cell: *719-555-0188*   WK: *719-555-0178*

Employer: *Bill's Bar and Grill*   Occupation: *Bartender*

Business Address: *2376 15th St.*   City: *Mersonville*   State: *CO*   Zip Code: *88088*

Business Phone: *719-555-0178*   Business Victim: Yes (*No*)

V = Declined medical attention.

V = Bartender a few minutes ago a customer came in and punched me in the eye, and walked out.

Suspect Frank Davis

S = Davis has come in before and watched different sporting events on the large televisions. Screams at television but has S = never done anything like this before.

S = Davis was alone, but he wasn't watching a game or anything; he just came in and hit me and walked out.

S = 6' tall and weighs about 200 lbs. and he has dark hair and he is kind of muscular.

V = Didn't see what Susp. wearing

S = just walked around to the end of the bar and came up to Vic. and knocked him down.

Closed fist one time with (R) hand

Photograph of injured eye

       Re-contact after speaking to witness Carlton.

Knows S = wife Sara and admitted he has been seeing her on the side.

V = said that warning Carlton heard may have been said by Mr. Davis after punch.

V = Treated at Memorial Hospital by Dr. Arnold for Orbital fracture. V = Surgery to repair.

Case #: *13-28331*   Title: *Assault in the Second Degree*

Dispatch: Arrival: Cleared:

Date: Time: Offense Location:

Suspect/ Victim /(Witness)/Other:

Name: *Carlton, Sandra Leanne*

DOB: *11-20-58*   Race: *W*   HGT: *5'03"*   WGT: *115*   Hair: *BLO*   Eyes: *GRN*

POB: Sex: *Male* (*Female*)

Clothing Description:

Address: *5001 Tree Line Dr.*   City: *Mersonville*   State: *CO*   Zip Code: *88088*

Contact Numbers: Home: *719-555-0134*   Cell: WK:

Employer: Occupation:

Business Address: City: State: Zip Code:

Business Phone: Business Victim: *Yes*   *No*

W = Mrs. Carlton she is a regular

W = was sitting at the bar watching game when she saw the S = Davis walk behind the bar and hit

V = Clark in the face.

After S = warned Vic. and walked out.

Took Vic. a minute to get up W = had to go over and help him up.

W = heard warning as "Don't come around or call my wife anymore, or you'll get more of that!"

W = seen Suspect + wife come in bar before to watch games.

W = Describe S = as 6' or 6'2" muscular maybe 190lbs. with dark hair. Wearing a drk blu t-shirt and blu jeans

W = S = has a tattoo on the right side of his neck of a dragon.

W = Obsv. S Hit V one time.

Case #: *13-28331*   Title: *Assault in the Second Degree*

Dispatch: Arrival: Cleared:

Date: Time: Offense Location:

(Suspect)/ Victim / Witness /Other:

Name: *Davis, Franklin, Markus*

DOB: *02-13-1985*   Race: *W*   HGT: *6'01"*   WGT: *205*   Hair: *BRO*   Eyes: *BLU*

POB: Sex: (*Male*) *Female*

Clothing Description: *Blue t-Shirt and blue Jeans*

Address: *2345 W. Yampa St.*   City: *Mersonville*   State: *CO*   Zip Code: *88088*

Contact Numbers: Home: *719-555-0192*   Cell: *719-555-0235*   WK: *719-555-0278*

Employer: *Up-Front Deliveries*   Occupation: *Truck Driver*

Business Address: *3333 Elk Valley Dr.*   City: *Mersonville*   State: *CO*   Zip Code: *88088*

Business Phone: *719-555-0278*   Business Victim: *Yes* (*No*)

I Observed white male entering the bar matching suspect description.

I asked if he was Frank Davis.

S = "Yes, I guess you're here to arrest me for punching that piece of crap at the bar!"

S = Declined to make any further statement.

S = treated at hospital and later booked into MCJ on 11-21-2013.

MERSONVILLE POLICE DEPARTMENT COVER SHEET

Offense ☒	Supplement ☐	Other ☐	Case Number 13-28331

Offense Title	State/City Statute Number	Date of this Report
Assault in the Second Degree	18-3-203	11/21/2013

Zone/Sector		Date and time Reported				Date and time Reported			
		Month	Day	Year	Time	Month	Day	Year	Time
4	2	11	21	2013	1730	11	21	2013	1710

Victim's Name Last, First, Middle	Date of Birth	Age	Sex	Height	Weight	Build	Hair	Eyes	Race
Clark, Barry, Robert	06/15/71	42	M	6'00"	190	M	BRO	BRO	W

Residential Address	City	State	Zip Code	Home Phone	Cell Phone
4320 Forks Rd.	Mersonville	CO	88088	None	719-555-0188

Business Address	City	State	Zip Code	Business Phone	Occupation
2376 15th St.	Mersonville	CO	88088	719-555-0178	Bartender

Location of Offense	City	State	Zip Code
2376 15th St.	Mersonville	CO	88088

If a business is the victim complete the information below

Name of Business	Business Address	City	State	Zip Code	Business Phone

Codes RP = Reporting Party AV = Additional Victim LO = Law Enforcement Officer W = Witness S = Suspect A = Arrestee O = Other

Code	Last, First, Middle	Date of Birth	Age	Sex	Height	Weight	Build	Hair	Eyes	Race
S/A	Davis, Franklin, Markus	02/13/1985	28	M	6'01"	205	L	BRO	BLU	W

Residential Address	City	State	Zip Code	Home Phone	Cell Phone
2345 W. Yampa St.	Mersonville	CO	88088	719-555-0192	719-555-0235

Business Address	City	State	Zip Code	Business Phone	Occupation
3333 Elk Valley Dr.	Mersonville	CO	88088	719-555-0278	Truck Driver

Clothing Description	Alias
Blue t-Shirt and blue Jeans	

Identifying Marks	Summons Number
Dragon tattoo on right side of neck	

Narrative

On 11-21-2013 at approximately 1730 hours I, Officer Smith 1616P, was dispatched to 2376 15th St. in reference to an assault. Upon arrival I made contact with Barry Clark, the victim, who stated that a customer by the name of Frank Davis entered the bar and walked over to him. Mr. Davis then with a closed fist punched him in his left eye. Mr. Clark stated that after the one punch he fell to the floor and Mr. Davis left the bar.

Mr. Clark was treated by Dr. Arnold, an emergency doctor at Memorial Hospital, for an orbital fracture to the bones of the left eye. Mr. Clark underwent surgery on 11-21-2013 to repair the damage to his eye.

Mr. Davis was contacted walking back into the bar and taken into custody. He was later treated for a fractured hand at Memorial hospital before being taken to Mersonville Criminal Justice Center.

Suspect information: Yes and arrest made.
Witness information: Yes
Evidence: Yes, photos of the victim's injury were taken.
Photos of the suspect's injuries were also taken.
See Supplement for more information.

Report Completed by:	Signature:	
Officer Smith 1616P	*Michael Lewis 1616P*	Page 1 of 3 Page
Report Completed by:	Signature:	
Sgt. Lynn 0123S	*David Lynn 0123S*	

Mersonville Police Department Supplement Report									
Offense Title		State/City Statute		Date of this Report			Case Number		
Assault in the Second Degree		*18-3-203*		*11-21-2013*			*13-28331*		

Codes RP=Reporting Party AV= Additional Victim LO= Law Enforcement Officer V=Victim W=Witness S=Suspect A=Arrestee O=Other

Code	Name: Last, First, Middle	Date of Birth	Age	Sex	Height	Weight	Build	Hair	Eyes	Race
W	*Carlton, Sandra, Leanne*	*11-20-1958*	*55*	*F*	*5'03"*	*115*	*S*	*BLO*	*GRN*	*W*

Residential Address	City	State	Zip Code	Home Phone	Cell Phone
5001 Tree Line Dr.	*Mersonville*	*CO*	*88088*	*719-555-0134*	
Business Address	City	State	Zip Code	Business Phone	Occupation

Clothing Description	Alias
Identifying Marks	Summons Number

Narrative

Victim Statement:

Clark, Barry, Robert
DOB: 06-15-71
Mr. Clark stated that on 11-21-2013 at approximately 1710 hours he was working at Bill's Bar and Grill as the bartender located behind the bar when Mr. Davis entered the establishment. Mr. Clark said that he observed Mr. Davis enter the bar and then observed Mr. Davis walk toward him behind the bar. Once behind the bar Mr. Davis used his right hand and struck him in the left eye with a closed fist. Mr. Clark said that the punch forced him to the floor. Mr. Clark said that the punch to his face caused him pain.

Mr. Clark did not know why Mr. Davis assaulted him. Mr. Clark said that Mr. Davis is a regular customer and has come into the bar previously with other people to watch sporting events but he has never done anything like this before. Mr. Clark said that at the time of the assault Mr. Davis was not in the bar as a customer and that he had just walked in alone and punched him in the eye and then walked out.

Mr. Clark denied knowing why Mr. Davis punched him. Mr. Clark described Mr. Davis as a muscular man who was approximately 6' tall and weighed approximately 200Lbs. with dark hair. Mr. Clark did could not recall what Mr. Davis was wearing.

Mr. Clark said that Sandra Leanne Carlton, a regular customer, was in the bar at the time of the assault.

Witness Statement:

Carlton, Sandra, Leanne
DOB: 11-20-1958
Mrs. Carlton stated that she was in the bar watching a game when she observed Frank Davis enter the bar and punch Mr. Clark one time in the face knocking him to the floor. Mrs. Carlton said that she knew Mr. Davis and had observed him in the bar previously with his wife watching games. Mrs. Carlton also heard Mr. Davis warn Mr. Clark after punching him. Mrs. Carlton said she heard Mr. Davis say "Don't come around or call my wife anymore, or you'll get more of that!" Mrs. Carlton then watched Mr. Davis walk out of the bar at which time she walked over and helped Mr. Clark up off the floor.

Mrs. Carlton described Frank Davis as being 6' to 6'02" tall and weighing approximately 190 lbs. with dark hair and wearing a dark blue t-shirt and blue jeans. Mrs. Carlton also said that Mr. Davis has a tattoo of a dragon on the right side of his neck.
See Continuation.

Report Completed by:	Signature:	Page 2 of 3 Pages
Officer Smith 1616P	*Michael Lewis 1616P*	
Report Reviewed by:	Signature:	
Sgt. Lynn 0123S	*David Lynn 0123S*	

Mersonville Police Department Supplement Report											
Offense Title *Assault in the Second Degree*			**State/City Statute** 18-3-203		**Date of this Report** 11-21-2013				**Case Number** 13-28331		
Codes RP=Reporting Party AV= Additional Victim LO= Law Enforcement Officer V=Victim W=Witness S=Suspect A=Arrestee O=Other											
Code	**Name: Last, First, Middle**	**Date of Birth**	**Age**	**Sex**	**Height**	**Weight**	**Build**	**Hair**	**Eyes**	**Race**	
Residential Address			**City**	**State**	**Zip Code**	**Home Phone**		**Cell Phone**			
Business Address			**City**	**State**	**Zip Code**	**Business Phone**		**Occupation**			
Clothing Description				**Alias**							
Identifying Marks				**Summons Number**							

Narrative

<u>Officer Statement</u>:

I walked through the bar and spoke to other customers who were there but did not locate anyone else who witnessed the altercation.

Mr. Clark was able to provide some personal information about Mr. Davis from the bar tab that he sometimes keeps with Bill's Bar and Grill.

When I spoke to Mr. Clark once more and asked if Mr. Davis had hit him over a relationship he was possibly having with Mr. Davis's wife, he told me that Mr. Davis and his wife, Sara, were having problems and that he had been seeing her on the side. I asked Mr. Clark if Mr. Davis could have said "Don't come around or call my wife anymore, or you'll get more of that!" after he hit him and he replied "he could have."

Mr. Clark declined medical treatment on scene but eventually decided to seek medical attention for his injury at Memorial Hospital.

While at Memorial Hospital with Mr. Davis who was being treated for his fractured hand I observed Mr. Clark in another patient room where he was being treated for his injured eye.

Mr. Clark's treating physician was Dr. Arnold who stated that Mr. Clark had an orbital fracture to his left eye and needed surgery to repair the damage. Dr. Arnold said that the injury was consistent with being struck with a closed fist.

While at the hospital I took photos of Mr. Davis's hand that was treated by Dr. Arnold as well. Dr. Arnold stated that Mr. Davis had a fracture of the fourth metacarpal bone of his right hand, commonly known as a Boxers Fracture, which was consistent with punching someone or something with a closed fist.

Mr. Davis declined to make any further statement. Mr. Davis was taken into custody and charged with Assault in the Second Degree 18-3-203 after being treated for his fractured hand.

<u>Evidence</u>:

Photos of Mr. Clark's injured eye and Mr. Davis's hand were placed into evidence at Mersonville Police Station on 11-21-2013.

Suspect:
Franklin Markus Davis
DOB: 06-15-71
Mr. Davis was advised of his Miranda Rights and was booked into the Morris County Jail.
No further information.

Report Completed by: Officer Smith 1616P	Signature: *Michael Smith 1616P*	Page 3 of 3 Pages
Report Reviewed by: Sgt. Lynn 0123S	Signature: *David Lynn 0123S*	

EXERCISE

1. In this exercise you will watch a video involving a domestic assault *(Domestic Assault Video 11.2)*. You need to take notes and then complete the case report. Use the interview sheets and domestic violence report form that can be found in the Appendix to complete this exercise. Additional information:

    Case number: 14-56090

    Call screen number: 908970

    Zone: 4

    Sector: 3

    Date: The current date

    Time: The time announced in the video

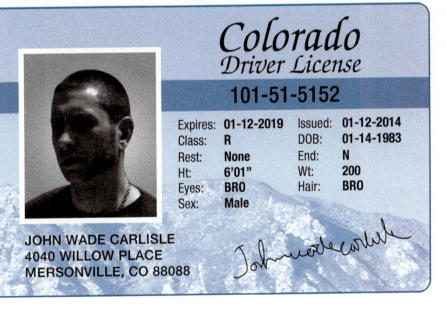

Colorado
Driver License
553-18-2461

Expires:	09-10-2019	Issued:	09-10-2014
Class:	R	DOB:	09-10-1975
Rest:	None	End:	N
Ht:	6'02"	Wt:	185
Eyes:	BRO	Hair:	BRO
Sex:	Male		

TODD WILLIAM SMITH
3112 PINE RIDGE RD.
MERSONVILLE, CO 88088

Todd William Smith

12

DOCUMENTATION OF THE USE OF FORCE

LEARNING OBJECTIVES

- Understand why use of force forms are required.
- Identify the different types of use of force used by law enforcement professionals.
- Understand the three most critical elements in completing a use of force form.
- Understand the legal issues involved in the use of force by law enforcement professionals.
- Apply your knowledge to practical examples by successfully completing the chapter exercises.

INTRODUCTION

Probably the one area in law enforcement operations that receives the most attention from the public and the media is the "use of force" by law enforcement officers. Additionally, it is probably the number one source of citizen complaints and litigation against law enforcement agencies. When police officers use force, they are infringing on the citizen's Fourth Amendment rights, as it is a "seizure." The standard of the "necessary and reasonable" force clause of the Fourth Amendment applies under any seizure or use of force. That is, the officer must show the force that he/she used was reasonable and necessary based on the circumstances.

All law enforcement agencies will have extensive guidelines describing when it is appropriate to use physical force. Additionally, police officers will receive extensive training on the use of force and how it is to be applied. That being said, policy and procedure cannot dictate what level of force is applicable in each specific situation. This is where the officer's training and understanding of the general guidelines of the agency is essential. The basic tenet is "use the minimum force to control the situation." Use of excessive force could result in disciplinary action, civil liability, criminal charges, and perhaps termination.

Some of this material has already been covered. The material is repeated here for the sake of emphasizing the importance of the issues. In addition, this chapter is intended to introduce you to reports that are prepared in support of a use of force situation.

Best Practices: Situations that require the use of force can be fluid, dynamic, and ever-changing. Some of the nondeadly uses of force techniques can be used as deadly force or viewed by others as deadly force when deadly force was not the intent of the officer. Therefore, it is important to document your actions accurately by explaining your intent.

USE OF FORCE FORMS

Many agencies require a separate and distinct use of force form in addition to the standard narrative case report. Although some agencies do not use such a document, their policies and procedures will require extensive descriptions of what type of force was used and why. The agency's goal is to protect both you and the department from potential complaints and possible civil and/or criminal litigation. "As a former patrol division commander, I can assure you that the chain of command will scrutinize every use of force scenario; it is critical that these forms are thorough and complete."

The goal of the use of force report is to ensure that you documented all of the essential elements required when force is used on a citizen. You want the reader of the report to completely understand what you felt, why force was used, how you used force, and that you applied force properly. It is essential to trap critical information on the incident, as it will probably be an extended period of time before you are required to testify in court on the details of the case. You will be able to articulate the facts of the incident with a well-written case report. Always remember that your professionalism and demeanor in handling the incident will affect the people who read these reports.

USE OF FORCE DEFINED

First, it is best to describe what we mean by use of force. All agencies describe what force is available in their policies and procedures manual. Most agencies explain the levels of force available to an officer as a force continuum. The force continuum chart or graph is simply a listing of the types of force to be used as the specific situation and incident require. As stated earlier, the appropriate force to be utilized in every situation is the minimum force necessary to control the situation. Here is an example of a force continuum chart:

Physical Presence: Just by being present, in uniform, you can exert control of citizens. An example of physical presence is when an officer simply raises his/her hand and jesters to the person to stop. Another example is calling for more backup officers at a scene to "show force" in order to control a potentially volatile situation.

Verbal Commands: You can exert force by using your voice to give commands to control the situation. There may be repeated verbal commands employed. Document what words you used and their frequency.

Empty Hand Submission Techniques: One empty hand "soft technique" is the pressure point control technique. Empty hand "hard techniques" include strikes with the hand or foot.

Intermediate Weapons: These less-than-lethal techniques include PR-24, baton, pepper spray, Taser, and beanbag rounds.

Deadly Force: Lethal force can be exerted with the officer's sidearm, rifle, shotgun, or other weapons.

The force continuum chart is designed to give you an idea of what type of force is available when the situation dictates a use of force. What the chart does not define is *when or how much* force to use in performing your duties. This is where the officer *must document* that the force used was reasonable and necessary given the circumstances of the incident. This is probably one of the most essential elements of writing a good case report and completing the use of force form. The legal standard here is defined as simply using the "minimum amount of force necessary to control the situation."

In applying any use of force, it is critical that you document each step. That does not mean that you have to use every level of force in every situation. For example, if you arrive at a scene and the individual has a gun pointed at you, you obviously need to take cover, draw your sidearm, and neutralize the situation. In this scenario, you may have time to issue verbal commands to "put down the weapon," but this is not always the case. The key thought is following department guidelines, using common sense, and relying on your training.

CONTENT OF THE REPORT

The content of the use of force form must be explicit and thorough. Cutting corners gets you into big trouble. Take the time and do it right the first time. If any degree of force is used, most agencies require that the officer complete the narrative report and the use of force form prior to going off shift. This restriction is to ensure critical documentation is captured while the incident is still fresh in your mind. It also sends a message to the officers that using any degree of force is a serious event and should be thoroughly explained. As an aside, if you take an individual into custody without any use of force, some departments require you to write, "no force was used in securing the suspect into custody." It is never a bad idea to document that the arrest was accomplished without the use of force.

Describing the scene in your use of force form is critical. Vague and ambiguous terms do not belong in a case report, especially for any incident that involves a use of force. Be descriptive and never assume that the reader will understand the situation by using vague and ambiguous terms. You want the reader to feel what you felt. If the suspect used profanity, use the exact words that the subject spoke. This is not the time for censorship or being afraid of offending the reader. Capture the scene! You have to show in this report that the force you used was reasonable and necessary given the specific circumstances.

Oftentimes, I have reviewed reports that simply state, "Mr. Jones appeared belligerent and was yelling profanities at me." That is simply unacceptable. What do you mean by "belligerent"? What do you mean by "profanities"? The proper way of stating this incident might be as follows:

> Upon arriving at 2242 Glenwood Circle, I observed Mr. Jones, who was standing in the driveway, shaking his fists in the air and pacing back and forth. I observed that his face was red flush colored, and he began shouting at me, "Shitface, what are you doing here? Shitface, get in your car and go get a donut."

In this example, you can see the difference in describing an incident. You want to capture the feelings of the moment regarding the incident. It is perfectly acceptable to use the exact improper language or profanity in your case report. This is not only a true reflection of what occurred, but it also captures the tenor and severity of the incident.

The three most critical elements in completing a use of force form are:

1. **Document the subject's behavior thoroughly.**
2. **Identify the need for a response.**
3. **Document the type of response you applied.**

All of the above three elements will now be discussed in detail.

Document the subject's behavior thoroughly. As stated earlier, this is not the place for vague or ambiguous language. Simply stating that the subject "appeared angry" tells the reader nothing. What made you think this person was angry? Use terms that clearly describe the subject's behavior. Instead of "angry," use descriptive words such as "flushed face, pacing back and forth, clenching his fists, punching the wall, and so on." Document the exact words the subject used that led you to the conclusion that he was "angry." If he used any fighting words or profanity, capture those exact words in your use of force report. Use specific terms and actions to justify your actions.

The following is the El Paso County Sheriff's Office's SOP on how to determine if physical force is required:

> A   CONSIDERATIONS SURROUNDING THE ELEMENTS OF THE USE OF NON-DEADLY PHYSICAL FORCE:
> 1. **Ability.**   Does the violator possess the apparent capacity to resist you or a third party, or to cause you or third party harm?
> 2. **Opportunity.**   Does the violator have the opportunity or apparent opportunity to resist you or a third party, or to cause you or a third party bodily harm?
> 3. **Jeopardy.**   Does the violator place you or a third party in danger of a hazard, threat, or peril, or perceived hazard, threat or peril?

Source: El Paso County Sheriff's Office Policy and Procedure Manual. Used by permission by the El Paso County Sheriff's Office.

Identify the need for a response. You need to document why you used this specific type of force on the subject. Was the force you used necessary and appropriate given the circumstances of the incident? That is the critical question that must be answered. You must document why the use of force was reasonably necessary in the moment the incident occurred. Answer this question: what are the defining circumstances, at that specific moment, that caused you to use force on the subject? Focus on the relevant moment that caused you to act.

Please note that there may be many shifts in dealing with the subject's behavior during an incident. You need to take the time to define and describe each of these shifts of the subject's behavior. Be sure and note exactly what caused you to escalate and/or de-escalate your use of force in each significant moment of the incident. You are painting the picture of possibly many particular moments or events in the incident that caused you to conclude in a reasonable and necessary manner to act in a specific way. Your trained perceptions of behavior have to be thoroughly documented.

Document the type of response. What specific actions did you take? Was it an arm bar control technique? Perhaps you used a pressure-point control technique. If so, document exactly what you did. Avoid terms that make you look like a prizefighter. Do not use phrases such as "I threw him to the ground." State the technique you have been trained to use, not some vague phrase such as "I threw him to the ground." An example of this might be, "Using the Georgia State Patrol takedown, I took Mr. Smith to the ground and secured him in handcuffs. At that point Mr. Smith became compliant and additional force was neither required nor used."

The type of response you may use in dealing with an incident may change at any time. You need to describe each level of force, at each specific moment, and why it was necessary. Be sure and document your suspicion factors. You may start out with simple verbal commands. You need to document that the subject did not respond to these verbal commands, which forced you into a higher level of force. If you gave repeated verbal commands, document that fact and the language you used in giving those commands. This documents the fact that lower levels of force failed, requiring an escalation of force to control the situation. Be sure to end the description of force by writing that you used the minimum force necessary to control the situation.

Best Practices: An appropriate use of non-deadly force with an impact weapon may be to strike the upper shoulder blade of an offender, but if the offender moves and the strike is delivered to the back of the head of the offender, it could be viewed as deadly force. The officer's intent to strike the upper shoulder blade must be documented in the report accurately along with the explanation of why the offender was struck in the head and not the upper shoulder blade.

MEDICAL IMPLICATIONS

While documenting the type of physical response you utilized, never forget to include any medical considerations if they are appropriate. If, in the course of deploying physical force, the subject is injured and you feel that medical attention is required, call for a medical response as soon as possible. If the subject refuses medical attention and, in your opinion, there is a need for medical attention, call for a medical response anyway. The subject still can refuse medical attention anyway—that is the individual's right—but this shows that, in good faith, you were trying to take appropriate and prudent care of the situation. Many agency policy and procedures manuals dictate the circumstances under which a medical response is mandatory. Know your agency guidelines regarding medical responses.

OTHER INVOLVED OFFICERS

Especially with regard to use of force situations, you *must* obtain written supplements from every officer involved in the incident. As with obtaining medical assistance, obtaining written supplements from all involved officers is normally a mandatory agency requirement. Additionally, most states have passed laws making reporting of use of force by all involved police officers mandatory under the penalty of law. Here is one such example, from Colorado:

> DUTY TO REPORT USE OF FORCE BY PEACE OFFICERS: 18-8-802 C.R.S. (1) (a) A peace officer who, in pursuance of such officer's law enforcement duties, witnesses another peace officer, in pursuance of such other peace officer's law enforcement duties in carrying out an arrest of any person, placing any person under detention, taking any person into custody, booking any person, or in the process of crowd control or riot control, uses physical force which exceeds the degree of physical force permitted pursuant to section 18-1-707 C.R.S. must report such use of force to such officer's immediate supervisor.
>
> Source: *El Paso County Sheriff's Office Policy and Procedure Manual.* Used by permission by the El Paso County Sheriff's Office.

LEGAL ISSUES

The law authorizes law enforcement officers who are trained in the use of force to use force in specific circumstances where the use of force is necessary and appropriate. Specifically, the landmark Supreme Court case that describes the use of force is *Graham v. Connor*, 490 U.S. 386 (1989). This ruling held that "when engaged in situations where the use of force is necessary to effect an arrest, or to protect an officer's life or that of another, a law enforcement officer must act as other reasonable officers would have acted in a similar, tense, rapidly evolving situation." This case implies the "reasonableness standard," which basically states that the actions that the officer took in the legal performance of his duties were necessary and reasonable given the circumstances.

Additionally, in the *Graham v. Connor* case, the Supreme Court defined the use of force by police officers whereby the "objectively reasonable" standard was defined. This is the term created by the courts as the standard by which an officer's actions will be evaluated in use-of-force situations. The court ruled that, because law enforcement officers are often forced to make split-second judgments about the amount of force that is necessary in circumstances that are frequently tense, uncertain, and rapidly evolving, the reasonableness of the officer's belief as to the appropriate level of force should be judged from the on-scene perspective and not by using the "20/20 vision of hindsight." The proper application of "objectively reasonable" requires

> "careful attention to the facts and circumstances of each particular case, including the severity of the crime at issue, whether the suspect poses an immediate threat to the safety of the officers or others, and whether he is actively resisting arrest or attempting to evade arrest by flight."

Subsequent Supreme Court cases have further defined the use of force and what standard of care a police officer must follow in using force against a citizen.

Once the incident goes to court, your narrative case report and your use of force form will become valuable tools in obtaining a conviction. Defense attorneys will attempt to attack your credibility. If your use of force was inappropriate, the defense attorneys will then go after the substantive other criminal matters of the case. For example, if you failed to accurately document your use of force, the subject's defense counsel will then attempt to demonstrate it was an improper drug seizure or search warrant. The defense counsel will try to make you look bad and shift the focus from the guilt of his/her client to your incompetence.

While testifying in court, the force used must be shown to have been necessary and reasonable for the situation. Do not forget that fear is a major contributing factor in deploying force. Fear is an element of a crime in many cases. Your report should contain language that clearly describes impending danger. For example, imagine the scenario where you had to use your baton on a subject who attacked you. Your report may contain things (if appropriate) such as how unexpected the attack was, how the subject quickly gained the upper hand, how your shirt was torn, how much bigger than you the subject was, and, perhaps, how you were in danger of retaining control of your firearm. These are all elements of a crime that need to be brought out in court. Again, you are painting the picture for the court by detailing why the actions you took were legal and proper.

Do not forget that, if a subject assaults you, that you are both a police officer and a victim. Proper investigative procedures should be followed in preserving case evidence if such an assault occurs. For example, your torn shirt should be placed into evidence and preserved for future presentation in court. If you sustained any injuries, document, photograph, and include a hospital report of the injuries, if applicable. These items provide valuable physical evidence of the severity of the incident.

While on the subject of "fear," be sure and describe in your report how the suspect reacted to the physical controls you utilized. For example, you want to demonstrate, if appropriate, how lower levels of force failed or perhaps the suspect defeated one of your lower-level compliance techniques. It is OK to admit that the subject was gaining the upper hand if that is what happened. This helps clarify to the court why you had to escalate your use of force to a higher level. Again, the ultimate goal is to capture the moment of your use of force and why the actions you took were reasonable and necessary.

THE *RIGHT* WAY TO *WRITE*

Although most of the elements of writing a typical narrative report apply to the documentation of use of force, there are some subtle points of emphasis you want to be sure to cover. The most notable "how" exception is that it is perfectly acceptable to document your feelings in these types of reports. For example:

> As Mr. Jones approached with the butcher knife, fearing for my safety, I drew my sidearm and ordered him to drop the knife.

This writing style incorporates your feelings at the time of the situation, which is a departure from the typical objective style of report writing.

The "how" or "what" to write when completing a use of force report must follow the standard of the "necessary and reasonable" force clause of the Fourth Amendment that applies under any seizure of a citizen or use of force. That is, the officer must show that the force used was reasonable and necessary based on the circumstances. Take the time to describe what force you used and why by reviewing the guidelines contained in this chapter.

The other most notable departure of use of force reports is that most agencies will require additional documentation or perhaps a separate cover sheet whenever force is used against a citizen. Typically, these additional types of forms simply require a few more details and filling in blanks on the forms. In the narrative portion of the use of force report, certain phrases are appropriate. Here is one example:

> *Using the minimum force necessary to control the individual, I . . .*

You want to be sure to document that you followed departmental guidelines in using the appropriate force required regarding the incident.

TIPS FOR DOCUMENTATION OF THE USE OF FORCE

Document the following in the report:

- Offender injuries (name, date, and time)
- Officer/deputy injuries (name, date, and time)
- Supervisor notified (name, date, and time)
- Officers on scene (name)
  - Supplements need to be completed by all officers on scene
- Other witnesses (names and contact information)
  - Statements need to be collected form anyone who observed the use of force
- Hospital/medical personnel attending to injured parties if treated
  - Physician/paramedic and statements identifying the injury severity
  - Photos of all injuries

SUMMARY

Public opinion condemns excessive violence by police officers against members of the public. Law enforcement supervisors have adopted a zero-tolerance stance toward excessive force by their officers. Every law enforcement agency has mandatory requirements whenever force is used against a citizen. Additionally, the Supreme Court has given us very specific guidelines as to how police officers must conduct themselves when using force.

Besides the narrative case report, many agencies require a separate and distinct use of force form to trap additional information. By using force, police officers must justify their actions. The standard of law requires that the force was "reasonable and necessary" in that specific instance. The use of force is normally outlined by agency policy and procedure describing the force available on a continuum depending upon the circumstances. Great care should be taken when preparing a case report where force was utilized. Always review and know your agency's policy and procedures regarding the use of force.

On the following pages is an attached sample use of force form from the El Paso County Sheriff's Office for you to review.

Use of Force Database Data – Entry From

When a use of force incident is documented, this form will be completed by the involved staff member and forwarded through the appropriate channels for review. Supervisors will ensure this form is complete and a copy of the report and other required documentation is attached. Once the form and documentation have been reviewed, the Bureau Chief or his/her designee will forward it to a designated staff member for data entry.

PART A – General Incident Information

Sergeant			# of Deputies Involved	
Case #	Date of Incident	Location	District	Grid
Time Incident Started	Assigned Shift	Incident Title:		
Circumstances/Comments				

PART B – Individual Officer Information

EID #		Name			☐ Physical Force
					☐ Spikes
Race	Gender	Rank	Years of Service	Assignment	☐ Electronic Device
					☐ Impact Force
Deputy's Age		Was Deputy injured? If yes, describe.	Was Deputy Killed? If yes, describe.		☐ Firearm
					☐ O.C.
Deputy Yrs Education					☐ K-9
					☐ Other:_____

EID #		Name			☐ Physical Force
					☐ Spikes
Race	Gender	Rank	Years of Service	Assignment	☐ Electronic Device
					☐ Impact Force
Deputy's Age		Was Deputy injured? If yes, describe.	Was Deputy Killed? If yes, describe.		☐ Firearm
					☐ O.C.
Deputy Yrs Education					☐ K-9
					☐ Other:_____

EID #		Name			☐ Physical Force
					☐ Spikes
Race	Gender	Rank	Years of Service	Assignment	☐ Electronic Device
					☐ Impact Force
Deputy's Age		Was Deputy injured? If yes, describe.	Was Deputy Killed? If yes, describe.		☐ Firearm
					☐ O.C.
Deputy Yrs Education					☐ K-9
					☐ Other:_____

PART C – Individual Officer Information

Animal ? ☐	Name					SSN	☐ Physical Force
Race	Gender	Date of Birth	Age	Height	Weight		☐ Spikes
							☐ Electronic Device

Was subject:

☐ Injured _____

☐ Killed _____

Was subject using:

☐ Drugs _____

☐ Alcohol _____

☐ Physical Force
☐ Spikes
☐ Electronic Device
☐ Impact Force
☐ Firearm
☐ O.C.
☐ K-9
☐ Other:_____

Animal ? ☐	Name					SSN	☐ Physical Force
Race	Gender	Date of Birth	Age	Height	Weight		☐ Spikes

Was subject:

☐ Injured _____

☐ Killed _____

Was subject using:

☐ Drugs _____

☐ Alcohol _____

☐ Physical Force
☐ Spikes
☐ Electronic Device
☐ Impact Force
☐ Firearm
☐ O.C.
☐ K-9
☐ Other:_____

Animal ? ☐	Name					SSN	☐ Physical Force
Race	Gender	Date of Birth	Age	Height	Weight		☐ Spikes

Was subject:

☐ Injured _____

☐ Killed _____

Was subject using:

☐ Drugs _____

☐ Alcohol _____

☐ Physical Force
☐ Spikes
☐ Electronic Device
☐ Impact Force
☐ Firearm
☐ O.C.
☐ K-9
☐ Other:_____

PART D – Individual Third Party Information

Name						SSN	☐ Physical Force
Race	Gender	Date of Birth	Age	Height	Weight		☐ Spikes

Was subject:

☐ Injured _____

☐ Killed _____

Was subject using:

☐ Drugs _____

☐ Alcohol _____

☐ Physical Force
☐ Spikes
☐ Electronic Device
☐ Impact Force
☐ Firearm
☐ O.C.
☐ K-9
☐ Other:_____

Name						SSN	☐ Physical Force
Race	Gender	Date of Birth	Age	Height	Weight		☐ Spikes

Was subject:

☐ Injured _____

☐ Killed _____

Was subject using:

☐ Drugs _____

☐ Alcohol _____

☐ Physical Force
☐ Spikes
☐ Electronic Device
☐ Impact Force
☐ Firearm
☐ O.C.
☐ K-9
☐ Other:_____

EXERCISES

1. What information do you feel would be useful to include in the use of force form supplement?

2. List and explain the many reasons why documenting the use of force is absolutely critical in the law enforcement profession.

3. Once again, to become a better writer, you should be able to recognize bad writing. Officer E. Literate has been involved in a situation that required him to use force on an individual. Consider the following use of force report that Officer E. Literate completed. Read the report and try to find at least three mistakes.

   1. _____

   2. _____

   3. _____

Bristlecone Police Department
Documentation of the Use of Force
Form

When a use of force incident occurs, this form must be completed by the officer involved and it must be forwarded via the chain of command for review. Supervisors must ensure that this form is completed and a copy of the report and all other documentation is attached. Once the chain of command has reviewed this report, it must then be forwarded to the supervisor of data entry, who will assign it to a data entry specialist, who will enter it into the Use of Force database.

PART 1 – General Information

Supervisor		Number of officers Involved	
William Jones 3409P		2	
Case Number	Date of Incident	Location	
15-34765	*01-15-2015*	*2908 N. Cedar Rd.*	
Shift	Time of Incident	Incident Title	
2	*1535*	*Resisting Arrest*	
Circumstances			
Subject came at me in an aggressive manner and I tased him. See Part 5 of this report for more information.			

PART 2 – Officer Information

Officer Name			Badge Number		
E. Literate			*1789P*		
Race	Gender		Years of Service		Assignment
W	*M*		*1*		*Patrol*
Officer Age	Officers Education Level		Was Officer Injured?		Was Officer Killed?
33	*High School Diploma*		*No*		*No*
Type of Force Used by Officer					
Physical Force	Impact Force	O.C	K-9	Taser	Firearm
				Yes	
Other Force used Explain:					

PART 2 – Officer Information

Officer Name			Badge Number		
J. Smith			*1616P*		
Race	Gender		Years of Service		Assignment
W	*M*		*12*		*Patrol*
Officer Age	Officers Education Level		Was Officer Injured?		Was Officer Killed?
40	*BS Degree*		*No*		*No*
Type of Force Used by Officer					
Physical Force	Impact Force	O.C	K-9	Taser	Firearm
Other Force used Explain:					

PART 3 – Subject Information

Animal	Name		Last	First		Middle
No			Markus	David		Howard
Race	Gender		Date of Birth	Age	Height	Weight
W	M		01-15-1985	35	6'01"	215 lbs.
Was Subject Injured	Was Subject Killed		Was Subject using Drugs?	Was Subject using Alcohol?		
No	No		No	Yes		
Type of Force Used by Officer						
Physical Force	Impact Force	O.C	K-9	Taser	Firearm	
				Yes		
Other Force used Explain:						

PART 3 – Subject Information

Animal	Name		Last	First		Middle
Race	Gender		Date of Birth	Age	Height	Weight
Was Subject Injured	Was Subject Killed		Was Subject using Drugs?	Was Subject using Alcohol?		
Type of Force Used by Officer						
Physical Force	Impact Force	O.C	K-9	Taser	Firearm	
Other Force used Explain:						

PART 4 – Witness Information

Name						
None						
Race	Gender		Date of Birth	Age	Height	Weight
Physical Address						
City			State		Zip Code	
Home Phone			Cell Phone		Work Phone	

PART 4 – Witness Information

Name						
Race	Gender		Date of Birth	Age	Height	Weight
Physical Address						
City			State		Zip Code	
Home Phone			Cell Phone		Work Phone	

PART 5 – Details of Incident

On 01-15-2015 at approximately 1530 I, Officer E. Literate 1789P, was dispatched to 2909 N. Cedar Rd. in reference to a disturbance. Upon arrival I heard people screaming at a male individual who was pacing back in forth in front of the steps to the residence. I asked him if he could tell me what was going on in the house. He then became belligerent and aggressive while using offensive and threatening language as he screamed at me.

I told him to calm down and he said more profanities and then came at me in a very aggressive manner. I ordered him to stop but he did not, so I drew my Taser, aimed it at him, and then shot it at him. He screamed and fell over onto the ground shaking violently. The Taser leads hit him square and after a few seconds I tased him again. The man was still not behaving so I ended up tasing him 10-20 times before cover arrived.

When Officer Smith, my cover, arrived the male was placed into handcuffs for his and our safety. The male complained of a headache from falling onto the sidewalk but did not appear to be bleeding. I pulled the taser leads out of the subject.

As I took the leads out of the suspect he kicked toward me, so I defended myself by kicking him in the face.

It was determined that this male individual had been drinking and smoking marijuana inside the residence all afternoon. He was eventually asked to leave by the owner of the house because he began to fight and argue with other guest.

The male individual was identified as Markus David Howard and was taken to Morris County Criminal Justice Center and charged with Disturbing the Peace and Resisting Arrest on Summons #19087465. See Case Report Number 15-34765 for more information on these charges.

No further information.

13

PROBABLE CAUSE AFFIDAVITS, ARREST WARRANTS, AND SEARCH WARRANTS

LEARNING OBJECTIVES

- Understand the difference between a probable cause affidavit and an arrest warrant.
- Identify the correct contents of the probable cause affidavit, the arrest warrant, and the search warrant.
- Understand the importance of correctly identifying the property to be searched during the issuance of a search warrant.
- Apply your knowledge to practical examples by successfully completing the chapter exercises.

INTRODUCTION

No textbook chapter dealing with arrest and search warrants would be complete without first presenting what is required by our U.S. Constitution, as detailed in the Fourth Amendment. The Fourth Amendment states:

> *The right of the people to be secure in their persons, houses, papers and effects against unreasonable searches and seizures, shall not be violated, and no warrant shall issue, but upon probable cause, supported by oath or affirmation particularly describing the place to be searched and the persons or things to be seized.*

Legal Information Institute: https://www.law.cornell.edu/constitution/billofrights#amendmentiv

The Fourth Amendment basically states that the burden of proof shall be *probable cause*, which is supported by a law enforcement officer's oath or affirmation, which specifically describes the place to be searched and the persons or things to be seized. Search warrants are issued by either a magistrate or a judge who must determine if that probable cause exists. The rationale is that a neutral or disinterested party (the magistrate or judge) reviews the facts of the case to determine if the issuance of a warrant is appropriate and proper.

The information contained in your affidavit supporting a search warrant must provide a comprehensive and thorough documentation of the facts of the incident.

These facts must rise to the level of probable cause, which will ultimately be determined by the magistrate or judge. Put simply, upon reading your sworn affidavit, the judge will conclude—based on the facts contained in your sworn statement—that a crime has been committed and that the persons and/or items sought are at the location described in the affidavit. Upon reaching this decision, a warrant will be issued.

One major part of the law enforcement professional's duties is to arrest any individual suspected of committing a crime. The probable cause affidavit (PC affidavit) is a document that contains the information about the elements of the crime, the suspect's participation in the crime, and an explanation by the affiant (i.e., the officer requesting the warrant) supporting the probable cause for an arrest, or why a specific person should be charged with the crime.

Probable cause exists when the facts or circumstances of a crime, within the officer's (the affiant's) knowledge, would lead a reasonable person to believe that the person listed in the affidavit (as the suspect) committed the crime.

The affidavit is a signed statement by the affiant that, under the penalty of perjury, asserts that the facts of the crime and the suspect's participation in that crime are true.

The affiant completing the PC affidavit is usually the investigating officer who has direct firsthand knowledge of the crime. The PC affidavit is normally completed upon the arrest of an individual, a short time after the crime is committed, and, in most circumstances, the person being arrested has already been taken into custody for that crime.

Once the person is arrested, he or she will have his or her first day in court, during which the court of jurisdiction will review the PC affidavit and determine if probable cause exists to hold the arrested person over for trial.

When completing the PC affidavit many officers make the mistake of just cutting and pasting the entire case into the affidavit. This can create a multiple page document that has to be read by supervisors, prosecutors, and judges.

Best Practices: From this author's experiences, supervisors, prosecutors, and judges do not like reading multiple pages looking for your probable cause; just state the facts in the affidavit. The case report you write will be reviewed later by the prosecution if they decide to move forward with the case.

In Figures 13.1 and 13.2 you will be able to review the PC affidavit that was completed for the arrest of an individual charged with the crime of robbery. The PC affidavit has only the information to support the crime of robbery and does not include the victim, witness, or additional officer statements.

The PC affidavit starts out with the deputy establishing the venue/jurisdiction of the crime, which must be identified in the affidavit.

Law enforcement professionals will also complete arrest warrants when the facts or circumstances of a crime, within the officer's (affiant's) knowledge, would lead a reasonable person to believe that the person listed as the suspect in the arrest warrant committed the crime.

You may have noticed that the requirements for an arrest warrant, as listed previously, are the same as the requirements for a PC affidavit. In both documents; probable cause must be established to support the charges, as well as the venue or jurisdiction where the search or crime was committed.

The arrest warrant is usually completed by a law enforcement professional when he or she does not have the person who committed the crime in custody, or if the investigating

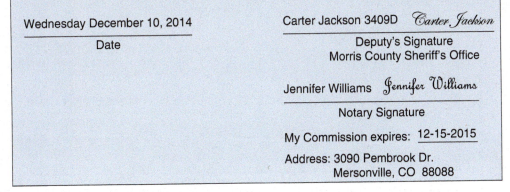

PROBABLE CAUSE AFFIDAVIT

The following affidavit is submitted to the Court to document the probable cause in support of the arrest of **Warren Michael Smith** DOB: **09-23-1966** SSN: **123-45-6789** on the charge(s) of: Robbery 18-4-301.

On 12-10-2014 I, Deputy Jackson your affiant, was dispatched to a reported Robbery at the Smoker Haven Tobacco Shop located at 3090 N. Washington Street which is located in the city of Mersonville, county of Morris, and state of Colorado. Upon my arrival I made contact with Michelle Tonya Jennings who told me that she was working in the store on this day at approximately 12:30 PM when a man, later identified as Warren Michael Smith, entered the store through the front entrance and walked up to the counter where she was standing and quickly pulled from his waistband a knife and demanded she hand him the money from the register. Mrs. Jennings complied by handing him the money from the register and as Mr. Smith turned to run out the door with the money he was knocked to the ground by John Benjamin Walters who was a customer who was already inside the store shopping for cigarettes prior to Mr. Smith's entry. Mrs. Jennings called the police while Mr. Walters held Mr. Smith on the ground until deputies arrived and took him into custody. Mrs. Jennings provided me with a video recording, from the stores surveillance cameras, supporting the facts asserted in this affidavit. Additional information concerning this case can be found in Morris County Sheriff's Office Case # 14-39087.

I would respectfully request that probable cause be found that Warren Michael Smith did commit the offense(s) of Robbery 18-4-301 in violation of the Colorado Revised Statutes.

Wednesday December 10, 2014

_____
Date

Carter Jackson 3409D   *Carter Jackson*

_____
Deputy's Signature
Morris County Sheriff's Office

Jennifer Williams   *Jennifer Williams*

_____
Notary Signature

My Commission expires: 12-15-2015

Address: 3090 Pembrook Dr.
Mersonville, CO 88088

Figure 13.1   *Probable Cause Affidavit*

agency would prefer to have the court of jurisdiction review the warrant prior to making an arrest to ensure that probable cause exists. If the person who committed the crime is in custody, then the PC affidavit is usually all that is needed, and an arrest warrant is normally not required. All arrest warrants should be accompanied by a PC affidavit, but PC affidavits do not need an arrest warrant.

Best Practices: If the person you are charging with a crime is in custody, then the PC affidavit is all that needs to be completed to book them into jail. If the person is not in custody, then the PC affidavit needs to be completed as well as the arrest warrant.

Every agency has its own policies regarding PC affidavits and arrest warrants, and you should always follow your agency's policy regarding these two documents.

In Figures 13.3, 13.4, and 13.5, you will be able to review an arrest warrant that was completed for the arrest of an individual charged with assault in the first degree. The arrest warrant, like the PC affidavit, has only the information to support the crime of assault in the first degree. It does not include the victim, witness, or additional officer statements.

IN THE DISTRICT COURT WITHIN AND FOR
THE COUNTY OF MORRIS AND STATE OF COLORADO
Criminal Action No._____
Division No._____

THE PEOPLE OF THE STATE OF COLORADO,

         Plaintiff

         vs.   Date of Birth

Warren Michael Smith   **09-23-1966** INFORMATION FOR
_____ PRELIMINARY PROCEDURE
_____
_____
_____

       Defendant _____.
The above named Defendant(s) was/were arrested on the <u>10</u> day of <u>December, 2015,</u>
on charges of: Robbery 18-4-301

The following bonding information is to be considered by the Judge in setting bail on the
defendant(s).

<u>STANDARD BAIL</u>

                           Carter Jackson
               _____
          Signature of Peace Officer who furnished
               the above information.

             Morris Sheriff's Office
            _____
                Agency

Figure 13.2 *Probable Cause Affidavit*

The arrest warrant starts out with the deputy establishing the venue or jurisdiction of the crime, which must be identified in the warrant.

The last affidavit left to be discussed in this chapter is the search warrant. Law enforcement professionals may also be required to complete search warrants when the facts or circumstances of a crime, within the affiant's knowledge, would lead a reasonable person to believe that the items listed in the application for the search warrant will be found at a specific location.

You may have noticed that the requirements for a search warrant are similar, once again, to that of the arrest warrant and probable cause affidavits described in this chapter. In all three documents, probable cause must be established to support the charges, as well as the venue or jurisdiction, where the search or crime was committed.

The search warrant is usually completed by a law enforcement professional when he or she has probable cause to believe that an item was stolen; designed to commit a crime; used in the commission of a crime; is illegal to possess; would be material evidence in a subsequent criminal prosecution; is required, authorized, or permitted by a statute of the state; or is kept, stored, transported, sold, dispensed, or possessed in violation of a statute of the state under circumstances involving a serious threat to the public safety, order, or to the public health.

ARREST WARRANT

(DISTRICT)(COUNTY) COURT, MORRIS COUNTY, STATE OF COLORADO
WARRANT NUMBER **14-34980**

The People of the State of Colorado, Plaintiff

V.

Joseph Michael Thompson, 03-23-1980, 6'01," 190 lbs, Brown, Brown, Defendant

Whereas **David Lincoln** has made an Application and Affidavit to the Court for the issuance of an Arrest Warrant, and; Whereas the application is in proper form and probable cause is found to believe that the person named in the application has committed the offense(s) of:

18-3-202 Assault in the First Degree

in violation of Colorado Revised Statutes within the County of Morris and State of Colorado; THEREFORE, any peace officer into whose hands this Arrest Warrant shall come is hereby ordered to arrest: **Joseph Michael Thompson, 03-23-1980, 6'01," 190 lbs, Brown, Brown** and bring him without unnecessary delay before the nearest Judge of the County or District Court.

It is further ordered that Bond is set in the amount of:

Standard Bond   dollars

Done this 7th day of December, 2014.
Time 1:00 p.m.

BY THE COURT:

                              Steven J. Parker

JUDGE
RETURN AND SERVICE: I have duly served this Arrest Warrant by arresting the aforementioned Defendant
as required on the _____ day of _____, 20__.

Signed: _____
                              Law enforcement agency: Morris County Sheriff's Office

Figure 13.3 *Arrest Warrant*

The address or description of the property to be searched in the search warrant should be described in the warrant so that it cannot be confused with other property within the same vicinity, which may be similar in size, shape, or appearance.

Every agency has its own policies regarding search warrants, and you should always follow your agency's policy regarding these documents.

In Figures 13.6 to 13.11, you will be able to review a search warrant that was requested to search a residence and a truck that were possibly used in the commission of a crime. Once again, the application for the search, or the search warrant, does not include the entire report, only the facts that are needed to establish probable cause.

Similar to the arrest warrant, the search warrant starts out with the deputy establishing the venue or jurisdiction of the crime, which must be identified in the warrant, which is then followed by the facts of the case.

(DISTRICT) (COUNTY) COURT, MORRIS COUNTY, STATE OF COLORADO
WARRANT NUMBER 14-34980

APPLICATION AND AFFIDAVIT FOR ARREST WARRANT

The People of the State of Colorado, Plaintiff

V.

Joseph Michael Thompson, 03-23-1980, 6'01," 190 lbs, Brown, Brown, Defendant

The undersigned, a peace officer as defined in 16-2.5-101, C.R.S. 1973, as amended, being first duly sworn on oath moves the Court to issue an Arrest Warrant for:

Joseph Michael Thompson, 03-23-1980, 6'01," 190 lbs, Brown, Brown

as provided in Rule 4.2 of the Colorado Rules of Criminal Procedure.

As GROUNDS THEREFORE, the undersigned applicant states that the facts submitted in support of this request are set forth in the accompanying attachment designated as Attachment "A" which is attached hereto and made a part hereof and that probable cause exists to believe that the aforementioned person has committed the offense(s) of:

18.3.202 Assault in the First Degree

in violation of C.R.S. 1973, as amended within the County of Morris and State of Colorado.

It is respectfully requested that bond on this Arrest Warrant be set in the amount of:

Standard Bond

David Lincoln

Applicant

Morris County Sheriff's Office

Deputy Sheriff
Sworn and subscribed before me this 7th day of December, 2014.

Judge: *Steven J. Parker*

Figure 13.4   *Application and Affidavit for Arrest Warrant*

THE *RIGHT* WAY TO *WRITE*

This chapter describes probable cause affidavits, arrest warrants, and search warrants. All of these are unique documents that require specific techniques. Although some of the required verbiage may vary from state to state, there are many commonalities in the preparation of these forms, which were presented in this chapter. With regard to how and what writing style to use in preparing these legal documents, your agency's policy and procedure manual, or standard operating procedures, will offer specific guidelines on preparing these documents. Follow the general guidelines offered in this chapter and then apply the appropriate jurisdictional or agency requirements, and you will be in compliance with the requirements of this task.

ATTACHMENT "A"

Your Affiant is Deputy David Lincoln, a regularly employed Deputy Sheriff for the County of Morris, the State of Colorado and is currently assigned to the Patrol Division of the Morris County Sheriff's Office.

On 12-07-2014 at approximately 0130 hours I, Deputy Lincoln 3487D, was dispatched to a reported assault at the Weehawken Night Club located at 3838 North Academy Drive which is located in the city of Mersonville, county of Morris, and state of Colorado. Upon arrival I made contact with Tina Marie Pendleton who told me that her boyfriend Alexander William Hamilton were at the night club with friends and at 0115 hours she and Mr. Hamilton decided to leave and go home. In the parking lot of the night club Mrs. Pendleton and Mr. Hamilton were approached by Aaron Richard Burr, Mr. Hamilton's old business partner, who started accusing Mr. Hamilton of stealing money from him six months ago. Mrs. Pendleton stated that the argument turned physical when Mr. Burr pushed Mr. Hamilton into the drivers' side of his car at which point Mr. Hamilton pushed Mr. Burr back causing him to fall backward to the ground where Mr. Burr then reached into his right coat side pocket and pulled out a black in color pistol and pointed it at Mr. Hamilton as he stood up. Mrs. Pendleton said that is when Mr. Hamilton called Mr. Burr a coward for pulling a gun on him to which Mr. Burr responded by yelling he was no coward and stepped forward toward Mr. Hamilton at which point the gun was fired once and after which Mr. Hamilton fell to the ground.

Mrs. Pendleton stated that she dropped to the ground to help Mr. Hamilton while Mr. Burr ran toward his Chevrolet Corvette that was parked nearby and drove out of the parking lot north-bound on North Academy Drive.

Mrs. Pendleton stated that she knows and is familiar with Aaron Richard Burr personally because Mr. Burr and Mr. Hamilton were business partners in a landscaping business that the two owned and operated for many years and where she was employed by them as their accountant. She was also familiar with the car Aaron Richard Burr owned and drove day to day.

Mrs. Pendleton stated that she is positive and has no doubt that it was the person she knows as Aaron Richard Burr that approached her and Alexander William Hamilton in the parking lot and shot Alexander William Hamilton and then fled the parking lot in the Chevrolet Corvette.

Dr. Hosack was the attending surgeon at Memorial Hospital who performed emergency surgery on Alexander William Hamilton and he confirmed that the gunshot wound to Alexander William Hamilton met the definition of serious bodily injury as it is defined in the Colorado Revised Statute.

Therefore, based on the above described facts and circumstances, Your Affiant respectfully moves this Honorable Court for issuance of an arrest warrant naming **Joseph Michael Thompson, 03-20-1980, 6'01," 190 lbs. Brown hair and Brown eyes** as defendant for the crime(s) of:

18.3.202 Assault in the First Degree
C.R.S. 1973, as amended.

David Lincoln   12-07-2014
Affiant   Date

Steven J. Parker   12-07-2014
Judge   Date

Figure 13.5   *Attachment to Arrest Warrant*

SEARCH WARRANT

IN THE (DISTRICT) (COUNTY) COURT, MORRIS COUNTY, STATE OF COLORADO
CRIMINAL ACTION NUMBER **14-32090**

Whereas **Smith, Robert** has made an Application and Affidavit to the Court for the issuance of a Search Warrant, and;

Whereas the application is in proper form and probable cause is found for the issuance of a Search Warrant to search the person(s) and or premises specified in the application.
THEREFORE, the applicant, and any other peace officer into whose hands this Search Warrant shall come, is hereby ordered, with the necessary and proper assistance, to enter and search within the next ten (10) days the person, premises, location and any appurtenances thereto, description of which is: **1030 Harmony Ct. Mersonville, Colorado 88088 and a White in color 2010 Ford F150, bearing Colorado Plate "1BADGUY" with vehicle identification number 1224557890DRK184D**

The following person(s), property or thing(s) will be searched for, and if found seized:

_____

See Attachment "B"

_____

as probable cause has been found to believe that it:

(X)   Is stolen or embezzled, or
(X)   Is designed or intended for use in committing a criminal offense, or
(X)   Is or has been used as a means of committing a criminal offense, or
(X)   Is illegal to possess, or
(X)   Would be material evidence in a subsequent criminal prosecution, or required, authorized or permitted by a statute of the State of Colorado, or
(X)   Is a person, property or thing the seizure of which is expressly required, authorized or permitted by a statute of the State of Colorado, or
(X)   Is kept, stored, transported, sold, dispensed, or possessed in violation of a statute of the State of Colorado under circumstances involving a serious threat to the public safety, or order, or to the public health.
(Mark "X" according to fact)

Furthermore a copy of this warrant is to be left with the person whose premises or person is searched along with a list of any and all items seized at the time of its execution. If said person cannot be located or identified, a copy of this Search Warrant and a list of the property seized shall be left at the place from which the property was taken.
Further, a return shall be promptly made to this Court upon the execution of this Search Warrant along with an inventory of any property taken. The property seized shall be held in some safe place until the Court shall further order.

Done by the Court this 14th day of December, 2014.
Judge: Henry K. Franklin

Figure 13.6   *Search Warrant*

The forms presented in this chapter are specific and technical types of documents. Be aware of the subjective nature of each state's requirements for the completion of these documents. This chapter places more emphasis on providing you with generic examples of each of the forms to demonstrate the appropriate techniques and structures of the verbiage. The rationale behind these examples was to provide instruction by example. Warrants and affidavits are formulaic documents; that is, there is a certain type of foundation and formation that must be established in their completion. Carefully study the examples given in this chapter to get an insight into their formation, structure, and tone. Practice and feedback are essential learning tools for these types of documents.

(DISTRICT) (COUNTY) COURT, MORRIS COUNTY, STATE OF COLORADO
CRIMINAL ACTION NUMBER 14-32090

APPLICATION AND AFFIDAVIT FOR SEARCH WARRANT

The undersigned, a peace officer as defined in 18-1-901 (3) (1), C.R.S. 1973 as amended, being first duly sworn on oath moves the Court to issue a Warrant to search those person(s) and/or premises known as: **1030 Harmony Ct. Mersonville, Colorado 88088 which is described as a brown in color house with a red in color door facing Harmony Ct. and the numbers 1030 clearly displayed on the left side of the red in color door. I also request to search a white in color 2010 Ford F150, bearing Colorado Plate "1BADGUY" with vehicle identification number 1224557890DRK184D**

The undersigned states that there exists probable cause to believe that the following person, property or thing(s) to be searched for, and if found, seized will be found on the aforementioned person(s) and or premises and are described as follows:

See Attachment "B"

The grounds for the seizure of said person(s), property or thing(s) are that probable cause exists to believe that it:

(X)   Is stolen or embezzled, or
(X)   Is designed or intended for use in committing a criminal offense, or
(X)   Is or has been used as a means of committing a criminal offense, or
(X)   Is illegal to possess, or
(X)   Would be material evidence in a subsequent criminal prosecution, or required, authorized or permitted by a statute of the State of Colorado, or
(X)   Is a person, property or thing the seizure of which is expressly required, authorized or permitted by a statute of the State of Colorado, or
(X)   Is kept, stored, transported, sold, dispensed, or possessed in violation of a statute of the State of Colorado under circumstances involving a serious threat to the public safety, or order, or to the public health.
        (Mark "X" according to fact)

The facts submitted in support of this application are set for in the accompanying attachment designaed as Attachment "**A**" which is attached hereto and made a part hereof.

Applicant: *Robert Smith 1616D*
Morris County Sheriff's Office
Deputy Sheriff

Sworn and subscribed before me this 14th day of December, 2014.
Judge: *Henry K. Franklin*

Figure 13.7   *Application and Affidavit for Search Warrant*

TIPS FOR PROBABLE CAUSE AFFIDAVITS, ARREST WARRANTS AND SEARCH WARRANTS

- These forms will be viewed by a judge or magistrate. Take your time and do a professional job when completing these types of forms.
  - You, as the affiant, will have direct contact with the on-call judge who will review the document prior to issuance. The document will be scrutinized.
  - Often your supervisor will not be able to review this document prior to your contact with the judge; it is often up to you to get it right.
  - If the judge finds flaws with your document, don't argue with the judge. Use his/her comments constructively and learn from the experience.

ATTACHMENT "A"

Your Affiant is Deputy David Lincoln, a regularly employed Deputy Sheriff for the County of Morris, the State of Colorado and is currently assigned to the Patrol Division of the Morris County Sheriff's Office.

On 12-13-2014 at approximately 1900 hours I, Deputy Smith 1616P the Affiant, was dispatched to 5809 N. Washington St. apartment # 125, which is located in the City of Mersonville, County of Morris, and the State of Colorado. The call for service was in reference to a reported home invasion robbery. Upon my arrival I made contact with Amanda Maria Tanner who told me that she and her boyfriend John William Carlisle were relaxing and watching MMA Fighting on their television set in their apartment when someone knocked on the apartment door.

Mr. Carlisle went to the door and upon opening the door a man wearing a ski mask pushed his way into the apartment and demanded that she and Mr. Carlisle lay on the floor as he pointed a black in color semi-automatic pistol at the two of them. Mrs. Tanner told me that she and Mr. Carlisle complied with the intruder's demand and laid down on the floor next to the kitchen.

The intruder then knelt down just above Mrs. Tanner and held the barrel of the gun to her head and asked Mr. Carlisle where the money was. Mr. Carlisle told the intruder that all the money they had was in the freezer of the refrigerator inside an old box of ice cream sandwiches. The intruder then stood up and ran into the kitchen and opened up the freezer door and grabbed the box of ice cream sandwiches and after looking inside the box he ran out the rear door of the residence carrying the ice cream box.

Mr. Carlisle attempted to follow the intruder after retrieving his own gun from the bedroom but could not catch him. Mr. Carlisle did observe a white in color Ford F150 pick-up truck with an unknown Colorado Plate and tinted windows speeding out of the apartment complex. Mr. Carlisle believed the vehicle belonged to one of his employee's brothers who he had met once before at a company party he had at a lake this past summer.

Mr. Carlisle stated that this past summer he had a company party and invited all of his employees from his stucco business to attend this event. Mr. Carlisle stated that one of his employees named Hector Martinez Gonzalez came to the party in a white in color Ford F150 pick-up truck with his brother Jose Martinez Gonzalez and that the Ford F150 pick-up truck had a large dent in the front right fender over the wheel.

Mr. Carlisle told me that he believes that the white in color Ford F150 pick-up truck that sped out of the parking lot was the same one driven by Jose Martinez Gonzalez because it also had a large dent in the right front fender over the wheel.

Mr. Carlisle described the intruder as possibly Hispanic male, about 5' 08" tall, approximately 150 lbs., wearing a white t-shirt with long sleeves, blue jeans, and a black ski mask.

Mrs. Tanner told me that the intruder was about 5'09" tall, approximately 155 lbs., and was wearing a white t-shirt, blue jeans, and a ski mask. Mrs. Tanner also said that she observed the intruder's feet when he knelt beside her and that he was wearing white laced up tennis shoes unknown brand.

Mrs. Tanner also said that she observed a tattoo on the intruder's left hand when he knelt beside her. She described the tattoo as the number "18" with the word "Mafia" just above the left thumb on the back portion of the hand.

Figure 13.8   *Attachment A*

- Remember that these types of documents are official orders from the court and, as such, they require a specific type of writing style.
- When in doubt while completing these types of documents, consult an experienced officer for help.
- These types of documents require facts, not opinions; never use any type of subjective inferences or deductions in your affidavits.

Mrs. Tanner and Mr. Carlisle both confirmed that the money inside the freezer was for their wedding and honeymoon that they were planning for next summer. Both Mrs. Tanner and Mr. Carlisle told me that they have shared their plans about the wedding and honeymoon with co-workers and other people. Both Mr. and Mrs. Carlisle stated they have told several people that they were saving money for the wedding and honeymoon, but neither could recall if they ever mentioned to anyone that their money was kept in their apartment.

Both Mr. Tanner and Mr. Carlisle confirmed that there was $10,000 inside the freezer that the intruder stole and that the $10,000 was all in $100 dollar denominations of U.S. currency wrapped in $2,000 dollar increments held together with a paper band marked with "$2,000 Supreme Bank and Loan." They also told me that the ice cream sandwich box was a "Kenny's Chocolate Ice Cream Sandwiches" brand box.

On 12-13-2014 at approximately 2230 hours I completed a Colorado Registration check through the Colorado Department of Revenue for a Jose Martinez Gonzalez and discovered that there was one listing for a Jose Martinez Gonzalez who had registered a white in color 2010 Ford F150 pick-up truck at 1030 Harmony Ct. in Mersonville, CO 88088 and I also discovered that this particular vehicle had been involved in a crash on 06-30-2014 with damage to the right front fender being reported.

I was also able to locate a copy of the traffic crash report case #14-23090 that listed Jose Martinez Gonzalez as one of the drivers in that crash with a Colorado Driver's License #123-56-9087, Date of Birth of 01-22-1980, with an address of 1030 Harmony Ct. in Mersonville, CO 88088.

On 12-13-2014 at approximately 2315 hours, I along with other deputies drove over to 1030 Harmony Ct. where I discovered a white in color Ford F150 parked on the street in front of the residence with a dent on the right front fender. Upon walking up to the F150 I observed in plain view in the bed of the truck that there was a "Kenny's Chocolate Ice Cream Sandwiches" brand box next to a paper band marked with "$2,000 Supreme Bank and Loan". This type of paper banding is commonly used to secure U.S. currency together which were both consistent with the box that Mrs. Tanner and Mr. Carlisle described that they kept their money in as well as the bank band that was used to secure their money in $2,000 increments by their bank.

On 12-13-2014 at approximately 2320 hours I along with other deputies contacted Jose Martinez Gonzalez, Date of Birth of 01-22-1980, at his residence located at 1030 Harmony Ct. which is located in the City of Mersonville, County of Morris, and State of Colorado. Mr. Gonzalez was alone and allowed deputies into his residence but denied knowing anything about the robbery.

I noticed that during this contact with Mr. Gonzalez in his residence that he had a tattoo on his left hand of a number "18" with the word "Mafia" just above the left thumb on the back portion of the hand which was consistent with the tattoo Mrs. Tanner observed on the intruder earlier in the evening.

Based on the facts contained in this affidavit for a search warrant I request that probable cause be found to support a search inside the residence located at 1030 Harmony Ct. which is located in the City of Mersonville, County of Morris, and the State of Colorado for Mrs. Tanner's and Mr. Carlisle's $10,000 that was taken from them. I also request permission to search for a black in color ski mask and a black in color semi-automatic pistol that were used by the intruder during the commission of the crime of robbery that occurred on 12-13-2014 at approximately 1845 hours at 5809 N. Washington St. apartment # 125 which is located in the City of Mersonville, County of Morris, and the State of Colorado.

Figure 13.9   *Attachment A* (*continued*)

SUMMARY

Preparing a legal affidavit is a skill that must be mastered by the law enforcement professional. Unlike the typical case report, these are legal documents that must contain certain legal verbiage. The requirements of these types of documents are based on the Fourth Amendment of the U.S. Constitution. The composers of the Constitution imposed specific safeguards to protect citizens from unreasonable searches and/or seizures by members of the government. Preparing these types of documents will require both narrative and technical skills.

The residence identified by county records as 1030 Harmony Ct. is a brown in color dwelling with the numbers 1030 on a pole on the right side of the porch as one looks at the residence from the street. The residence of 1030 Harmony Ct. sits between two other residences with the address of 1028 on the residence on the left side and 1032 on the residence on the right side as one looks at it from the street. The utility records for 1030 Harmony Ct. indicate that Jose Martinez Gonzalez, Date of Birth of 01-22-1980 is the person responsible for the utilities.

I would also request that probable cause be found to search a white in color 2010 Ford F150 pick-up truck with a dent on the right front fender bearing Colorado Plate 1BADGUY with vehicle Identification # 1224557890DRK184D registered to Jose Martinez Gonzalez, Date of Birth of 01-22-1980 at 1030 Harmony Ct. Mersonville, Colorado 88088.

Therefore, based on the above described facts and circumstances, Your Affiant respectfully moves this Honorable Court for issuance of a search warrant for search of those person(s) and or premises known as:

1030 Harmony Ct. Mersonville, Colorado 88088 which is described as a brown in color house with a red in color door facing Harmony Ct. and the numbers 1030 clearly displayed on the left side of the red in color door. I also request to search a white in color 2010 Ford F150, bearing Colorado Plate "1BADGUY" with vehicle identification number 1224557890DRK184D. The person(s), property, or things(s) to be search for are contained in Attachment "B".

Robert Smith 1616D
_____   *12-14-2014*
Affiant   _____
                                                                          Date

Henry K. Franklin
_____   12-14-2014
Judge   _____
                                                                          Date

Figure 13.10   Attachment A (*continued*)

The mechanics of the affidavit are pretty straightforward. The affiant takes an oath swearing that the facts show probable cause for his or her belief that a crime has been committed, and that the person(s) or things sought are at the location to be searched. The affiant must state the facts upon which the affiant's belief is based. These facts are brought before a magistrate or judge for an impartial review. At this point, the magistrate or judge will determine if probable cause for arrest is appropriate, and if so, the arrest order will be signed and delivered to the law enforcement officer to execute.

Preparing probable cause affidavits, arrest warrants, search warrants, and other related court orders is among the myriad duties you will face as a law enforcement professional. Although completion of these forms may seem intimidating and tedious at times, they are simply another essential requirement you must perform on a routine basis. These types of

ATTACHMENT "B"

The following items are to be searched for and, if found, seized:
1. $10,000 U.S. Currency in $100 denominations secured together by a bank band marked $2,000 Supreme Bank and Loan.
2. Black in color ski mask.
3. Black in color semi-automatic pistol.

Figure 13.11   Attachment B

forms require a little more technical expertise than the typical case report. However, with practice, preparing affidavits is a skill that you can master. Adhere to the basic principles as presented in this chapter, seek review and advice from trusted colleagues, and take the time to do it correctly and you will be fine!

EXERCISES

1. In Chapter 10, you watched a video and completed a report for a theft that was committed, now it is time to complete the PC affidavit for the person who was charged. You may need to watch the video once more and review your report to refresh your memory (*Theft Video 10.2*). Use the probable cause form that can be found in the Appendix of this book to complete this exercise.

2. In Chapter 11, you watched a video of an assault that was committed in a bar, now it is time to complete the arrest warrant for the person that was charged. In this chapter you will watch the same video except that you will not be able to locate the suspect therefore requiring you to complete an arrest warrant for the person who committed the assault. You need to watch video titled *Assault Video 11.1* and complete the arrest warrant. Use the arrest warrant form that can be found in the Appendix of this book to complete this exercise. All additional information can be found in the report in Chapter 11.

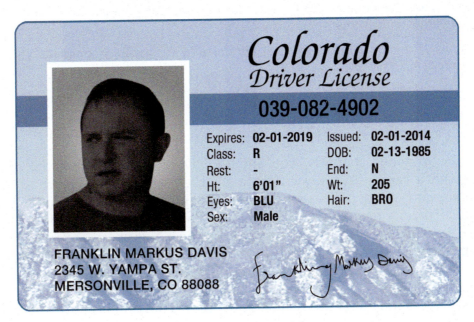

14

MISCELLANEOUS FORMS

LEARNING OBJECTIVES

- Recognize the many other different forms and reports that may need to be completed during the documentation of an incident that you are investigating.

- Be familiar with the NCIC system and gathering information for "pick-ups" for individuals with warrants and how stolen property information is entered into the NCIC system.

- Be able to complete the chain of custody sheet and other forms needed to ensure the proper procedure for collecting evidence.

- Recognize the various procedural issues in completing the custody sheet when placing an individual under arrest.

- Apply your knowledge to practical examples by successfully completing the chapter exercises.

INTRODUCTION

In the previous chapters, you should have discovered that the individual who chooses a career as a law enforcement professional will be required to complete numerous types of police reports. In this chapter, you will be introduced to additional miscellaneous reports and forms that all law enforcement professionals across the nation complete during their assigned duties. Not every organization requires the same reports, nor do they require a report for every situation. Your agency policy and procedure manual and SOPs will dictate when these various forms should be utilized.

This chapter will cover some of the more common types of miscellaneous forms you will be required to complete. Be cognizant that the forms presented in this chapter are by no means intended to be an all-inclusive list. There are many other agency forms that may be authorized. The forms in this chapter are simply the more frequently occurring forms found in all law enforcements agencies. This chapter will present some general guidelines that can be applied to most of the common miscellaneous forms that you will encounter.

"PICK-UP" OR A NCIC WANT FOR A PERSON WITH A WARRANT

This form is used when a law enforcement professional investigates a crime where there is probable cause to make an arrest, but the officer cannot locate the offender. The officer will complete what is commonly referred to as a "pick-up" for the wanted person.

The pick-up is a form that has all the case information regarding the wanted person, the crime severity, and any other information that could be used to locate the suspect. The information from the pick-up is then typically entered into the National Crime Information Center (NCIC) by a records specialist. Once the wanted person's information is entered into NCIC, every law enforcement agency in the nation will have access to this vital information.

If the wanted person is contacted in another state during a traffic stop, or during any other contact with law enforcement, that person's name will usually be entered into NCIC by the contacting agency, which will discover that the individual is wanted by another agency in another jurisdiction.

The pick-up is the data entry form that will be accompanied by a summons/ticket, signed complaint, or the warrant for the wanted person. The records section will keep all copies of the summons/ticket, signed complaint, and warrant as well as the pick-up form that was used to enter the information into NCIC.

Best Practices: It is important to note that a pick-up in any format is not a universal form, and it should not be confused with an arrest warrant, probable cause affidavit, or writ of commitment. The pick-up is nothing more than an agency form that is used to help expedite the processing of the information in an arrest warrant, probable cause affidavit, or writ of commitment into the NCIC database by data entry professionals.

In Figure 14.1, you will see an example of a pick-up for an individual who is wanted by the Bayou Township Police Department for the charge of harassment, 18-9-111. The pick-up was completed by Officer Smith, 1616, but it was entered into NCIC by Wendy Carter, 4090D.

"PICK-UP" OR WANT FOR A VEHICLE

The information on the vehicle pick-up form for a vehicle is similar to a pick-up form for an individual. This form is also completed by a law enforcement agency in an effort to locate a vehicle that is stolen, used in the commission of a crime, or simply might belong to a missing person. Once the determination has been made by the law enforcement agency to place a vehicle pick-up, it is essentially the same process that is used for the pick-up of an individual. The law enforcement agency completes the form and then turns it over, along with a copy of the report, to the records section, which, in turn, enters the information into the NCIC system.

The use of a pick-up for a person or a vehicle is associated with the commonly known police announcement of "Be on the Look Out" (BOLO). The BOLO term has been used in law enforcement for decades and is still used today. The pick-up process triggers the broadcast of the BOLO's information to all appropriate law enforcement agencies.

A pick-up can be used for many items that law enforcement may be trying to locate across the country. The two pick-ups covered in this chapter are simply the most common forms you will utilize. In Figure 14.2, you will find a pick-up for a stolen vehicle.

NCIC WARRANT FOR ARREST PICK-UP SHEET

FELONY ☐	MISDEMEANOR ☒	PETTY OFFENSE ☐

DATE WARRANT ISSUED	TIME WARRANT ISSUED	CASE #
02/13/2014	2030	14-34890

AGENCY	OFFICER/DEPUTY	BADGE #
Bayou Township PD	Smith	1616

WANTED PERSON INFORMATION   MALE ☒   FEMALE ☐

NAME (LAST)	FIRST	MIDDLE	SUFFIX
Williams	David	Carl	Jr.

DOB MM/DD/YYYY	BUILD	SKIN TONE
09/25/1970	Medium	Light

ALIAS	SCARS/MARKS	TATTOOS
None known	None known	Wolf on left arm

DRIVER LICENSE STATE	DRIVER LICENSE #	SOCIAL SECURITY #
LA	234-0900-8907	123-45-6789

HEIGHT	WEIGHT	HAIR	EYES	RACE
6'0"	180 Lbs	BRO	BRO	White

LAST KNOWN ADDRESS	LAST KNOWN PHONE
3030 Decatur Dr.	

CITY	State	Zip Code
Bayou Township	LA	88088

LAST KNOWN BUSINESS ADDRESS
45509 Royal Rd.

CITY	State	Zip Code
Bayou Township	LA	88088

BUSINESS NAME	BUSINESS PHONE
Walter and Wayne Shoes	504-555-0199

CRIME	CITY/STATE STATUTE
Harassment	18-9-111

CRIME OF VIOLENCE   YES ☐   NO ☒   HOMICIDE ☐   ASSAULT ☐

FIREARM USED ☐   EDGED WEAPON USED ☐   OTHER WEAPON USED ☐

ADDITIONAL INFORMATION
Mr. Williams pushed another person down in a parking lot and ran away. Mr. Williams was identified by store security as working in the mall. Mr. Williams could not be located see summons # 10009000345 for more information.

DATE ENTERED INTO NCIC M M/DD/YYYY	TIME	BY:	ID #
02/13/2014	2100	Wendy Carter	4090D

DATE ENTERED INTO NCIC M M/DD/YYYY	TIME	BY:	ID #

Figure 14.1   *"Pick-up" Sheet*

EVIDENCE CHAIN OF CUSTODY SHEET AND EVIDENCE TAGS

Another important task associated with report-writing is the collection and documentation of evidence that is used in the commission of a crime. The law enforcement professional must maintain the chain of custody of an item that he or she has collected from a crime scene. Once an item has been photographed, collected, and tagged, it is then itemized and described on the Evidence Chain of Custody Sheet. In Figures 14.3 and 14.4, you will find various items that were photographed, tagged, and itemized on a chain of custody sheet.

STOLEN VEHICLE PICK-UP FORM FOR NCIC DATA ENTRY		
CASE NUMBER 14-32908	AGENCY Corn County SO	DATE OF REPORT 11/14/2014

VEHICLE YEAR 2011	VEHICLE MAKE Acura	VEHICLE MODEL TL	VEHICLE COLOR BLK

VEHICLE IDENTIFICATION NUMBER 123456789MDHE9876	VEHICLE TYPE Sedan	DAMAGED None

LICENSE STATE AL	LICENSE NUMBER 1-WINNER	LICENSE YEAR 2014

ANY OTHER IDENTIFIABLE MARKS/DAMAGE/CUSTOM PAINT/AFTER MARKET ITEMS ON PROPERTY
None

OWNER NAME (LAST) Smith	(FIRST) Steven	(MIDDLE) Wayne

OWNER ADDRESS: 1414 N. Elm St.	CITY Tombigbee	STATE AL	ZIP CODE 88088

OWNER HOME PHONE 251-555-0909	OWNER WORK PHONE 251-555-0890	OWNER OTHER PHONE 251-555-0188

ADDRESS STOLEN FROM 1414 N. Elm St.	CITY Tombigbee	STATE AL	ZIP CODE 88088

DATE STOLEN 11/14/2014	DATE RECOVERED	OWNER NOTIFIED YES ☐ NO ☐	OWNER NOTIFIED BY:
TIME STOLEN 0830	TIME RECOVERED	DATE OWNER NOTIFIED	TIME OWNER NOTIFIED
LOCATION WHERE RECOVERED		TOWED BY:	TOWED TO:

ARREST MADE: YES ☐ NO ☐	NAME OF PERSON ARRESTED
USED IN ANOTHER CRIME YES ☐ NO ☐	LOCATION	CRIME COMMITTED
KEPT AS EVIDENCE YES ☐ NO ☐	INSURED BY:

ADDITIONAL INFORMATION
Mr. Smith started his 2011 Acura TL and left it running in his driveway on 11/14/2014 at approx. 0830 and when he came back outside to go to work he discovered it stolen. For more information see case # 14-32908

DATE ENTERED INTO NCIC M M/DD/YYYY 11/14/2014	TIME 0945	BY: Barnett	ID # 0909
DATE ENTERED INTO NCIC M M/DD/YYYY	TIME	BY:	ID #

Figure 14.2   *"Pick-up" for a Stolen Vehicle*

The two photos presented in Figure 14.3 and Figure 14.4 are of a pistol and the rounds found inside it when it was seized during a consent search of a residence. In Figure 14.5, you will find the evidence tags along with the chain of custody sheet for both items.

Best Practices: Make sure all firearms are unloaded and safe when placed into evidence. This is to ensure that the weapon will not discharge accidentally when it is moved or handled by others.

The evidence tag would be affixed to Item 1, the firearm, but Item 2, the bullets taken out of Item 1, would be placed into an evidence bag, which would display the same information as an evidence tag. Figure 14.6 is an example of the front of an evidence bag, which would be completed for Item 2, the bullets, which were removed from the cylinder of Item 1.

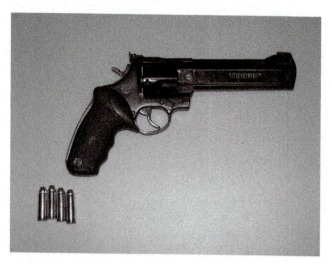

Figure 14.3 *Item 1*
(*Photo by: Michael Merson*)

Figure 14.4 *Item 2*
(*Photo by: Michael Merson*)

Make: Taurus

Type: Raging Bull

Caliber: 454

Serial # 4567809T (Real Serial number intentionally not displayed)

Four: 454 caliber bullets discovered loaded inside cylinder of Item #1

Brand: Unknown

Now that both items from the case have been properly tagged, the chain of custody sheet is ready to be completed. In Figure 14.7, the chain of custody sheet is completed for Items 1 and 2. This will provide you with a reference document for future use.

CUSTODY SHEET/REPORT

The custody sheet is usually required for booking someone into jail on a specific criminal charge. The custody sheet is not normally used if an individual is released on a summons, or when a juvenile is released to the custody of the parent or guardian. In Figure 14.8, you will find a completed custody sheet.

EVIDENCE/PROPERTY TAG			
CASE # 14-35890	ITEM # 1	DATE OF REPORT 12/01/2014	TIME COLLECTED *at approx. 0230*
Description *Black in color Taurus Brand "Raging Bull" 454 caliber pistol Serial #4567809T*			
Address or location where item was collected from *45789 New Haven Dr. Goldfinch, WA 88088*			
Evidence ☒	Found/Other Property ☐		Placed for Destruction ☐
Victim Name *Williams, Mary*		Suspect Name *Williams, Franklin*	
Owner Name *Williams, Franklin*	Owner Address *45789 New Haven Dr.*		Owner Contact Number *206-555-0199*
Agency *Goldfinch Police Department*	Officer/Deputy *Davis*		Badge # *8907P*

Figure 14.5 *Evidence/Property Tag*

EVIDENCE/PROPERTY TAG

CASE # 14-35890	ITEM # 2	DATE OF REPORT 12-01-2014	TIME COLLECTED *at approx. 0230*

Description:
Item #2 - four bullets, 454 caliber, unknown make recovered from the cylinder of Item #1 on

12-01-2014 at approx. 0230. Nothing Follows

Address or location where item was collected from

45789 New Haven Dr. Goldfinch, WA 88088

Evidence ☒	Found/Other Property ☐	Placed for Destruction ☐

Victim Name *Williams, Mary*		Suspect Name *Williams, Franklin*	

Owner Name *Williams, Franklin*	Owner Address *45789 New Haven Dr.*	Owner Contact Number *206-555-0199*
Agency *Goldfinch Police Department*	Officer/Deputy *Davis*	Badge # *8907P*

Figure 14.6   *Evidence/Property Bag*

THE *RIGHT* WAY TO *WRITE*

This chapter covers miscellaneous forms. It is not meant to be an all-inclusive list of forms. The types and volumes of forms will vary from agency to agency. The how and/or what to write regarding these types of forms will also vary significantly from agency to agency. This chapter attempted to give you some generic examples of these forms. Again, your agency's SOPs will provide you with the best guidelines and directions on completing these forms. The service situations you encounter will dictate your jurisdictional responses to these types of incidents and the specific forms that will be required.

Property/Evidence Report

Goldfinch Police Department Property/Evidence Report	Criminal Case Number 14-35890
Property Evidence Number	Traffic Crash Number
Storage Location	Summons Number

Officer Badge/ID # *Davis 8907P*	☒ Evidence ☐ Personal Property ☐ Found Property	Date Placed into Evidence 12-01-2014

Address Location Recovered From
45789 New Haven Dr.   Goldfinch, WA   88088

Victim (Last, First, Middle) *Williams, Mary, Anne*	Address (City, State, Zip Code) *45789 New Haven Dr. Goldfinch, WA 88088*	Contact Phone *206-555-0199*
Victim (Last, First, Middle)	Address (City, State, Zip Code)	Contact Phone

#	Suspect (Last, First, Middle)	DOB	Address (City, State, Zip Code)	Offense
1	*Williams, Franklin*	*01-12-1970*	*45789 New Haven Dr. Goldfinch, WA 88088*	*Menacing 18-3-206 (Felony 5)*

Item #	Quantity	Linked to Suspect #	Article Description (Make, Model, Serial #, Vin#)	Property Technician Use Only
1	1	1	*Black in color Taurus Brand "Raging Bull" 454 caliber pistol Serial #4567809T recovered from under suspect's mattress in suspect's bedroom on 12-01-2014 at approx. 0230. By: Officer Davis 8907 P*	
2	4	1	*Four quantity bullets, 454 caliber, unknown make recovered from the cylinder of Item #1 on 12-01-2014 at approx. 0230. By: Officer Davis 8907 P.*	

Approving Supervisor *Carl 0230P*	Placed in Locker Number : 234	By Officer: *Davis 8907 P*

Date Received	Technician Receiving Items	Locker Number	Page 1 of 1

Figure 14.7   *Chain of Custody Sheet*

TIPS FOR MISCELLANEOUS FORMS

- As in writing a good case report, most of the forms you complete could be subpoenaed into a court of law. The same basic principles of proper report writing apply to these forms.
- Every judicial district has slightly different requirements for completing various forms and other legal documents.
  - Specific instructions on completing the various forms will be documented in your agency's policy and procedure manual and/or its SOPs.

☒ Adult ☐ Juvenile	Agency MPD		**Custody Report**		Agency Case Number 14-90875	

Custody Date 02-02-2014	Custody Time 0245	Custody Location 3020 N. Barnes Dr.		Zone 4	Sector 5	Booking Number 56890

Subjects Name (Last) Smith	(Middle) Michael	(First) Steven	DOB MM-DD-YYYY 05-05-1974	Age 39

Address 3640 Backbone Mountain Dr.	(City) Rockfish	(State) MD	Zip Code 88088	Home Phone 410-555-0195

Employer Name Mike's Appliances	Address 40040 Mills Rd.	(City) Rockfish	(State) MD	(Work Phone) 410-555-0176	Zip Code 88088	Cell Phone 410-555-0177

Place of Birth City/State Hobbs, NM.	Race W	Sex M	Height 5' 10"	Weight 180	Hair BRO	Eyes BLU	SSN 123-45-6789

Scars/Marks/Tattoos
Octopus Right shoulder

Subject Resisted ☐ Yes ☒ No	Subject Armed ☐ Yes ☒ No	Alias/Nickname ☐ Yes ☒ No If yes, Alias or nickname

CODES: A = Accomplice   S = Spouse   P = Parent   G = Guardian   O = Other

Code S	Name (Last, First, Middle) Smith, Vera	Address 3456 Backbone Mountain Dr. Rockfish, MD 88088	Home Phone 410-555-0184	Other Phone
Code	Name (Last, First, Middle)	Address	Home Phone	Other Phone

Injury/Illness None	Treated ☐ Yes ☐ No	Where Treated:	Date and Time Treated	Treated By:

☐ Injury Result of Subject Resisting During Arrest   ☐ Injured Prior to Law Enforcement Contact   ☐ Injured While in Custody

Morris County Jail Number	State or City Statute Number	Title of Offense	Warrant Number	Summons Number
45789	18-9-111	Harassment	NA	100090032
48902	18-4-301	Robbery	348908	NA

Disposition	☒ Held in Custody ☐ No Formal Charge ☐ Released on Bond ☐ Charges Dropped by Police ☐ Released on Own Recognizance ☐ Turned over to Another Agency ☐ Deceased

Narrative
Mr. Smith was taken into custody after slapping another customer at the Dew Drop Inn Bar and Grill located at 3020 N. Barnes Rd.

Mr. Smith was intoxicated, belligerent, and refused to leave in a taxi. Mr. Smith was administered a portable breath test that revealed a possible BAC of .18

Mr. Smith was charged with Harassment 18-9-111 after officers spoke to the victim. See Case # 14-90875 / Summons # 100090032

Mr. Smith also had a warrant for Failure to Appear (FTA) for Robbery see Warrant # 348908 No further Information

Vehicle Year	Vehicle Make	Modle	Body Style	Vehicle Color	License Number	State	Location of Vehicle

Arresting Officer Davis	ID # 1616	Arresting Officer	ID #
Morris County Intake Deputy Williams			ID # 1301

Figure 14.8   *Completed Custody Sheet*

SUMMARY

As law enforcement professionals, we live and work in a world characterized by technical jargon, specialized forms, and intense judicial scrutiny. Knowing which form to use and how to complete the document correctly is a critical skill that you must master. As a law enforcement professional, you are frequently expected to complete numerous types of miscellaneous forms. These forms are technical documents, and most address search and seizure elements of the Fourth Amendment of our Constitution. As such, be aware that these forms are often presented in a court of law.

This chapter gave just a few examples of various types of miscellaneous forms that you will encounter in the performance of your assigned duties. The forms presented in this chapter contain the basic common elements found in the various forms within your particular area of operation. The chapter was designed to give you an overview of what to expect and how to complete several types of commonly used forms. The chapter presented general guidelines regarding miscellaneous forms, which can be applied to any agency. Every jurisdiction will have specific nuances in regard to these types of forms. Be aware of these differences and simply adjust the general concepts you learned in this chapter to the requirements of your specific jurisdiction.

EXERCISES

1. In this exercise you need to complete a pick-up for the described person. Use the pick-up arrest form that can be found in the Appendix of this book to complete this exercise.

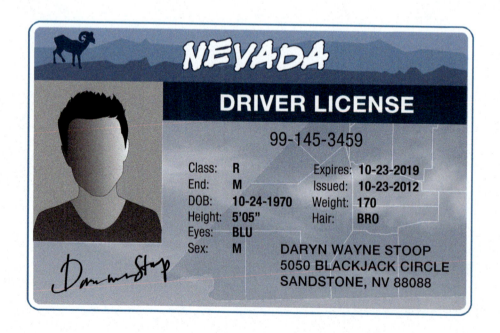

Case #: 15-34980		Title: Assault in the First Degree 200-471 and200-481
Dispatch: 2340	Arrival: 2350	Cleared: 0400
Date: Today's Date	Time: 2330	Offense Location: 5050 Blackjack Cir

(Suspect)/ ~~Victim /Witness/Other:~~

Name: Daryn Wayne Stoop

DOB: 10-24-70   Race: W   HGT: 5'05"   WGT: 170   Hair: BRO   Eyes: BLU

POB: Sandstone, NV   SEX: (Male) ~~Female~~

Clothing Description: White short sleeved buttoned shirt and blue jeans

Address: 5050 Blackjack Cir	City: Sandstone	State: CO	Zip Code: 88088
Contact Number: Home: 702-555-0187	Cell: 702-555-0158		WK: 702-555-0199
Employer: Bill's House of Cards	Occupation: Card Dealer		
Business Address: 1212 Desert Way	City: Sandstone	State: CO	Zip Code: 88088
Business Phone:	Business Victim: Yes No		

Date of Warrant: Today's Date / Subject's Alias: "21"

Time of Warrant: 1200 or 12:00 PM / Subject's Build: Large / Subject's Skin Tone: Light

Scars/Marks: Scar over left eye / Tattoos: Tattoo of ace of spades on right shoulder

Subject's Driver's License State NV#9633-098-12390 / Subject's Social Security Number: 789-56-1234

Crime of Violence: Yes / Weapon Used: Machete

Mr. Stoop was having a card game at his home when he believed the victim was cheating. Mr. Stoop pulled a machete from under the table and cut the victim's hand off. Stoop left before police arrived and could not be located. See case # 15-34980 for more information.

Date Entered into NCIC: Today's Date / Time Entered into NCIC: 0800 OR 8:00 AM

Entered by: Class Instructor

2. In this exercise you need to complete a pick-up for the stolen vehicle described in the provided documents. Use the pick-up stolen vehicle form that can be found in the Appendix of this book to complete this exercise.

OKLAHOMA REGISTRATION/OWNERSHIP TAX RECEIPT

TYPE	PLATE	TAB/VAL	VIN	EXPIRE
PAS-REG	GON4EVR	A934567	90467523KLOE984MD	11/2015

TITLE	YEAR	MAKE	BODY	CWT/PAS	T/C	FLEET	FUEL	PREV EXP
Y231	2012	ACURA	CP	35	C		G	

PUR DATE	PUR PRICE	ORIGINAL TAXABLE VALUE	BUS DATE	CO#	UR/CODE
11/15/2014	55,000	53,000	11/21/2014	11U	0001

EM FEE	TITLE FEE	PRIOR O.T.	OWN TAX	LIC FEE	ROAD FEE	BRIDGE FEE
0.00	0.00	0.00	850.00	120.00	23.00	13.50

RTD TAX	COUNTY TAX	CITY/DIS TAX	STATE TAX	SPECIAL FEE	OTHER FEE
0.00	50.00	30.00	25.00	0.00	0.00

UNIT	GVW	MILES	HT GVW	HC DATE

OWNER MAILING ADDRESS

FEES IN BOLD INCLUDED IN UC FEE
E09933456 4356

STORY, MELANIE
23560 N. REDBUD ST.
HONEYBEE, OK 88088

SIGNATURE REQUIRED ON REVERSE SIDE

VALIDATION	LN		TOTAL
PAID MORRIS	24	11/23/2012	

MOTOR VEHICLE INSURANCE IS COMPULSORY IN OKLAHOMA, NON-COMPLIANCE IS A MISDEMEANOR TRAFFIC OFFENSE

3. In this exercise, you will need to complete an evidence tag and the property evidence report for the evidence that was collected and listed on the following pages. Use the evidence tag and property evidence report forms that can be found in the Appendix of this book to complete this exercise. The additional information for the felon/suspect is as follows:

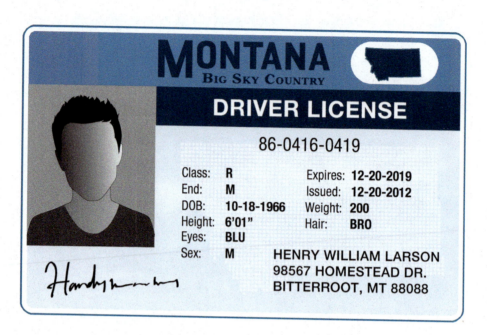

Case #: 15-34210   Title: *Possession of a weapon by a previous offender*

Dispatch: *1300*   Arrival: *1310*   Cleared: *1530*

Date: *Today's Date*   Time: *1330*   Location: *98567 Homestead Dr.*

Suspect / Victim /Witness/Other:

Name:

DOB: *10-18-66*   Race: *W*   HGT: *6'01"*   WGT: *200*   Hair: *BRO*   Eyes: *BLU*

POB: *Hobbs, NM*   SEX: (Male) Female

Clothing Description:

Address: *98567 Homestead Dr.*   City: *Bitterroot*   State: *MT*   Zip Code: *88088*

Contact Number: Home: *406-555-0145*   Cell: *406-555-9009*   WK: *406-555-0876*

Employer: *Best Sports Store*   Occupation: *Clerk*

Business Address: *3030 Texhoma Dr.*   City: *Bitterroot*   State: *OK*   Zip Code: *88088*

Business Phone: *719-555-0186*   Business Victim: Yes (No)

Information from an informant led to a knock and talk at suspect's home. Suspect consented to search of home. During the search I discovered the below listed items under a couch in the living room of the suspect who is a convicted felon. Approving Supervisor is class instructor.

Items placed into locker 43 at the Bitterroot Police Department

(Photos by: Michael Merson)

Item 1:

Make: Ruger Mini 14
Type: AR15
Caliber: 5.56
Serial number: 8790457RM (real Serial number intentionally not displayed)
Found under the couch next to Item 2.

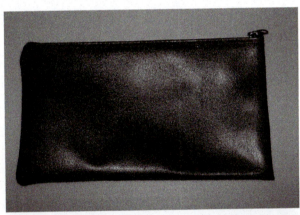

(Photos by: Michael Merson)

Item 2:

Make: Unknown
Type: Plastic
Description: Red in color 6″ × 10″ bag commonly used to transport currency found under the couch next to Item 1.

(Photo by: Michael Merson)

Item 3:

Make: U.S. Currency

Dollar amount: $1,000

Description: U.S. currency, 10 quantity of $100 dollar bills found inside of Item 2 with various serial numbers.

4. Complete a custody sheet for the individual listed below. Use the custody report form that can be found in the Appendix of this book to complete this exercise.

Case #: 14-098745   Title: *Assault in the First Degree 18-3-202*

Dispatch: *0940*   Arrival: *0950*   Cleared: *1145*

Date: *Today's Date*   Time: *0930*   Offense Location: *4300 N. Flathead Ave.*

(Suspect) / ~~Victim~~ / ~~Witness~~ / ~~Other~~:

Name: *Robert Michael Gray*

DOB: *10-24-68*   Race: *W*   HGT: *6'03"*   WGT: *220*   Hair: *BRO*   Eyes: *BRO*

POB: *Phoenix, AZ*   SEX: (Male) ~~Female~~

Clothing Description: *Black pants and a red shirt with a green dragon design that goes around it.*

Address: *34098 Fourth St.*   City: *Bitterroot*   State: *MT*   Zip Code: *88088*

Contact Number: Home: *406-555-0145*   Cell: *406-555-0156*   WK: *406-555-0902*

Employer: *West Side Auto Graphics*   Occupation: *Detailer*

Business Address: *4589 West 3rd St.*   City: *Bitterroot*   State: *MT*   Zip Code: *88088*

Business Phone: Business Victim: *Yes* (No)

Location of Custody: 4300 N. Flathead Ave. Bitterroot, MT 88088

Date of Custody: Today's Date

Time of Custody: 2200 or 10:00 PM

Zone: 5 Sector 8

Booking # 45678

Gray's Social Security Number: 987-65-4321

Scars/Marks/Tattoos: Large cross on his back

Gray was not armed nor resisted, and he does not have a nickname

Gray's point of contact for emergencies is his mother: Julia Terry Gray

Mothers Contact Information: 34098 Fourth St. Bitterroot, MT 88088

Mother's Home Phone Number: 406-555-0124

No injuries/illness: None

Frank County Jail Number   4390-909

Subject's Charges: Assault in the First Degree 18-3-202 or your states charge for felony assault.

Subject was held in custody

Mr. Gray was having a party and during the party he and another individual had a verbal argument that turned physical when Mr. Gray pushed the victim and then used a knife to stab the victim in the stomach. See case # 14-098745 for more information.

No Vehicle was involved

You are the arresting officer and the intake deputy is your instructor.

Agency: Bitterroot Police Department

15

CORRECTIONAL FORMS AND REPORTS

INTRODUCTION

This chapter is intended to acquaint the student with the various forms and procedures in the field of corrections. The good news is that the majority of the concepts in this textbook apply as directly to correctional operations as they apply to the patrol function. It is simply a matter of adjusting your skills to different sets of paperwork. Interestingly, in many sheriff's departments, jail officers are also certified patrol deputies. This makes the transition from one assignment to the other relatively smooth and operationally sound as members of the department are cross-training in both disciplines. Again, the real operational differences of correctional or patrol paperwork are minimal.

CORRECTIONAL INCIDENT REPORT

Probably the backbone of jail or prison written report forms is the incident report. The incident report is a written narrative that can be applied to a myriad of incidents. Some examples of when an incident report would be written are escape attempts, inmate disciplinary infractions, hunger strikes, inmate/staff injuries, discovery of contraband, visitor infractions, intelligence information, building maintenance concerns, damage to jail or prison property, and so on. The incident report form is the most common form that will be used in any correctional setting.

Incident reports serve a variety of purposes. They serve to document significant events (incidents) that need to be communicated to other correctional staff members. Most correctional facilities will require a completed incident report when any of the following events have occurred:

- Use of less-than-lethal devices to control inmates
- Discharge of a firearm or other weapon
- Use of force to control inmates
- Staff or inmate injury
- Inmate suicide or suicide attempt

Additionally, the incident report can be used to document any inmate disciplinary infraction. In effect, the incident report then mirrors the information commonly found in a law enforcement case report. Instead of the elements of a crime (as found in a law enforcement case report), the incident report would document the rule infraction violated. The same techniques and procedures for the narrative of the law enforcement case report apply to the correctional incident report.

The correctional incident report form normally contains a face sheet followed by a written narrative. Some incident report forms' face sheets are more detailed than others. Again, as in law enforcement case reports, there is no nationally recognized standard form. Each agency will personalize parts of their specific incident report form. Regardless of agency individuality, all incident report forms contain the same basic structure and information. The same concepts as the law enforcement written case report apply to the correctional incident report. Some of the major principles are:

- Use proper English. Be aware of sentence and paragraph structure.
- Be careful of punctuation and grammar.
- Keep it simple. Be aware of who the potential reader may be.
- Keep things in chronological order. You are telling a story, so start from the beginning and proceed on to the conclusion.
- Don't forget to include who, what, when, where, how, and why.
- Ask the question, "How did you know?" when interviewing victims, witnesses, or suspects. This will pay dividends in later courtroom testimony.
- Keep things in chronological order. Be thinking about how you would describe all of the activities that took place.
- Don't neglect your agency's requirements when dealing with issues such as format and style.
- Use clear and concise wording.
- Avoid abstract words.
- Keep things in the active voice.
- Use the first person singular.
- Keep things in the past tense.
- Use the involved persons' names. Don't get trapped into using "victim 1," "victim 2," and so on.

- Use the surnames (e.g., "Mr. and Mrs.") when referring to victims, witnesses, and suspects.
- Use factual statements; don't guess or use deductive statements.
- Be sure and include your observations.
- Use quotations sparingly.
- There are only two kinds of writers in this world: those who use too many commas, and those who don't use enough commas. Be aware of this dilemma and adjust your style as needed.
- Avoid run-on sentences.
- Don't use police jargon.
- Avoid abbreviations.
- Check for spelling and grammatical errors.

Best Practices: The documentation of an incident in a correctional facility is very important, as this report could be used later to charge an inmate for a criminal offense. Therefore, the incident report must be accurate and free of any grammar, spelling, or word use errors.

INMATE DISCIPLINARY FORM

For anyone working in a correctional facility, the inmate disciplinary form will probably be the second most common form used on a regular basis. Correctional facilities house inmates; some of them are not so nice. Disciplinary infractions are commonplace, and there are certain procedures and forms that must be completed when inmate infractions occur. There are several Supreme Court decisions that dictate what types of documentation must occur when imposing discipline on an inmate. The Court has also ruled that there are certain "due process" guarantees for all incarcerated individuals. Most of these Constitutional due process issues require extensive and precise documentation.

It is important to note that the inmate disciplinary process is an administrative process, not a judicial process. The purpose of this administrative process is to secure the good order of the institution. In other words, sometimes inmates need to be disciplined to maintain the security and control of the facility. For more severe inmate disciplinary infractions, criminal charges can also be filed. Thus an inmate could face a correctional disciplinary punishment as well as criminal prosecution for a single incident. This is not considered double jeopardy, as a disciplinary board sanction is an administrative process and a criminal prosecution is a judicial process.

In all correctional incidents resulting in a request for disciplinary action, documentation must include, but not be limited to, the following information:

Specific institutional rule violated

A formal statement of the charge

Any unusual inmate behavior

Any staff witness

An explanation of the event that includes:

People involved

Events that transpired

Time and location of the occurrence

Any physical evidence and its disposition

Any immediate action taken, including the use of force

Reporting staff member's signature and date and time of report

The correctional agency's policy and procedure manual will dictate specific guidelines regarding the proper format and structure of the inmate disciplinary infraction forms. Standardized forms will be used. The restriction of an incarcerated individual and the denial of certain privileges given to all inmates in the general population require specific due process guarantees and precise documentation. Inmates are typically very litigious individuals who will not hesitate to file legal actions against anyone, if they feel that their Constitutional rights have been violated. As in all aspects of the criminal justice system, take the time and do things in a professional manner.

THE PRE-SENTENCE INVESTIGATION REPORT

When an offender is found guilty or pleads guilty to an offense, the court of jurisdiction will usually have a pre-sentence investigation report (PSIR) completed by an officer of the court or a parole officer. The PSIR is the history of the offender that may be used by the judge in determining whether or not other factors influenced the offender during the commission of the crime. The judge may consider the factors listed in the PSIR and the recommendations by the parole officer completing the PSIR in his or her decision during the sentencing of the offender.

The PSIR will usually have some or all of the following information:

Age

Social information

Personal information

County of conviction

Evaluation of recommendation

Description of the current offense

Criminal history

Summary of all previous community placements and terminations/conclusions (probation, Intense Supervised Probation (ISP), treatment providers)

Victim impact statement

Initial needs assessment

Level of supervision inventory (drug addiction assessment, sex offender assessment)

Any other documents that may be needed in determining decision

Figure 15.1 is an example of a PSIR.

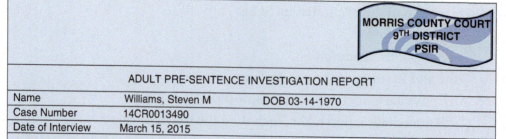

ADULT PRE-SENTENCE INVESTIGATION REPORT

Name	Williams, Steven M	DOB 03-14-1970
Case Number	14CR0013490	
Date of Interview	March 15, 2015	

Details of case:

According to the Mersonville Police Department report, on November 28, 2014, officers responded to Big Mike's Camping Emporium at 3333 N. Willow Dr. to investigate a reported theft. The investigation by the responding officers revealed that an employee observed Steven M. Williams select a Greenwich brand watch from the jewelry counter and then conceal it in his right coat pocket. Mr. Williams then was observed leaving Big Mike's Camping Emporium through the front entrance without paying for the Greenwich brand watch at the registers located near the front entrance. Mr. Williams was contacted by security officers employed by Big Mike's Camping Emporium who identified themselves and asked Mr. Williams to accompany them back to the store security office. Mr. Williams refused to go back inside the store and pushed one security officer to the ground and punched the other with a closed fist causing bodily injury. Mr. Williams was finally subdued with the help of other store employees who held him in the parking lot until the Mersonville Police Officers arrived and took him into custody.

Defendant's statement or comments:

"I was having a really bad time because I got fired at the car wash for showing up late. I had to walk home and after about an hour I had to use the bathroom so I walked into Big Mike's Camping Emporium. I used the bathroom and when I was leaving I stopped to look at some watches and I guess I put one in my pocket and forgot to pay for it. The security guys came outside and tried to manhandle me and it pissed me off. I tried to run and one guy fell down and the other one grabbed me by my neck and started to choke me so I punched him. I did not know I hit him that hard. I guess I broke the bone around his eye or something. I think they should have just asked me to go back inside!"

Disposition of co-defendants:

There are no co-defendants.

Circumstance of victim:

John Carter Jackson was injured during the confrontation with Mr. Williams and has lost time at work and has medical bills exceeding $10,000. Mr. Jackson currently experiences frequent headaches and now has a visible scar over his left eye from the surgery that was necessary to repair the damaged to the bones that were a result of being punched by Mr. Williams.

The Greenwich brand watch valued at $49.99 that Mr. Williams stole was returned to the Big Mike's Camping Emporium.

Prior criminal record:

The following sources were used to determine the defendant's criminal history: NCIC, CBI, Statewide Index, DMV records, and arrest records from the Mersonville Police Department. All entries occurred in Morris County unless otherwise noted.

- 03-08-1992, Case # 92-11908, Damage to Private Property, sentence 6 months' probation and restitution in the amount of $400.00.
- 02-15-1993, Case # 93-12983, Burglary, sentenced to 90 days and 6 months' probation.
- 03-13-1994, Case # T94-13023, DUI, Leaving the Scene of an Accident, and Failure to Report. Sentence 180 days and 1 year probation.
- 08-11-1995, Case # 95-34589, Menacing (F5) Sentence 90 days and 2 years' probation.
- 10-31-1998, Case # 98-54090, Second Degree Assault (F3) Sentence 180 days and 2 years' probation.
- 11-14-1999, Probation revoked for failure to comply with probation conditions.
- 11-14-1999, Case # 99-51067, Revocation of Probation on Case # 98-54090. Sentence 180 days, and 1 year probation.
- 06-27-2002, Case # 02-32457, Assault in the Third Degree (M3) case dismissed by DA.
- 08-26-2002, Case # 02-43870, Assault in the Second Degree (F3) sentence 2 years DOC.
- 12-21-2005, Case # T63049, Vehicular Homicide, DUI, Leaving the Scene of an Accident, and Failure to Report. Sentence 8 years DOC.
- 04-13-2014, Case # 14-23876, Theft (M3) case dismissed by DA.
- 05-13-2014, Case # 14-28098, Theft (M3) sentence to 180 days suspended with 2 year probation.

Figure 15.1 *Adult Pre-Sentence Investigation Report* (*continued on next page*)

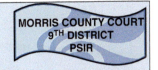

MORRIS COUNTY COURT
9TH DISTRICT
PSIR

Family background:

Mr. Williams is single and the only child of his divorced parents. Mr. Williams denies having any children of his own and does not have contact with either one of his parents. Mr. Williams was born in Sacramento, California but moved to Mersonville, Colorado after his parents divorced when he was 10 years of age.

Mr. Williams reports that his mother was an alcoholic and had many boyfriends when he was growing up. Mr. Williams also reports that his mother has never had a long term relationship nor employment and usually works as a bartender.

Mr. Williams believes that his father is still in California but he does not know for sure as the two have not spoken to each other since Mr. Williams was arrested for Vehicular Homicide in 2005.

Mr. Williams denies being in a current relationship but admits to having various girlfriends in the past. Mr. Williams believes that his longest relationship lasted 1 year from 1994 to 1995.

Education:

Mr. Williams attended Mersonville High School and dropped out of school in the 12th grade and did not graduate. While in DOC from 2006–2013 he completed his GED and received a Certification in Welding.

Employment:

Mr. Williams has worked sporadically since the age of 18 at various occupations but self identifies as a laborer and sometimes welder but most recently he has worked as a car detailer at a local car wash.

Mr. Williams's longest term of employment was 1 year from 1994 to 1995 at Dirt Work Landscaping Co. in Mersonville, Colorado.

Cost of care/financial condition:

Mr. Williams has no current source of income. He owns no significant property or possessions and does not own a vehicle. He relies on the bus system and walking for his transportation needs. He did not note any significant debt or collection agencies to which he owed money. He does not currently have any medical coverage.

Mental health issues:

Mr. Williams states he has never been diagnosed with a mental health issue. He has however admitted to being prescribed antidepressant medication while he was in DOC from 2006–2013.

Substance abuse:

Mr. Williams self identifies with being an alcoholic and admits that because of his drinking he has lost jobs, friends, and committed crimes while under the influence of alcohol. Mr. Williams stated that he started drinking alcohol occasionally at the age of 13 and that it progressed as he entered adulthood.

Mr. Williams admits to experimenting with marijuana around the age of 15 but was not a regular user of marijuana until it was made legal in Colorado recently. Mr. Williams admits that he smokes marijuana or drinks alcohol every day.

Mr. Williams denies using or experimenting with any other street or prescription drugs.

Mr. Williams believes the longest he has ever been sober was during his time in DOC from 2005–2013.

Additional information:

Mr. Williams believes that he can get a job working in landscaping with the spring and summer months approaching.

Mr. Williams believes his strengths are:

Hard working

Responsibility

Honesty

Mr. Williams does not have any long term friendships. He has never been associated with any gangs or gang activity.

Mr. Williams believes that probation can assist him by requiring sobriety which will lead to steady employment so that he can pay restitution back to the victim in his current case.

Figure 15.1   *Adult Pre-Sentence Investigation Report* (*continued on next page*)

MORRIS COUNTY COURT
9TH DISTRICT
PSIR

Recommendations:

Steven Williams is a 45-year-old male currently before the Court on a charge of Second Degree Assault (F3). This is his sixth felony conviction. Parties stipulated to community corrections. If he is not accepted at community corrections then, the sentence will be the Department of Corrections. He is currently in custody at the Morris County Jail awaiting sentencing.

According to his history he has served time in the Department of Corrections previously. He has an extensive criminal history and has served time in the Department of Corrections on two different occasions. He has violated probation previously as well. Mr. Williams is currently on probation on Case # 14-28098, Theft (M3).

Mr. Williams's current case involves an assault with bodily injury to another. Mr. Williams has been arrested for crimes of violence 4 previous times for situations involving assaults, menacing and once for vehicular homicide. Mr. Williams admits to punching the victim during the theft and is willing to pay financial restitution.

Mr. Williams was cooperative and forthcoming during the presentence interview. He expressed frustration over his inability to maintain a stable lifestyle. He believes that alcohol and marijuana abuse has played a significant role in his extensive criminal history. Mr. Williams acknowledges that he needs counseling to overcome his addictions, which he believes would help him to finally obtain a stable lifestyle.

I agree with Mr. Williams's assessment of his risks/needs. He requires structure and accountability and may not perform well without it. He requires outpatient substance abuse therapy as well as a stable and predictable environment. He also requires cognitive skills in order to assist with his thinking errors and life job courses to assist with employment. Additionally, a mental health evaluation would be helpful in treating any undiagnosed conditions. All of these interventions can be provided to the defendant in a community corrections setting.

Probation is not recommended for Mr. Williams as it would not provide the necessary structure, accountability, and monitoring he requires.

According to standardized assessment tools utilized by the Probation Department, Mr. Williams is a maximum risk to reoffend criminally. Chief areas of concern relate to antisocial cognitive/attitude/beliefs, antisocial personality pattern, employment/education, and substance abuse.

Based on the above report, I respectfully recommend that Mr. Williams be sentenced to community corrections for a period of time to be determined by the Court. If Mr. Williams is rejected from community corrections, it is recommended he be sentenced to the Department of Corrections due to the significant role in his extensive criminal history. Mr. Williams acknowledges that he needs counseling to overcome his addictions, which he believes would help him to finally obtain a stable lifestyle.

_____   Approved by: _____

Michael Smith
Probation Officer

Gary Warrens
Investigation Supervisor

Figure 15.1   *Adult Pre-Sentence Investigation Report*

Best Practices: Some PSIRs are completed with the help of the original police report. The case report may be helpful in completing the PSIR, but do not copy and paste it directly from the report into the PSIR without proofreading it for accuracy. The practice of copying and pasting can cause errors in the appropriate use of tenses.

THE *RIGHT* WAY TO *WRITE*

Correctional forms and reports are very similar to law enforcement documents. In fact, they often overlap. Consider a statutory crime, like an assault, that occurs in a correctional institution. The investigation and subsequent narrative report prepared by the correctional officer will mirror a report taken by a patrol officer. The only real difference in this scenario is that the offender could be additionally charged with an institutional disciplinary violation that will require additional documentation (i.e., the facility's disciplinary infraction form). The point here is that the same general principles describing law enforcement report writing apply to correctional officers. Although some of the correctional forms are unique, there is a great commonality in the preparation and completion of these documents.

This chapter's emphasis on writing style reinforces the need for effective writing skills in various criminal justice settings. The good news is that, despite different nomenclature and forms found in other areas of the criminal justice system (e.g., corrections, probation, and parole), the same general principles and techniques can be applied to these documents. In general, correctional writing should be the same as law enforcement writing: clear, purposeful, and concise. Regardless of the professional setting, good writing is good writing!

TIPS FOR CORRECTIONAL FORMS

- In most instances, correctional paperwork and forms will resemble law enforcement paperwork and forms.
- The same basic principles and writing style presented for law enforcement report writing in this textbook apply to correctional paperwork.
- Every correctional, probation, or parole agency will have some minor modifications regarding their specific paperwork. It is just the nature of the criminal justice system.
- Review and be familiar with your agency's policy and procedure manual and standard operating procedures regarding all professional written correspondence.
- Remember, anything written that involves someone under custodial/correctional care can be subpoenaed into a court of law.

SUMMARY

The profession of corrections is an integral component of the criminal justice system. It doesn't matter what aspect of corrections you participate in (prisons, jails, probation, parole). The basic structure and format of the paperwork involved entail extensive similarities with the paperwork generated by the law enforcement component of the criminal justice system. Put simply, the same principles apply to both components of the criminal justice system.

Correctional professionals are often the most overlooked and underappreciated criminal justice professionals. Many correctional officers work one of the nation's most dangerous and challenging beats. Ensuring security and order in an environment characterized by society's highest-risk criminals, correctional professionals are legally mandated to maintain their professional composure and accomplish their mission in a humane and safe manner.

The authors of this textbook would like to thank them all for their mastery of complex skills, their dedication, and their professionalism.

EXERCISES

In this exercise two inmates were involved in a verbal argument in the Crofton Correctional dining facility. The Crofton Correctional Facility Disciplinary/Report on the following pages contains many errors, and it is up to you to identify at least five of those errors. List the mistakes here:

1. _____

2. _____

3. _____

4. _____

5. _____

Crofton Correctional Facility
Disciplinary/Incident Report
Part I

Inmates Name (Last, First, Middle) Carter, David, Charles		Inmates Registered Number 190875	
Date of Incident 01-24-2015		Time of Incident 12:30	Location of Incident Dining Facility
Inmates assignment at time of incident Eating lunch			Housing Unit A1
Incident Verbal Alteration			
Prohibited Act Code (s)			

Brief Description of incident:

On 01-24-2015 at approximately 12:20 PM I, Officer Smith 1616C, was assigned to the dining facility to monitor inmates. It was during this time that I observed inmate David Carter (190709) walk over to inmate Gary Jackson (190875) who was eating alone at a table near the south wall. Once at the table Mr. Carter said something to Mr. Jackson and then using his right hand he slid Mr. Jackson's tray of the table onto the floor. Mr. Carter then yelled "what the fuck are you going to do about it?" at which time he clenched his fist an took a fighting stance across from Mr. Jackson while inviting him to fight by yelling "Come on, you wanted this, now is your chance!"

I along with other Officers ran over too Mr. Carter and upon reaching him I ordered him to turn around and cuff up. Mr. Carter did not comply with my order. After I told Mr. Carter that I was going too pepper spray him if he did not comply he looked at me, dropped his hands to his side, and than turned around and allowed me to cuff him.

Mr. Carter was taken to segregation an refuse to speak about the incident.

Mr. Jackson denied knowing why Mr. Carter was angry with him.
No further information.

Name of Employee Reporting Incident (Last, First, Middle) Smith, Michael Robert	Employee # 1616C
Name of Employee/Witness Reporting Incident (Last, First, Middle) Williams, Shawn, David	Employee or Inmate # 1890C
Date Incident Reported to Above Employee 01-24-2015	Time Incident Reported to Above Employee 12:30 PM

Crofton Correctional Facility
Disciplinary/Incident Report
Part II
Committee Action

Inmates Explanation to Committee Regarding Incident

Inmate Jackson has been telling people he was going to get me for a week now and I was tired of looking over my shoulder. I decided to give him his chance

The Committee did find that the inmate:

1.   _x_ Committed the Prohibited Act identified in Part I
2.   _____ Did not commit the Prohibited Act identified in Part I
3.   _____ Committed Prohibited Act Code (s) _____

The Committee

1.   _____ is referring this to the Division of Investigations for possible criminal charges.
2.   _x__ advised the inmate of its finding and of the right to file an appeal within 30 days.

The Committee decision was based on the following evidence:

Inmate Carter's admission to the incident as well as video surveillance from the dining facility.

Date Committee Made Decision 01-27-2015	Time Committee Made Decision 1:45 PM
Committee Chairman Frank Lincoln	Signature *Frank Lincoln*
Committee Member Wyatt Burns	Signature *Wyatt Burns*
Committee Member Samuel Donaldson	Signature *Samuel Donaldson*

Crofton Correctional Facility
Disciplinary/Incident Report
Part II
Investigation

Investigator Name (Last, First, Middle) *Carter, David, Charles*	Investigator/Employee *0349C*

Date Investigation Began *01-24-2015*	Time Investigation Began *12:30*

Inmate advised of Right to Remain Silent: You are advised of your right to remain silent at all stages of the discipline process. Your silence may be used to draw an adverse inference against you at any stage of the discipline process. Your silence alone may not be used to support a finding that you have committed a prohibited act.

Inmate advised of above right by: <u>*Lincoln, Frank, Michael*</u>   Inmate Initials: <u>*DCC*</u>

Inmate Statement

Inmate Carter stated that he was upset over Inmate Gary Jackson's comments an it finally reached a boiling point and he reacted in a way he should not have. Inmate Carter takes full responsibly and understands that this incident will become part of his permanent record.

Other Facts about the incident. Statements of other witnesses and possible evidence.

Inmate Gary Jackson denied that he made any comments or threatened Inmate Carter in any way. No other witness were found to collaborate either inmates accusations about what happened prior to Inmate Carter confronting Inmate Jackson in the dining facility.

Investigators Comments

The incident in the dining facility was definitely in regards to comments Inmate Carter acclaims Inmate Jackson had said previously. No evidence could be found to support Inmate Carter's accusations about Inmate Jackson's alleged comments.

Disciplinary Action Taken

Inmate Carter was paced into isolation following the incident for 24 hours. He was informed that the behavior in the dining facility would became part of his permanent record and that any similar future behavior could lead to new criminal charges.

Date and Time Investigation Completed	Date *01-24-2015*	Time *4:30 PM*

Printed Name and Signature of Investigator

Printed Name *Lincoln, Frank, Michael*	Signature *Frank Lincoln 0349C*	Title *DOC Investigator*

16

PUTTING IT ALL TOGETHER

LEARNING OBJECTIVES

- Understand the unique style, flow, and content of a law enforcement written report.
- Understand the various forms needed to complete a police report.
- Identify the information that needs to be collected for the report by following the crime scene checklist.
- Understand the dynamics involved in courtroom testimony.
- Demonstrate your acquired knowledge by completing the report for one of the most challenging incidents—a homicide case report!

INTRODUCTION

In this final chapter, courtroom testimony will be discussed. Additionally, a final case report exercise, involving an alleged homicide scenario, will be presented. Presentation of your case report in a court of law is the culmination of a phenomenal amount of police work. Most law enforcement officials do not look forward to appearances in court. Usually these appearances require extensive preparation, often occur on your time off, and frequently involve delays or postponements. As mentioned in prior chapters, your testimony in court may appear many months, or even years, after the incident has occurred. That being said, courtroom testimony is a fact of life in the duties of every law enforcement professional.

COURTROOM STRATEGY

The key to successful courtroom testimony is preparation. Your best source of reference for your testimony is your completed case report. Review your case report extensively prior to arrival in court—know your case! Prepare a list of key elements in your case. Be thinking about evidence; that is, the facts that prove your case. Review your state's revised statutes regarding the legal elements of the crime involved. Bring a copy of your case report with you to court. It is OK to highlight or mark specific parts of your case report for easy reference.

For most cases, especially cases involving major felonies, meet with the prosecutor prior to your testimony in court. Don't assume that he or she will know all of the facts of the case. Remember, you were the first officer on the scene and you know more about this case than anyone else. Make sure that the prosecutor knows all of the key elements of your testimony. Be sure and communicate to the prosecutor all of the strengths and weaknesses of this specific case. Anticipate tough or sensitive questions. Let the prosecutor know what your concerns about the case are and seek advice on how best to neutralize any weaknesses. Meeting with the prosecutor prior to your appearance in court is a perfectly acceptable legal practice.

Before court begins, familiarize yourself with the courtroom layout. This familiarization will allow you to walk confidently to the witness stand when called. Arrive at your court appearance early. Be sure to contact the prosecutor and let him/her know that you have arrived and that you are ready to present your testimony. Dress professionally. For males, this means a conservative business suit or duty uniform. A conservative blue or brown business suit works best. For females, the proper dress is business formal or your duty uniform. A conservative pantsuit or dress works best for most female officers. Do not wear excessive or flashy jewelry. For both sexes, minimize accessories, be well groomed, and look professional.

When waiting to be called to the witness stand, you will be typically be seated in the gallery in the courtroom. Be attentive. People (perhaps even jurors) will be watching your demeanor, especially if you are in uniform. Always be aware of your body language. Pay close attention to the court proceedings. Be aware of "hallway conversations." Many times, officers are talking freely to other officers or perhaps to the prosecutor in the hallway prior to their testimony. Don't say anything in the hallway that you would not want repeated on the witness stand. Always assume that people are listening in on your conversations.

Upon taking the witness stand, remember that all eyes in the courtroom are now focused on you. Know how to pronounce the names of the defendant and any other "player" in the case. Speak loudly and confidently. Always begin your remarks facing the questioner and then turn and face the jury when giving the bulk of your statements. Although this seems awkward at first, it is the proper courtroom etiquette when presenting your testimony. Make eye contact with the jurors. Always pause just a few seconds before answering any question. There are two reasons for this pause: first, it allows your counsel to object if it is an improper question, and second, it gives you a brief moment to collect your thoughts on the question.

Your court testimony will normally begin with what is termed "direct testimony." Direct testimony is when your counsel is asking the questions (typically the prosecutor). You will normally be asked open-ended questions (e.g., "Explain to the court what happened when you arrived at the scene."). This is your chance to present all of the evidence to support the criminal charge against the defendant. Your role is to present testimonial evidence to convince the fact finder (usually the jury) of the integrity and strength of the evidence and the appropriateness of the charge. Listen to all questions carefully and make sure you understand the question before you answer.

Once you have completed your direct testimony, it is time for the opposing counsel to question you. This phase is called "cross examination." Typically, the defense counsel will ask you closed-ended questions (e.g., requiring "yes" or "no" responses). The objective in cross examination is to attack your credibility or impeach your testimony in any way permissible by law. Always think carefully before you answer any question. If the question cannot be answered in one word, state that fact to the judge for ruling. Never guess or speculate when giving any response on the witness stand.

Upon completion of the cross-examination phase of your testimony, your counsel now shifts into redirect testimony, which often allows you to clarify any responses you may have given during the cross-examination phase. This is often referred to as "damage control." Your counsel will typically ask you open-ended questions at this point in your testimony. The focus here is explaining your cross-examination testimony a little further. Normally, you will be dismissed from the witness stand after completion of redirect testimony.

This short synopsis of courtroom testimony is in no way intended to be an all-inclusive listing of your strategies and performance techniques for testifying it court. Instead, it is intended to give you a brief overview of what to expect in a courtroom setting. Courtroom testimony, like so many other tasks in law enforcement, improves with experience. You will hone your courtroom skills as your career progresses. Always remember that, without a good case report, your chances of a successful prosecution are limited.

Best Practices: In Chapter 1, under the topic "Importance of the Case Report," you read "If it isn't written, it doesn't exist." On the day of court, when you're sitting in the witness box, these seven words will ring true as you're being questioned by the defense attorney about the information he or she has discovered to be missing from your report. Missing information, no matter how slight, could provide the defense the reasonable doubt they need for a not guilty verdict by the jury.

THE *RIGHT* WAY TO *WRITE*

The conclusion of the textbook contains some tips on courtroom testimony, a crime scene checklist, and a practical exercise. Regarding the right way to write, this is where it all comes to a conclusion. Apply all of the concepts discussed in the previous chapters to the homicide scenario. Critique both yourself and other students. Compare your writing style and format to those used by others in the class. Practice and feedback are the best learning tools to hone your writing skills in a professional manner. Good luck!

TIPS FOR SUCCESSFUL COURTROOM TESTIMONY

- Tell the truth.
  - Nothing is worth giving perjured testimony in court. Lying in court will ruin your career!
  - Avoid the temptation of embellishing the truth; let facts stand on their own
  - Always testify HONESTLY!

- Don't guess or speculate. If you don't know the answer, tell them you don't know.
- Speak loud and clear.

- Listen to the question, formulate an answer, and answer only that question.
- Don't look around the courtroom for assistance. Be confident and in control of your testimony.
- Be courteous and polite. Use "yes sir" and "no sir." Use "Mr." and "Mrs."
- Appear and act professionally. You never know who is watching you.
- Don't memorize your testimony. It looks too rehearsed. Know the facts, but use your own words and adjust to the questioning.
- Sit up straight and keep your hands on your lap or on the witness stand table.
- If you make a mistake, acknowledge it. Don't get caught trying to cover up a mistake. It makes it look like you are untruthful.
- Avoid looking at your attorney or around the courtroom when testifying. This looks like you are asking for help.

SUMMARY

Over the course of their careers, all law enforcement officials, regardless of rank, are going to find themselves testifying in court; it is simply the nature of the job. Courtroom testimony can be a challenging aspect of your career as a law enforcement official. The courtroom is a formal, structured type of environment. It can be intimidating, especially if it is your first appearance. Law enforcement officer testimony is one of the most important elements of any criminal prosecution. Prior preparation of your courtroom testimony is the key to a successful prosecution. Law enforcement officials need to feel confident and prepared when they are subpoenaed into a court of law.

Remember that everything you do in your official capacity as a law enforcement officer may result in being called into court. What you want to communicate on the witness stand is that you are just doing your job, and that job entails assisting the criminal justice system with truthful and accurate information. You are there to communicate your actions and observations regarding a violation of the law. While on the witness stand, you will be in the spotlight. Additionally, you will be cross examined by the opposing counsel. Be honest, neutral, and above all be yourself!

EXERCISES

1. To finish up this textbook, a hypothetical homicide case is presented. The rationale for a homicide exercise is simple. A homicide practice scenario is appropriate because these types of major cases utilize practice on numerous types of writing techniques, procedures, and forms presented throughout this textbook. Homicide cases are high-profile cases, which generally entail lots of public media attention and scrutiny from both the public and your superior officers. Do the little things right, and the big things will follow. This final exercise is a chance to prove your understanding of all of "the little things" presented in this textbook.

Prior to reviewing the homicide scenario, review the following major case checklist for tips. Although investigating a homicide may seem a long way down the road in your law enforcement career, even a rookie police officer can stumble into a homicide case. Your actions as the first officer on the scene are critical in a successful resolution to a major incident.

This checklist is given as a general guideline to help you gather notes for your case report. This crime scene checklist presents some of the basic principles of the first officer at a crime scene. Additionally, many agencies issue their officers a crime scene log or a crime scene guide to be followed when arriving at a major crime scene. These documents are great references to help you process the crime scene in a methodical fashion.

TIPS FOR PROCESSING A MAJOR CRIME SCENE: A CHECKLIST

(There is an assumption that crime scene technicians will be responding to the scene for photography, evidence collection, etc.)

- Arrival
  - Do you need a search warrant?
  - Render aid to the injured, if it is necessary.
  - Make sure the scene is safe.
  - Set up a perimeter.
  - Keep critical witnesses separate.
  - Obtain license numbers of vehicles in the area.

- Notifications
  - Notify supervisor(s).
  - Who are the detectives?
  - Who are the crime scene examiners?
  - Who else is assigned?
  - Obtain a case number.

- The crime scene
  - Is the scene safe?
  - Watch where you walk and what you touch.
    - Try to keep contamination to a minimum.
    - If you have to move an object, note this in your notepad.
  - Is the crime scene perimeter defined and secured?
  - Note any transient evidence (e.g., cigarette smells, footprints in the snow, etc.)

- Victim/Witnesses/Suspect
  - Are they separated and controlled?
  - Who is assigned to interview them?
  - Do you need to arrange transportation to the police station?
  - Will you be assigned any follow-up interviews?
  - Is a neighborhood canvass necessary?

- Notating critical times in your notepad
  - When did you arrive on scene?
  - When did you notify your supervisor?
    - When did he/she arrive/depart?
  - When did other officers, medical staff, public information officers, or other key individuals arrive?
  - When did you contact victim(s), witness(es), suspect(s), and so on?

- Miscellaneous notes
  - Make sure you have the exact location/address of the crime scene, all victims, witnesses, suspects, and so on.
    - Copy this information from the individual's photo ID and ask if "this information is currently correct?"
  - If you are the first officer on the scene, note the time when you briefed your superior and the time that this individual assumed command of the scene.
  - Note any spontaneous or incriminating statements of the suspect(s).

- Leaving the crime scene
  - Try to minimize movement of objects. Leave the scene in some semblance of order.
  - Turn off all unnecessary lights.
  - Lock all windows and doors.
  - Remove all animals from the scene.
  - Dispose or refrigerate perishable items.
  - If returning to the scene is an option, place evidence tape on the doors and/or ensure an officer is assigned to protect the scene from contamination.

Keep in mind that these are just some generalized items to consider if you are the first officer on the scene of a major crime. Successful homicide investigations rely heavily upon the initial actions taken by the first officer on the scene. Initially, anything and everything should be considered as evidence. Your focus should be on securing the scene and protecting evidentiary items before they can be altered, destroyed, or misplaced. All evidence must be noted, preserved, and brought to the attention of the detectives assigned to the crime scene. Remember, as the first officer on the scene, you know this scene better than anybody else. Take your time and be professional!

Now on to your last scenario!

In this exercise, you will watch a video involving a homicide (**911 Hang-up**). Then you must complete your notes and the correct report forms. Use the interview sheets, face sheet/cover sheet, and supplement/continuation report forms that can be found in the Appendix of this book to complete this exercise.

Additional Information:

- Case Number: 14-28342
- Zone: 4
- Sector: 2
- Date: Your current date
- Time: The time announced in the video

Information for Johnson:

David William Johnson

Home Phone Number: 719-555-0909

Cell Phone Number: 719-555-0945

Work Phone Number: 719-555-0176

Place of Employment: J&B Automotive

     Address: 3030 North Park Rd.

     Mersonville, CO 88088

Occupation: Mechanic

Social Security Number: 333-55-9999

Information for Benson

Wendy Samantha Benson

Home Phone Number: 719-555-0999

Cell Phone Number: 719-555-0178

Work Phone Number: 719-555-0188

Place of Employment: Wendy's Boutique

     Address: 4132 East Beech St.

     Mersonville, CO 88088

Occupation: Hair Stylist

Social Security Number: 111-22-8888

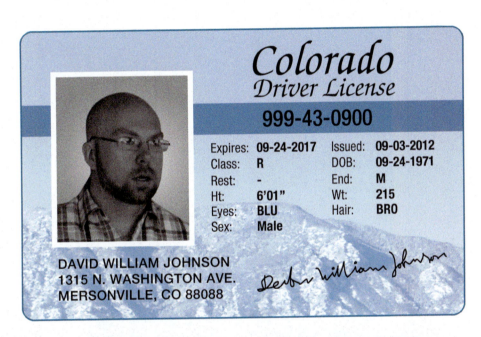

Colorado *Driver License*

999-43-0900

Expires:	09-24-2017	Issued:	09-03-2012
Class:	R	DOB:	09-24-1971
Rest:	-	End:	M
Ht:	6'01"	Wt:	215
Eyes:	BLU	Hair:	BRO
Sex:	Male		

DAVID WILLIAM JOHNSON
1315 N. WASHINGTON AVE.
MERSONVILLE, CO 88088

Colorado *Driver License*

888-09-4444

Expires:	08-23-2019	Issued:	08-23-2013
Class:	R	DOB:	06-18-1974
Rest:	None	End:	N
Ht:	5'03"	Wt:	120
Eyes:	BLU	Hair:	BRO
Sex:	Female		

WENDY SAMANTHA BENSON
1313 N. WASHINGTON AVE.
MERSONVILLE, CO 88088

Appendix

SAMPLE FORMS

Case #:   Title:

Dispatch: Arrival: Cleared:

Date: Time: Offense Location:

Suspect/ Victim/Witness/Other:

Name:

DOB: Race: HGT: WGT: Hair: Eyes:

POB: SEX: Male   Female

Clothing Description:

Address: City: State: Zip Code:

Contact Number: Home: Cell: WK:

Employer: Occupation:

Business Address: City: State: Zip Code:

Business Phone: Business Victim: Yes   No

MERSONVILLE POLICE DEPARTMENT COVER SHEET

Offense ☐	Supplement ☐		Other ☐	Case Number

Offense Title	State/City Statute Number	Date of this Report

Zone/Sector	Date and time Reported				Date and Approximate Time of Occurrence			
	Month	Day	Year	Time	Month	Day	Year	Time

Victim's Name Last, First, Middle	Date of Birth	Age	Sex	Height	Weight	Build	Hair	Eyes	Race

Residential Address	City	State	Zip Code	Home Phone	Cell Phone

Business Address	City	State	Zip Code	Business Phone	Occupation

Location of Offense	City	State	Zip Code

If a business is the victim complete the information below

Name of Business	Business Address	City	State	Zip Code	Business Phone

Codes RP = Reporting Party AV = Additional Victim W = Witness LO = Law Enforcement Officer A = Arrestee S = Suspect O = Other

Code	Name: Last, First, Middle	Date of Birth	Age	Sex	Height	Weight	Build	Hair	Eyes	Race

Residential Address	City	State	Zip Code	Home Phone	Cell Phone

Business Address	City	State	Zip Code	Business Phone	Occupation

Clothing Description	Alias

Identifying Marks	Summons Number

Narrative

Report Completed by:	Signature:	
		Page of Pages

Report Completed by:	Signature:

Mersonville Police Department Supplement Report

Offense Title	State/City Statute	Date of this Report	Case Number

Codes RP=Reporting Party AV= Additional Victim W=Witness LO= Law Enforcement Officer A=Arrestee S=Suspect O=Other

Code	Name: Last, First, Middle	Date of Birth	Age	Sex	Height	Weight	Build	Hair	Eyes	Race

Residential Address	City	State	Zip Code	Home Phone	Cell Phone

Business Address	City	State	Zip Code	Home Phone	Occupation

Clothing Description	Alias
Identifying Marks	Summons Number

Narrative

Report Completed by:	Signature:	
		Page of Pages
Report Reviewed by:		Signature:

Mersonville Property Supplement

Offense Title	State/City Statute	Date of this Report	Case Number

Victim's Name: Last, First, Middle	Date of Birth	Age	Sex	Height	Weight	Build	Hair	Eyes	Race

Residential Address	City	State	Zip Code	Home Phone	Cell Phone

Suspect's Name: Last, First, Middle	Date of Birth	Age	Sex	Height	Weight	Build	Hair	Eyes	Race

Residential Address	City	State	Zip Code	Home Phone	Cell Phone

Vehicle Property Information:

Stolen _____ Victim_____ Suspect_____ Local Recovery_____ Outside Recovery_____ Owner Notified_____

Vehicle Status:

Returned to Owner_____ Impounded_____ Placed into Evidence_____ Towed by: _____

Vehicle Year	Vehicle Color	Vehicle Make	Vehicle Model	Vehicle Style

License Plate Number	License Plate Type	License Plate Year	License Plate State	License Plate Color

Vehicle Identification Number	Insured by:

Vehicle Owner's Name: Last, First, Middle	Owner Notified of Recovery Yes_____ No_____ Date:_____

Vehicle Owner's Residential Address	City	State	Zip Code	Home Phone	Cell Phone

Pick-up Issued into NCIC for Above Vehicle Yes_____ No_____	Pick-up Cancelled in NCIC for Above Vehicle Yes_____ No_____

Firearm Property Information:

Stolen _____ Victim_____ Suspect_____ Local Recovery_____ Outside Recovery_____ Owner Notified_____

Firearm Status:

Returned to Owner_____ Placed into Evidence_____

Firearm Make	Firearm Model	Firearm Caliber	Firearm Serial Number	Firearm Color

Pick-up Issued into NCIC for Above Firearm Yes_____ No_____	Pick-up Cancelled in NCIC for Above Firearm Yes_____ No_____

Other Property Information

Stolen _____ Victim_____ Suspect_____ Local Recovery_____ Outside Recovery_____ Owner Notified_____

Property Status

Returned to Owner_____ Impounded_____ Placed into Evidence_____ Towed by: _____

Pick-up Issued into NCIC for Above Other Property Yes_____ No_____	Pick-up Cancelled in NCIC for Above Other Property Yes_____ No_____

Item #	Quantity #	Brand	Model	Serial #	Damaged Yes_____ No_____	Value
Description						

Item #	Quantity #	Brand	Model	Serial #	Damaged Yes_____ No_____	Value
Description						

Item #	Quantity #	Brand	Model	Serial #	Damaged Yes_____ No_____	Value
Description						

Any other Description Not Covered Above Vehicle_____ Firearm_____ Other property_____	Total Loss of All Property Listed:

Officer Completing Property Report and ID #	Supervisor Name and ID#	Page of Pages

MERSONVILLE DOMESTIC VIOLENCE REPORT

Summons Number 9002340

The People of the State vs.

Case Number _____

Defendant's Name: Last, First, Middle	Date of Birth	Age	Sex	Height	Weight	Build	Hair	Eyes	Race

Residential Address	City	State	Zip Code	Home Phone	Cell Phone

Business Address	City	State	Zip Code	Business Phone	Occupation

Location of Offense		City	State	Zip Code

Charge #1	Statute Number	Title

Description   Misdemeanor_____   Felony_____

Charge #2	Statute Number	Title

Description   Misdemeanor_____   Felony_____

Charge #3	Statute Number	Title

Description   Misdemeanor_____   Felony_____

Location of Custody	City	State	Zip Code

Custody Date	Custody Time	Did Suspect Resist Arrest? Yes____ No____

Defendant Weapon Use

Weapon Used _____   No Weapon Used _____   Weapon Displayed but Not Used ____

Assault With Weapon ____   Edged Weapon used _____   Firearm Used _____

Blunt Object Used _____   Description of Other Weapon Used_____

Defendant Drugs or Alcohol Use

Illegal Street Drugs Used or Suspected ____   Prescription Drug Used or Suspected _____

Alcohol Used _____   Other Unknown Substance Suspected____

Victim's Name: Last, First, Middle	Date of Birth	Age	Sex	Height	Weight	Build	Hair	Eyes	Race

Residential Address	City	State	Zip Code	Home Phone	Cell Phone

Business Address	City	State	Zip Code	Business Phone	Occupation

Victim also Defendant on Cross Complaint   Summons Number
          Yes____ No____   _____

THE UNDERSIGNED HAS PROBABLE CAUSE TO BELIEVE THAT THE DEFENDANT COMMITTED THE OFFESE(S) AGAINST THE PEACE AND DIGNITY OF THE PEOPLE OF THE STATE

Officer _____ID#_____Signature_____

Officer _____ID#_____Signature_____

Served By: Officer _____ ID#_____Signature_____

PROBABLE CAUSE AFFIDAVIT

_____

_____

_____

_____

_____

_____

_____

_____

_____

_____

_____

_____

_____

_____

_____

_____

_____

_____

_____

_____

_____

_____

_____

_____

_____

_____

_____

_____

_____

_____

UNDER PENALTY OF PERJURY, I AFFIRM THAT ALL THE INFORMATION CONTAINED UPON THIS DOCUMENT IS TRUE
AND CORRECT TO THE BEST OF MY KNOWLEDGE.

AFFIANT _____   PRINT NAME _____

On this date, The Affiant signed this Affidavit and swore to its truth

_____   _____   _____

Date   Notary Public Name   My Commission Expires

MERSONVILLE DOMESTIC VIOLENCE REPORT

Summons Number 9002340

Information on Victim

Case Number _____

Victim's Name: Last, First, Middle	Date of Birth	Age	Sex	Height	Weight	Build	Hair	Eyes	Race

Residential Address	City	State	Zip Code	Home Phone	Cell Phone

Business Address	City	State	Zip Code	Business Phone	Occupation

Victim also Defendant on Cross Complaint   Summons Number

Yes____   No____   _____

Children Present

Child Name	DOB	Address (If different from victim)	Did Child Witness Incident ____Yes ____No
Child Name	DOB	Address (If different from victim)	Did Child Witness Incident ____Yes ____No
Child Name	DOB	Address (If different from victim)	Did Child Witness Incident ____Yes ____No

Witness Information

Witness Name	DOB	Address	Home Phone	Other Phone
Witness Name	DOB	Address	Home Phone	Other Phone

Victim and Defendant Status

Married ____   Cohabitants ____   Separated/Divorced ____   Dating not Living Together ____

Active Restraining Order

____ Mandatory (72 hour)   ____ Temporary   ____ Permanent Case Number _____

Who Called?

____ Victim   ____ Family Member   ____ Neighbor   ____ Suspect   ____ Other ____

Victim Weapon Use

Weapon Used ____   No Weapon Used ____   Weapon Displayed but Not Used ____

Assault With Weapon ____   Edged Weapon used ____   Firearm Used ____   Blunt Object Used ____

Description of Other Weapon Used _____

Victim Drugs or Alcohol Use

Illegal Street Drugs Used or Suspected ____   Prescription Drug Used or Suspected ____

Alcohol Used ____   Other Unknown Substance Suspected ____

Medical Attention

Refused ____   Medical on Scene ____   Victim Hospitalized ____   Defendant Hospitalized ____

Victim Questions

Has the suspect ever done this before? _____ If yes, when? _____

Any previous violence with another person? ____ If yes, who? _____

Has suspect made threats? ____ If yes, what and to whom? _____

Were all the injuries caused by the suspect? ____ If not, by whom? _____

The above listed victim has requested that he/she be notified of the pending release of the defendant by Morris County Jail Authorities.

Victim Signature_____   Victim Notified by: _____   Date:_____

Victim Statement:_____
_____
_____
_____
_____
_____
_____

Victim Name (Print) _____   Victim Signature _____

AUTHORIZATION TO RELEASE MEDICAL RECORDS TO DISTRICT ATTORNEY AND LAW ENFORCEMENT

Patient/Victim's Name: _____

Patient/Victim's DOB: _____

Guardian's Name (If patient/victim is a minor) _____

Reports Relevant to Case Number _____

Any medical records relating to diagnosis or treatment of physical trauma associated with a crime of domestic violence, committed upon patient on _____ (MM/DD/YYYY).

I authorize all physicians and any other medical personnel to furnish copies of the reports indicated above to prosecutors or support staff of the district attorney's office. I further authorize said medical personnel to discuss all observations and perceptions arising from their contact with the above patient that might promote understanding of the mentioned crime(s).

In authorizing this disclosure, I am aware that the records and information released to the district attorney's office will be used in a criminal prosecution, and by the court rule, must be available by the district attorney to the accused person.

Patient Signature_____ Date_____ (MM/DD/YYYY)

Medical Response Company _____

Medical Response Report Number _____

Fire Response Engine/Unit Number _____

Treating Medical Facility _____

Treating Paramedic/EMT_____

Treating Paramedic/EMT_____

Doctor Treating Patient_____

MORRIS COUNTY DISTRICT ATTORNEY'S OFFICE PHYSICIAN'S STATEMENT

The Colorado Revised Statutes define "Serious Bodily Injury" as follows:

"*Serious Bodily Injury means injury which either at the time of the actual injury or at a later time, involves a substantial risk of death, a substantial risk of serious permanent disfigurement, a substantial risk of a protracted loss or impairment of the function of any part or organ of the body, or breaks, fractures, or burns of the second or third degree.*"

I, Dr. _____ (print), having read the definition of "Serious Bodily Injury" do state that the injuries of
_____ (patient's name), fit within the definition, and the patient did suffer Serious Bodily
Injury. The patient's diagnosis is:

_____
_____
_____
_____
_____
_____

These injuries involved (check as many as applicable):

_____a substantial risk of death

_____a substantial risk of serious permanent disfigurement

_____a substantial risk of protracted los or impairment of the function of any part or organ of the body,
specifically, _____

_____a break or fracture

_____a burn of the _____second or _____third degree

My reason for this diagnosis is:_____
_____
_____

Address: _____
Phone: _____
Physician Signature: _____
Officer: _____

VICTIM OF DOMESTIC VIOLENCE RIGHTS

IMPORTANT! VICTIM NOTICE

THE PEOPLE OF THE STATE V. _____

- You received this notice because you have been identified as a victim of a Domestic Violence Crime.
- You have the right to participate in this process.
- You have the right to speak to the judge and a Deputy District Attorney about bond/bail, plea offers, and sentencing.

> If you do not wish to appear in court, the District Attorney will speak on your behalf.
> If you do not appear, the District Attorney may have to proceed without your information.

☐ In cases involving misdemeanor charges:

- It is extremely important that you appear at the District Attorney's Victim Advocate Office at 3030 Pembrook Dr. Room 13 at 9:00 AM on _____ (MM/DD/YYYY). The District Attorney's Victim advocate needs to speak with you before the defendant appears in court.
- Once arrested, the Defendant will appear in court the following business day at 1:00 PM. You are encouraged to appear in court at that time.

> At that time the Court will: *advise the Defendant of his/her rights
> *advise the Defendant of the Mandatory Protection Order
> *Set bond or bail
> *Sentence the Defendant if a plea agreement is reached
> *Set a future court date if needed

> At that time the District Attorney will:
> *Meet with you to discuss the case
> *Request an appropriate amount of bail or bond
> *Meet with the Defendant to discuss the charges
> *Make a plea offer to the Defendant if applicable

> If you are unable to appear in person, it is very important you call 555-0199 and speak to the District Attorney's Victim Advocate.

☐ For cases involving felony charges call 555-0198 to obtain information about court appearances.

☐ For cases involving juvenile offenders call 555-0197 to obtain information about court appearances.

If the District Attorney's Office does not hear from you, a NO CONTACT ORDER, against the offender will be requested.

If the Defendant is released from jail on a weekend or holiday, you may pick up your copy of the Mandatory Protection Order at the Morris County Jail any time before the Defendant's first appearance.

To file a civil protection order, contact the office of Victims' of Domestic Violence at 555-0188

If you feel you are in danger call 911.

NCIC WARRANT FOR ARREST PICK-UP SHEET

FELONY ☐	MISDEMEANOR ☐		PETTY OFFENSE ☐
DATE WARRANT ISSUED	TIME WARRANT ISSUED		CASE #
AGENCY	OFFICER/DEPUTY		BADGE #

WANTED PERSON INFORMATION   MALE ☐   FEMALE ☐

NAME (LAST)	FIRST	MIDDLE		SUFFIX
DOB MM/DD/YYYY	BUILD	SKIN TONE		
ALIAS	SCARS/MARKS	TATTOOS		
DRIVER LICENSE STATE	DRIVER LICENSE #	SOCIAL SECURITY #		

HEIGHT	WEIGHT	HAIR	EYES	RACE

LAST KNOWN ADDRESS

CITY	STATE	ZIP CODE

LAST KNOWN BUSINESS ADDRESS

CITY	STATE	ZIP CODE
BUSINESS NAME	BUSINESS PHONE	
CRIME	CITY/STATE STATUTE	
CRIME	CITY/STATE STATUTE	

CRIME OF VIOLENCE   YES ☐   NO ☐   HOMICIDE ☐   ASSAULT ☐

FIREARM USED ☐   EDGED WEAPON USED ☐   OTHER WEAPON USED ☐

ADDITIONAL INFORMATION

DATE ENTERED INTO NCIC MM/DD/YYYY	TIME	BY:	ID #
DATE ENTERED INTO NCIC MM/DD/YYYY	TIME	BY:	ID #

STOLEN VEHICLE PICK-UP FORM FOR NCIC DATA ENTRY

CASE NUMBER	AGENCY	DATE OF REPORT

VEHICLE YEAR	VEHICLE MAKE	VEHICLE MODEL	VEHICLE COLOR

VEHICLE IDENTIFICATION NUMBER	VEHICLE TYPE	DAMAGED

LICENSE STATE	LICENSE NUMBER	LICENSE YEAR

ANY OTHER IDENTIFIABLE MARKS/DAMAGE/CUSTOM PAINT/AFTER MARKET ITEMS ON PROPERTY

OWNER NAME (LAST)	(FIRST)	(MIDDLE)

OWNER ADDRESS:	CITY	STATE	ZIP CODE

OWNER HOME PHONE	OWNER WORK PHONE	OWNER OTHER PHONE

ADDRESS STOLEN FROM	CITY	STATE	ZIP CODE

DATE STOLEN	DATE RECOVERED	OWNER NOTIFIED YES ☐ NO ☐	OWNER NOTIFIED BY:

TIME STOLEN	TIME RECOVERED	DATE OWNER NOTIFIED	TIME OWNER NOTIFIED

LOCATION WHERE RECOVERED	TOWED BY:	TOWED TO:

ARREST MADE: YES ☐ NO ☐	NAME OF PERSON ARRESTED

USED IN ANOTHER CRIME YES ☐ NO ☐	LOCATION	CRIME COMMITTED

KEPT AS EVIDENCE YES ☐ NO ☐	INSURED BY:

ADDITIONAL INFORMATION

DATE ENTERED INTO NCIC MM/DD/YYYY	TIME	BY:	ID #
DATE ENTERED INTO NCIC MM/DD/YYYY	TIME	BY:	ID #

Property/Evidence Report

Bitterroot Police Department Property/Evidence Report		Criminal Case Number
Property Evidence Number		Traffic Crash Number
Storage Location		Summons Number
Officer Placing Evidence:		
☐ Evidence ☐ Personal Property ☐ Found Property		
Date Placed Into Evidence MM/DD/YYYY		
Time Placed Into Evidence		
Address Location Recovered From		

Victim (Last, First, Middle)	Address (City, State, Zip Code)	Contact Phone
Victim (Last, First, Middle)	Address (City, State, Zip Code)	Contact Phone

#	Suspect (Last, First, Middle)	DOB	Address (City, State, Zip Code)	Offense

Item #	Quantity	Linked to Suspect #	Article Description (Make, Model, Serial #, Vin#)	*Property Technician Use Only*

Approving Supervisor	Locker Number :	By Officer:

Date Received	*Technician Receiving Items*	*Locker Number*	Page __ of __ Pages

EVIDENCE/PROPERTY TAG			
CASE #	ITEM #	DATE	TIME COLLECTED
Description			
Address or location where item was collected from			
Evidence ☐	Found/Other Property ☐		Placed for Destruction ☐
Victim Name			Suspect Name
Owner Name	Owner Address		Owner Contact Number
Agency	Officer/Deputy		Badge #

EVIDENCE/PROPERTY BAG

CASE #	ITEM #	DATE	TIME COLLECTED

Description:
_____
_____
_____
_____
_____
_____
_____
_____
_____
_____
_____
_____
_____
_____
_____
_____
_____
_____
_____
_____
_____
_____

Address or location where item was collected from

Evidence ☐	Found/Other Property ☐	Placed for Destruction ☐
Victim Name		Suspect Name
Owner Name	Owner Address	Owner Contact Number
Agency	Officer/Deputy	Badge #

☐ Adult ☐ Juvenile	Agency	**Custody Report**		Agency Case Number		
Custody Date	Custody Time	Custody Location		Zone	Sector	Booking Number

Subjects Name (Last)	(Middle)	(First)	DOB MM-DD-YYYY	Age

Address	(City)	(State)	Zip Code	Home Phone

Employer Name	Address	(City)	(State)	(Work Phone)	Zip Code	Cell Phone

Place of Birth City/State	Race	Sex	Height	Weight	Hair	Eyes	SSN

Scars/Marks/Tattoos

Subject Resisted ☐ Yes ☐ No	Subject Armed ☐ Yes ☐ No	Alias/Nickname ☐ Yes ☐ No If yes, Alias or nickname

CODES: A = Accomplice S = Spouse P = Parent G = Guardian O = Other

Code	Name (Last, First, Middle)	Address	Home Phone	Other Phone
Code	Name (Last, First, Middle)	Address	Home Phone	Other Phone

Injury/Illness None	Treated ☐ Yes ☐ No	Where Treated:	Date and Time Treated	Treated By:

☐ Injury Result of Subject Resisting During Arrest ☐ Injured Prior to Law Enforcement Contact ☐ Injured While in Custody

Frank County Jail Number	State or City Statute Number	Title of Offense	Warrant Number	Summons Number

Disposition ☐ Held in Custody ☐ No Formal Charge ☐ Released on Bond ☐ Charges Dropped by Police
☐ Released on Own Recognizance ☐ Turned over to Another Agency ☐ Deceased

Narrative

Vehicle Year	Vehicle Make	Model	Body Style	Vehicle Color	License Number	State	Location of Vehicle

Arresting Officer	ID #	Arresting Officer	ID #
Frank County Intake Deputy			ID #

State Department of Revenue
Traffic Accident Report

☐ Amended/ Supplement ☐ Under 1,000 ☐ Private Property ☐ Counter Report | Page __ of __

DOT CODE	DOR CODE	☐ Interstate HWY HWY Number ___ ___ ___ ☐ State HWY MILE Point ___ ___ ___.___ ___ ☐ City State County Road	Case Number

Date of Accident	City	State	Agency	County	County #

Time (24 Hour)	Officer Number	Officer Name	Officer Signature	Zone Sector/Detail

Date of This Report	Agency Code	Number Killed	Number Injured

Location Street, Road, Route _____ Miles _____ Feet ☐ North ☐ South ☐ East ☐ West of:
☐ At _____
Latitude _____   Longitude _____ _____ _____

Investigated at Scene ☐ Yes ☐ No	Total Vehicles	District Number	Bridge Related ☐ Yes ☐ No	Public Property or Employee ☐ Yes ☐ No	Railroad Crossing ☐ Yes ☐ No	Const. Zone ☐ Yes ☐ No	HWY Interchange ☐ Yes ☐ No	Photos ☐ Yes ☐ No

Vehicle 1 or _____	☐ Vehicle ☐ Parked ☐ Bicycle ☐ Pedestrian ☐ Non-Vehicle ☐ Non-Contact Vehicle	Vehicle 2 or _____	☐ Vehicle ☐ Parked ☐ Bicycle ☐ Pedestrian ☐ Non-Vehicle ☐ Non-Contact Vehicle

Last Name	First Name	MI	Last Name	First Name	MI

Street Address	Home Phone	Street Address	Home Phone

City	State	Zip	Other Phone	City	State	Zip	Other Phone

Driver License Number	CDL	State	Sex	DOB	Driver License Number	CDL	State	Sex	DOB

Primary Violation
☐ DUI | Primary Violation
☐ DUI

Violation Code	Citation Number	Common Code	Violation Code	Citation Number	Common Code

Year	Make	Model	Body Type	Year	Make	Model	Body Type

License Plate Number	State or County	Color	License Plate Number	State or County	Color

Vehicle Identification Number	Vehicle Identification Number

Vehicle Owner Last Name ☐ Same	First	MI	Vehicle Owner Last Name ☐ Same	First	MI

Address	City	State	Zip	Address	City	State	Zip

Towed due to damage ☐ By:
To: | Towed due to damage ☐ By:
To:

Slight = 1 Moderate = 2 Severe = 3 / Shade in areas of Damage | Slight = 1 Moderate = 2 Severe = 3 / Shade in areas of Damage

Insurance Company ☐ None ☐ No Proof Policy #	Exp. Date	Insurance Company ☐ None ☐ No Proof Policy #	Exp. Date

Owner Damage Property Last Name	First	MI	Address	City	State	Zip

TU #	Pos	Rest	Endo	Saf Eqp	Air Bag	Eject.	Susp Imp	Inj Sev	Age	Sex	Name/Address

Approved BY:	ID. #	Date

230

Case #	DOR CODE	Accident Date	Agency

Describe Accident

Details

Carrier Name	☐ US DOT ☐ ICC ☐ State DOT
Address	Carrier Identification #
Carrier Name	☐ US DOT ☐ ICC ☐ State DOT
Address	Carrier Identification #

Mersonville Police Department Summons and Complaint Penalty Assessment	MPD	☐ Mersonville Municipal Court ☐ Morris County Court ☐ Traffic ☐ Non-Traffic ☐ Other	Summons 1800900 Case Number

The People of State, City of Mersonville vs

First	Middle	Last		DOB
Residential Address			City	State	Zip Code

Residential Address					City	State	Zip Code

Drivers' License Number Presented ☐ Yes ☐ No		State	Race	Sex	HGT	WGT	Hair	Eyes	Alias
Home Phone	Cell Phone	Work Phone		Occupation				Employer	
Identifying Marks/Scars/Tattoos					Place of Birth				

Vehicle Information

License Plate Number	Vehicle Year	State	License Year	Last Four of Vehicle Identification Number	Evidence ☐ Yes ☐ No
Make	Model	Damage	Body Style	Color(s)	Traffic Crash ☐ Yes ☐ No	Photos ☐ Yes ☐ No

Towed ☐ Yes	Towed ☐ No	Towed By:	Towed To:

Charges

City/State Statute Number	Title	Fine	Surcharge	Points
Description			☐ Felony ☐ Misdemeanor	
City/State Statute Number	Title	Fine	Surcharge	Points
Description			☐ Felony ☐ Misdemeanor	
Approximate Location of Violation		Violation Date	Violation Time	
Custody/Service Location		Service Date	Service Time	

You are hereby directed to appear as indicated

☐ Morris County Court located at: Street Address, City, State, Zip

☐ Mersonville Municipal Court located at: Street Address, City, State, Zip

On the _____ day of _____ 20_____ at _____ AM/PM

To answer charges of violations of the ☐ 1970 CRS as Amended ☐ The Code of Mersonville 2014

☐ Non Payable Summons ☐ Traffic ☐ Criminal Without admitting guilt, I hereby promise to appear at the time and place indicated. Failure to appear constitutes a separate offense and will result in a warrant being issued.	☐ Payable Summons ☐ Traffic ☐ Criminal Upon signing below I promise to pay the assessed fine within 20 days to the County Treasurer's Office per the instructions on the reverse side. Further, upon payment of this Penalty Assessment I acknowledge guilt of all charges. I am aware that the Penalty Assessment must be paid within 20 days or it becomes by law a Summons and Complaint and REQUIRES my appearance before the court at the time and place indicated above.
X _____	X _____

☐ Defendant Held in Custody ☐ Morris County Justice Center ☐ Defendant Released

The undersigned have probable cause to believe that the defendant committed the offense(s) against the peace and dignity of the people of the State of Colorado; and that this summons and complaint was signed and served upon the defendant at the location and on the date referenced above

Officer: _____ Served by: _____ Complaining Witness _____

PROBABLE CAUSE AFFIDAVIT

_____
_____
_____
_____
_____
_____
_____
_____
_____
_____
_____
_____
_____

WEATHER: ☐ CLEAR ☐ CLOUDY ☐ RAIN ☐ SNOW ☐ FOG ☐ DAWN ☐ DUSK **ATTITUDE:** ☐ EXCELLENT ☐ GOOD ☐ FAIR ☐ POOR

TRAFFIC: ☐ VEHICLE ☐ PED ☐ BICYCLE ☐ ONCOMING ☐ SAME ☐ CROSS **SURFACE CONDITIONS:** ☐ DRY ☐ WET ☐ ICY ☐ SNOWPACKED

DIRECTION OF TRAVEL: ☐ NORTH ☐ SOUTH ☐ EAST ☐ WEST ☐ INTERSECTION ☐ CROSSWALK ☐ STOP BAR

RADAR: GUN NUMBER _____ TUNING FORKS _____ ☐ SPEED POSTED ☐ NOT POSTED ☐ SCHOOL ZONE

OFFICER(S) TO BE NOTIFIED FOR TRIAL

OFFICER _____ BADGE NUMBER _____

OFFICER _____ BADGE NUMBER _____

UNDER PENALTY OF PERJURY, I AFFIRM THAT ALL THE INFORMATION CONTAINED UPON THIS DOCUMENT IS TRUE AND CORRECT TO THE BEST OF MY KNOWLEDGE.

AFFIANT_____ PRINT NAME_____

ADDRESS_____

HOME PHONE_____ WK. PHONE_____
ON THIS DATE, THE AFFIANT SIGNED THIS AFFIDAVIT AND SWORE TO ITS TRUTH

NOTARY PUBLIC_____ MY COMMISSION EXPIRES DATE_____

PROBABLE CAUSE AFFIDAVIT

The following affidavit is submitted to the Court to document the probable cause in support of the arrest of _____
DOB: _____   SSN: _____   on the charge(s) of: _____

_____
Date

_____
Deputy's Signature
Morris County Sheriff's Office

Jennifer Williams   *Jennifer Williams*
_____
Notary Signature

My Commission expires: 12-15-2015

IN THE DISTRICT COURT WITHIN AND FOR
THE COUNTY OF MORRIS AND STATE
Criminal Action No._____
Division No._____

THE PEOPLE OF THE STATE,

Plaintiff
vs.

Date of Birth

_____

_____   INFORMATION FOR
                                            PRELIMINARY PROCEDURE
_____

_____

Defendant _____.
The above named Defendant(s) was/were arrested on the ___ day of _____, _____,
on charges of:

The following bonding information is to be considered by the Judge in setting bail on the
defendant(s).

STANDARD BAIL

_____
Signature of Peace Officer who furnished
the above information.

Morris Sheriff´s Office
_____
Agency

ARREST WARRANT

(DISTRICT)(COUNTY) COURT, MORRIS COUNTY, STATE WARRANT NUMBER

_____

The People of the State, Plaintiff

V.

_____ Defendant

_____

Whereas _____ has made an Application and Affidavit to the Court for the issuance of an Arrest Warrant, and; Whereas the application is in proper form and probable cause is found to believe that the person named in the application has committed the offense(s) of:

in violation of State Revised Statutes within the County of Morris and State; THEREFORE, any peace officer into whose hands this Arrest Warrant shall come is hereby ordered to arrest: _____
and bring him without unnecessary delay before the nearest Judge of the County or District Court.

It is further ordered that Bond is set in the amount of:

Standard Bond _____ dollars

Done this _____
Time _____

BY THE COURT:

Steven J. Parker

JUDGE

RETURN AND SERVICE: I have duly served this Arrest Warrant by arresting the aforementioned Defendant as required on the _____ day of _____, 20__.

Signed: _____ Law enforcement agency: Morris County Sheriff's Office

(DISTRICT) (COUNTY) COURT, MORRIS COUNTY, STATE WARRANT NUMBER:

_____

APPLICATION AND AFFIDAVIT FOR ARREST WARRANT

_____

The People of the State, Plaintiff

V.

_____ ,Defendant

_____

The undersigned, a peace officer as defined in _____, C.R.S. 1973, as amended, being first duly sworn on oath moves the Court to issue an Arrest Warrant for:

_____

as provided in Rule 4.2 of the State Rules of Criminal Procedure.

As GROUNDS THEREFORE, the undersigned applicant states that the facts submitted in support of this request are set forth in the accompanying attachment designated as Attachment **"A"** which is attached hereto and made a part hereof and that probable cause exists to believe that the aforementioned person has committed the offense(s) of:

_____

in violation of C.R.S. 1973, as amended within the County of Morris and State.

It is respectfully requested that bond on this Arrest Warrant be set in the amount of:
Standard Bond
_____

Applicant _____

Morris County Sheriff's Office

Deputy Sheriff
Sworn and subscribed before me this date_____ .

Judge: *Steven J. Parker*
_____

ATTACHMENT "A"

Your Affiant is Deputy David Lincoln, a regularly employed Deputy Sheriff for the County of Morris, the State and is currently assigned to the Patrol Division of the Morris County Sheriff's Office.

Therefore, based on the above described facts and circumstances, Your Affiant respectfully moves this Honorable Court for issuance of an arrest warrant naming _____ _____as defendant for the crime(s) of:

_____

C.R.S. 1973, as amended.

_____
Affiant

_____   Date

Steven J. Parker   12-07-2014
Judge   Date

Index